PENGUIN

THE UNFINISHED GLOBAL REVOLUTION

Mark Malloch-Brown was Minister of State at the Foreign and Common-
wealth Office, and has previously been United Nations Deputy Secretary-
General under Kofi Anna Head of the UN ment
Program (1999–2005
Bank (1994–9)
is now the , FTI Consulting.

MARK MALLOCH-BROWN

The Unfinished Global Revolution

The Limits of Nations and The Pursuit of a New Politics

PENGUIN BOOKS

PENGUIN BOOKS

Published by the Penguin Group
Penguin Books Ltd, 80 Strand, London WC2R ORL, England
Penguin Group (USA) Inc., 375 Hudson Street, New York, New York 10014, USA
Penguin Group (Canada), 90 Eglinton Avenue East, Suite 700, Toronto, Ontario, Canada M4P 2Y3
(a division of Pearson Penguin Canada Inc.)
Penguin Ireland, 25 St Stephen's Green, Dublin 2, Ireland (a division of Penguin Books Ltd)
Penguin Group (Australia), 250 Camberwell Road,
Camberwell, Victoria 3124, Australia (a division of Pearson Australia Group Pty Ltd)
Penguin Books India Pvt Ltd, 11 Community Centre,
Panchsheel Park, New Delhi – 110 017, India
Penguin Group (NZ), 67 Apollo Drive, Rosedale, Auckland 0632, New Zealand
(a division of Pearson New Zealand Ltd)
Penguin Books (South Africa) (Pty) Ltd, 24 Sturdee Avenue,
Rosebank, Johannesburg 2196, South Africa

Penguin Books Ltd, Registered Offices: 80 Strand, London WC2R ORL, England

www.penguin.com

First published in the United States of America by
The Penguin Press, a member of Penguin Group (USA) Inc., 2011
First published in Great Britain by Allen Lane 2011
Published in Penguin Books 2012

1

Copyright © Mark Malloch-Brown, 2011

Printed in England by Clays Ltd, St Ives plc

ISBN: 978-0-141-03537-6

www.greenpenguin.co.uk

MIX
Paper from
responsible sources
FSC™ C018179

Penguin Books is committed to a sustainable
future for our business, our readers and our
planet. This book is made from paper certified
by the Forest Stewardship Council.

To my mother, Ursula, who encouraged me go out
and discover the world; to Trish, my partner in everything;
and to our children, Madison, Isobel, George,
and Phoebe, who, with better grace than I deserved,
have put up with the global life.

CONTENTS

THE **UNFINISHED GLOBAL** REVOLUTION

INTRODUCTION: EVENTS

On the bright sunny morning of July 7, 2005, United Nations secretary-general Kofi Annan and I were in London, on our way to Scotland for the Gleneagles G8 summit. The gathering of the Western world's biggest economies plus Russia was expected to commit to an ambitious plan of international cooperation to halve global poverty by 2015 and tackle climate change. A strong commitment at Gleneagles would turn the whole international mood. I had just stepped down from the UN's top development job, administering the United Nations Development Program (UNDP), to become Annan's chief of staff, so I was as invested as anyone in trying to get the world to cooperate for global progress. Before we left our London hotel, I told a BBC interviewer that this was going to be a good day for international development, a chance to get the world back on track after Iraq and 9/11.

On the drive to Heathrow, I noticed that the Scotland Yard protection officer seated up front was growing increasingly agitated. He pressed one hand against an earpiece and used the other to muffle whispers into his cell phone. When we arrived at the airport, he raced us to a small government jet and seemed to relax only when we were airborne. Forty minutes later we landed in Scotland, and the officer turned to Annan. Bombs had gone off in London that morning, he said. Fifty-two commuters, we would later learn, had lost their lives as a result of coordinated terrorist attacks on London's public transport system.

Acts of violence big and small have sent the affairs of nations in new directions. The 1914 assassination of Austrian Archduke Franz Ferdinand set off World War I; the 9/11 attacks prompted controversial wars in Afghanistan and Iraq. Now, I feared, it seemed to be happening again.

My life as a journalist, political consultant, international official and later British minister had given me plenty of opportunity to observe the unpredictability of international events. I had seen close up the strange interplay between the big macro trends in world affairs and the role played by accident and personality. As a journalist I had covered a turbulent period in British politics as Margaret Thatcher ascended to power, and as a political adviser I seemed to be caught up in nearly every democratic revolution from the mid-1980s to the mid-1990s, from the Philippines to Peru to Russia. I became a senior official at the World Bank just as the markets were roiled by financial crisis and the institution was under siege from antiglobalization activists. I was the head of UNDP and then Kofi Annan's right hand in the years when the UN was straining to keep up with what was happening all around it. These positions meant that I often had a front-row seat for witnessing the turning points in the move from the divided world of the Cold War to a freer, faster, but so far less managed future.

At Gleneagles that day the macro, the accidental, and the personal were all on display. Our host, British prime minister Tony Blair, was hoping that Gleneagles could rehabilitate him with progressive opinion at home, which he had lost after siding with the United States in the Iraq War. The so-called development community—the nongovernmental organizations and agencies, development ministries, and developing countries themselves—was hoping that all the G8 countries would commit to do what Europe had already pledged to do: increase their development assistance to poor countries to 0.7 percent of their gross domestic product (GDP) by 2012. Many of us also hoped that in the summit's later stages, when prominent developing country leaders joined, we could achieve breakthroughs on climate change and trade.

For too long the global discussion had been mired in a pessimistic and defensive agenda addressing terrorism and Iraq. Back in 2000 trade, technology, economics, and social change had seemed to be driving governments everywhere into one another's laps, and global understanding and cooperation had begun to take root. Like it or not, it had seemed then, we had to find ways to address our shared problems. Poverty, global markets, and the spread of disease across borders (in an era of mass air travel) had become pressing issues everywhere. The increasingly urgent problem of climate change demonstrated that we were all in the small same lifeboat: if one side rocked it, through damaging carbon emissions, it put us all at risk.

Globalization—its threats and its opportunities—had come to dominate the political conversation. It seemed too powerful a force for politicians, whatever their political stripe, to resist. The new president in Washington, George W. Bush, initially appeared not to contradict the logic of global integration, and of America's role. In his inaugural address on January 21, 2001, he told the American people: "The enemies of liberty and our country should make no mistake: America remains engaged in the world by history and by choice, shaping a balance of power that favors freedom."[1]

I thought globalization was becoming the fundamental issue that would replace class and religion in politics. You would be for it or against it, depending on your economic interests. A businessman might support it for the trade opportunities it presented; a consumer might enjoy the cheaper goods it afforded; but a blue-collar worker and a small farmer might feel threatened by its disruptions as it moved their jobs elsewhere. The media commentary on the subject was interminable: in 1981 an electronic database of eight thousand newspapers contained just two references to *globalization*; in 2001 the figure had risen to more than fifty-seven thousand; then after 9/11 commentation took fright and it trailed off for a time.[2] In the West, globalization meant dislocation, as existing jobs were lost to foreign competition, but it also meant a higher standard of living, as consumers got better value from Chinese imports at Wal-Mart and other big stores, and as the comparative advantages of capital, labor, and innovation played out across the global economy.

Most participants in the global debate argued that this dynamic restructuring of the global economy, as long as it was well managed and well governed, could leave most people around the world better off. But it would have to be managed, they acknowledged, because change could not be left to the hidden hands of markets. Without regulation, nationalist political reactions might resist globalization by playing on the unfairness and human costs of arbitrary change. During earlier periods, long before the ungainly term *globalization* was first used in a European Commission document in 1979, the integration of world trade had blossomed.[3] But each time a political backlash had reversed it. For a brief period before World War I, international trade's share of global GDP was higher than it would be in 2000. But then nationalism and protectionism set in, and an assassination in a Sarajevo square ignited war.

In 2005 those of us who were passionate about good international public policy seemed to have everything to play for again. The world was more integrated than ever, yet less governed. Dramatic economic forces were redrawing the political landscape, in a vacuum of politics and public policy at the global level. To be sure, figuring out how any system of international policy or regulation would work is difficult, but the mantra of "leave it to the market" gave business a dangerously free hand to take the world economy anywhere it wanted. Momentum was the result of millions of disconnected actions. Chinese workers and entrepreneurs scrabbled out of poverty by working longer and harder for less money than others; their equivalents in Vietnam, Ghana, and Mexico scrambled to undercut them by working for even less; and CEOs in corporate suites responded to the free-for-all by dispersing investment, manufacturing, and assembly across the world in a quest for market share and comparative advantage.

This dynamic change that benefited worker and consumer alike would have been impossible if politicians and planners had protected the cozy economic status quo of nations' vested interests. International capitalism, with its disruptive power, was a critical agent of change. But such undirected change was so evidently unfair and painful to so many, who lost jobs and enterprises, that some way of managing these issues at a global level seemed necessary.

The failure to set up a framework for the fair management of global affairs invited a grassroots rejection of globalization, which seemed to be introducing insecurity into everyone's life. In September 1999 in Seattle, trade ministers tried to begin negotiating a new world trade agreement, but violent demonstrations disrupted their meeting. It was a wake-up call. Not everybody, apparently, viewed globalization as a benign force for greater prosperity and international cooperation. Globalization had to be managed better, or the backlash against it would grow.

Two years later, on September 10, 2001, the pollster Andy Kohut and his colleagues visited me in my office at the UNDP in New York. They were preparing to go out into the field to take a poll on international attitudes toward America. We agreed that despite Seattle they would likely uncover increasingly benign views. Despite skepticism toward the new president, the longer-term trend seemed clear: trade and information were flowing through porous modern borders, and the world was growing inexorably closer. This was going to be a sink-or-swim-together century.

In his subsequent book *America Against the World*, Kohut recalls our conversation that day, only hours before the attack on the World Trade Center changed the world.

> From an office overlooking UN headquarters with the New York skyline as a backdrop, we wondered aloud whether any conceivable event might radically change the world political landscape as had the fall of the Berlin Wall in 1989. Could anything supplant globalization as the top international issue in the foreseeable future? We agreed, after brief reflection, that no such cataclysmic change was on the horizon. Of course we could not have been more wrong. Literally overnight, on September 11, the terrorist attacks on the towers of the World Trade Center and the Pentagon changed the world as dramatically as it was changed on the event of our first international polling when the Iron Curtain rose unexpectedly.[4]

Later attacks in London, Madrid, and Bali did not have the same global public aftershock but reinforced a growing view that terrorism now stalked the world. September 11 changed everything. The warning in Bush's State of the Union address had been fulfilled: America would engage with the world, not least to defend itself. Globalization suddenly seemed to have a dark underside. International travel had increased, making it normal for young Saudi students, in the case of 9/11, to take courses in America—and rendering the West vulnerable. Globalization was moreover not just the enabler but in some ways the cause. The consumerism spread by Western commercial culture was a source of provocation to conservatives everywhere. The most extreme form that that reaction took was terrorism.

After both 9/11 and London's 7/7, I was struck by what might have been. On September 11, 2001, a senior Cuban official was visiting me at my New York office; we stood at the window, despairingly watching smoke rise from the site of the Twin Towers; then we too had to evacuate, in case the UN was the next target. Shaken, the Cuban observed that that day everybody sympathized with America and that everybody had to reach out to help. The French newspaper *Le Monde* echoed this sentiment a day later with its headline: "We Are All Americans."

Four years later at Gleneagles, the G8 leaders, by now hardened by earlier terrorist experiences, reacted swiftly and unequivocally to the London attacks, expressing solidarity with Tony Blair. Amidst the tragedy, it was one of Blair's best moments. A day later Annan and I found him in his shirtsleeves in the Gleneagles Hotel garden.

Leisurely bilateral talks had been scheduled for the hotel's spacious Victorian reception rooms, but because Blair had to rush to London to rally a shocked Britain, then dash back to keep the summit on track, the meetings had been moved to the garden so that Blair could move more quickly between the groups. If he had his way, Blair said, terrorists would not succeed in distracting the meeting from laying out the vital groundwork for an assault on global poverty. In the gardens, meeting rooms, and corridors, the brave buzz was that terrorists would not win. But in a way they already had.

Ah, what might have been. Blair had broken the rules of this stuffy club of world leaders and had welcomed to Gleneagles the entertainers Bono and Bob Geldof, of the development lobby's celebrity arm. In truth the G8 leaders were less and less representative of the global economy. Most of Blair's peers exhibited little real sympathy for the big cause of global poverty. Apart from the development leaders, his allies at Gleneagles were his official guests, like Annan and South African president Thabo Mbeki. Otherwise organizations like Oxfam and coalitions against third world debt and the destruction of rain forests appeared to speak for the wider world. Power was tangibly moving away from the state level, from the mostly white men of the old G8, to a newer, more diverse global leadership.

I recall Annan sitting at the foot of a Gleneagles hotel bed as Bob Geldof leaned over him and Bono squatted in front of him. Both had built reputations as champions of antipoverty issues on top of careers as rock stars. Richard Curtis, the filmmaker and master of modern

British romantic comedies (the man who has given Hugh Grant his best lines), hung back diffidently. As Geldof blustered on about the importance of not letting down "his people"—meaning the huge number of fans who had attended Make Poverty History rock concerts before the meeting—Bono, always the more practical, honed in on the possible. Implausibly, this unofficial trio, as much as the elected leaders, could claim to have a mandate from their fans and supporters to advocate for the poor.

Later, I saw the animated tag team of Geldof and Bono ambush a bemused President Jacques Chirac of France, who had been blocking concessions on European agriculture that would allow cheap food imports from developing countries that might hurt French farmers. As I went by, Geldof warned Chirac of a backlash if he held out against Geldof's French rock fans. Before an earlier G8 summit in France, I had irritated Chirac by pointing out that the daily European Union subsidy for one European cow was three times the size of the dollar a day, or less, that 1.2 billion people in the world survived on. But at Gleneagles, as before, not even pop stars could move him.

Agriculture might account for only about 2 percent of French employment,[5] but it remained a vital staple of national life and culture. Chirac was not budging. And his stand reflected the instinctive resistance of billions of global citizens to a helter-skelter integration that was throwing people together because it was good economics, without regard for how people chose to live their lives. While Blair was in London handling the aftermath of the terrorist attacks, Chirac took advantage of his absence to bully the British Foreign Office official who was standing in for him to limit discussion of the subject.

For all the celebrity lobbying, public concern, and anxious efforts of international development officials like myself, the world leaders at Gleneagles frankly lacked the will and imagination to summon up collaborative international action. They did promise more aid, pledging to meet an ambitious target over the following seven years, but this promise turned out to be empty for nearly everyone but the British hosts. Poverty could wait another day. Nor did they move on trade and the environment. Both are important to poverty reduction because one offers jobs and a foot in the door of the global economy and the other secures the forests and lands that are the basis of many of the poor's meager assets.

In a divided and distracted world, terrorists were not the only ones who stopped global integration. And in that sense the tragedy of 7/7 was not in the same league as other acts of political violence. It did not start a war or even depress the ambition of the Gleneagles summit. Indeed, leaders rallied to say the right things about standing together and not allowing terrorists to deflect them from their agenda. Rather, Gleneagles confirmed the disconcerting truth that those who had the power to make globalization work did not have the courage to do so, even as those who hated it were growing in their resistance. And the resisters had many faces. They were not just brutally violent bombers; they were also thoughtful and decent politicians, the leaders of social protest movements worldwide, academics, activists, and voters.

The battle lines were being drawn between the Globalists, who seemed to take for granted the inevitability of their eventual triumph, and the Nationalists, who, losing control over their own lives and economic fortunes, were preparing to fight back. Gleneagles was a skirmish. The longer war is still under way.

Gleneagles was a tableau of the new political actors. Countries that barely a generation before had been objects of sympathy as they apparently languished in unending poverty were prying power from the hands of the old Western political establishment. The development and environmental communities and their celebrity leaders, representing causes rather than countries, had also found their way to the table. But this exuberant and chaotic politics was being played out against the grim backdrop of terrorism, and it was not always played with courage and vision. Leaders, as creatures of their voters, did not often envision a world of shared purpose and mutual responsibilities. Factions not vision ruled, as the world began to grapple with life after the all-powerful nation-state.

This book attempts to explain why politics is migrating beyond the gray confines of national parliaments and cabinets to a global bazaar where rock stars may conduct deals on global debt with bankers and dictators and where emerging powers like China and India will seek to push aside former colonizers as they set up their stalls. The official platform for much of this pageant is the creaking boards of the United Nations, whose strained bureaucratic processes pale beside the pageant's vitality and activism.

For globalization is likely to become the twenty-first century's most local and most perennial political issue. It is not going to leave us alone. It has already thrown us together and made us dependent on one another for some common government of a shared world. But if we fail to recognize the profundity of this change, we will fail to equip ourselves with the global arrangements that might enable us to handle these shared responsibilities. As it stands now, national politics in much of the world is turning its back on the future, unable to embrace the concept that some parts of national power will have to be pooled with that of global neighbors.

The worldwide economic crisis that began in 2008 demonstrated that without effective global institutions to manage the fallout and regulate the financial sector, big fortunes as well as the small investor and the pensioner from the United States to China would be at risk. And for all of us, the crisis hit very close to home, while the solutions were beyond the reach of individual nations' politicians.

The second great crisis of globalization after terrorism was about money. That was appropriate: economics had become the primary engine and driving idea of global integration. It is generally agreed that financial markets must be prevented from ever again threatening global stability and prosperity. But now that the financial crisis has receded, even this apparently straightforward objective of shared economic security has proved elusive. Bankers are back to notching up profits and are largely resisting efforts to regulate their business. But their rescue, and that of the economies they threw into recession in 2008, has left deep political scars. Their follies cost too many jobs on Main Street.

Political leaders have begun to understand the vulnerability and exposure that people feel when they no longer control the fate of their jobs and communities and cannot understand who does. The hidden hand of the market seems to have returned in a manner that Karl Marx would recognize. In this book I describe people struggling to restore control over their lives, and to find structures of accountability, local and global, that work when the defenses of national politics are breached. They, far more than the politicians, have had the courage to seize this logic and fashion global solutions.

Hence the extraordinary rise of NGOs and civil society more broadly. Civil society figures are usually much more passionate and committed and inspirational in their political ambitions than old-style politicians. More Britons donate to Oxfam than belong to the leading political parties. People are attracted by global causes to which their political leaders often seem indifferent. From these early traces may emerge global political culture—the shared values of a new politics.

But the state is not dead—far from it. In our more crowded world with finite resources, the scramble to control energy and other commodities will only grow more intense. Winning this fight will require state power as well as commercial power. And the coming model of capitalism may not be the Western free market, which stumbled so badly during the global financial crisis, but the state-allied Asian one, which weathered it much better. China, to secure mineral and oil concessions in Africa, exerts diplomatic as well as commercial power.

Many believe that states will soon go to war with one another over access to fresh water. Controlling the natural resources that feed our industrial economies will, for better or worse, require the exercise of state as well as commercial power.

Globalization throws up so many problems that are beyond the reach of states alone to solve; yet far from withering, the state has gained a new rationale, both as the bulwark of the individual against disconcerting and dislocating global change and as the ally of its business sector in winning economic advantage in a competitive world.

Perhaps the real surprise in the pages that follow is the resilience rather than the disappearance of the old national political structures. In my fifty-something lifetime, global population has more than doubled; more people now live in cities than were alive when I was born. It is a crowded teeming world, younger than ever and more connected than ever. Yet despite this global revolution old structures—the Chinese Communist Party, the American Congress, and Britain's hidebound political system—persist relatively unchanged. The official world has proven resilient. My father, dead for many years, would recognize most of the official institutions that are still deemed to matter. Beyond their walls the world is utterly different, but somehow they have kept afloat amid the tumult, bobbing atop a teeming younger urbanized world. Somehow tradition has held on in unlikely places.

A career of observing and sometimes participating in a small way in these global changes has left me wary of making predictions. I have witnessed democratic revolutions, from bold initial hopes to the steady insidious return of the old order. I've seen brave attempts to restructure global institutions batted down by government representatives who prefer the status quo. And above all I have heard warnings that proved false: the Soviet Union will dominate a failing United States; America is in a state of imperial overstretch; Japan will rise to economic hegemony in the 1980s. (Japan subsequently suffered the longest economic stagnation of modern times.) In the 1990s many believed we had arrived at all the economic answers. The market had triumphed and that was the end of the matter.

Hubris is perhaps the inevitable companion of such revolutionary times. But we should not be driven by today's predictions of the rise of China to parity or more with the United States, or of the triumph of Asia and its economy at the expense of the West. What is certain is that revolutionary change will continue, bringing upsets and surprises and dashed predictions. For example, while Asia will continue to grow, it will likely also see its fair share of political and environmental conflict. Its full emergence may have to await the resolution of problems closer to home. What we need is a system of international institutions that has the strength and flexibility to handle the unexpected and ensure that change is managed peacefully. Such institutions would allow Asian countries a greater global role as they are ready and in the meantime bring help to bear on Asia's local problems.

While I argue for building the laws and institutions of a new global order that can manage the volcanic disputes that must lie ahead, I am wary then of predictions about the rise or fall of particular countries or even final solutions to the global problems crowding in on us.

One cannot make the case for such changes without attaching them to a wider purpose. At the close of the book I call for a global contract that builds on the emerging common values of solidarity and compassion in a shared world. We must harness globalization to a vision of bringing benefit to all, at least a basic threshold of human security, well-being, and opportunity. We must demonstrate that global governance can deliver economic fairness between nations; security for people from overbearing states; and agreed rules for sharing our finite natural resources, and above all the processes to manage global changes.

This book is finally about the pioneers, many of them friends, who have sought with mixed success to build a platform upon which we can peacefully resolve disputes and build a more just world. But it is an impatient book because if we insist on prevaricating and hiding behind national systems, we risk immolation. We need to get on with it.

CHAPTER ONE

HOME SCHOOLING

As a young political journalist in London in the late 1970s, I encountered an extraordinary economic reformer-leader: Margaret Thatcher. At the time I was *The Economist*'s junior political correspondent covering Westminster. Thatcher was the controversial leader of the opposition, feared more than admired for her hard-line views. She faced, however, a failing Labour government that by 1978 was beset by strikes and chronic economic difficulties. Although Labour seemed likely to lose the election due in 1979, only a handful of Thatcher's faithful would have predicted that she was about to launch the country on a thirty-year path of reform and economic success.

What Mrs. Thatcher was able to do for Britain demonstrated to me the impact that strong national leadership can have as well as its limits. Thatcher's Britain was not an island—it needed the rest of the world. She was no enthusiast for the state, which she always considered too big, but she was also a great British patriot. She believed in Britain the nation. That latter conviction would have made her despise the second half of my central proposition: that if we are to have much-reduced states, we will have to compensate with global government arrangements.

As opposition leader, Thatcher would talk to the Westminster press corps once a week on so-called lobby terms. The lobby was the stone-flagged hallway, adjacent to the House of Commons, where members of the press had traditionally been allowed to accost members of Parliament as they had entered or left the chamber. It was a rule of the House that all such exchanges were off the record. This meant that as a journalist you could not attribute what you heard to a specific politician. The rule had stayed, even as the briefings themselves had moved to a formal briefing room up in the roof of the rabbit warren of the Parliament buildings.

Normally the politicians who briefed us, protected by the nonattributable nature of the sessions, would trade waspish tidbits of gossip and talk tactics. But Margaret Thatcher relentlessly sought to educate us in grand strategy. Each week she would assault us with the advantages of privatizing state companies, selling public housing, and liberating enterprise by lowering taxes. My British journalist colleagues, who considered their skepticism a vital barrier against conviction or co-optation, would visibly squirm when we were subjected to these humorless broadsides. It was not how it was supposed to be done. We were there to trade information, they sniffed, not to be lectured.

While I relished Thatcher's conviction in the face of their limp cynicism, I nevertheless too found her impossibly strident. That stridency, along with her refusal to play by the clubbish rules of Westminster, or engage in the bitchy gossip of her male colleagues, would, I suspected, leave her as no more than an interesting footnote in British political history.

The 1979 election, however, followed a winter of trade union challenges to the Labour government that made her victory almost certain. The garbage had piled up, public transport had ground to a halt, and all sorts of other indignities had been visited on the British public. For middle-class voters, Labour had lost its rationale—the ability to manage workers' expectations in a way that kept the country going. The trade unions had brought a divided country to a halt, and Labour had clearly lost the authority to stop them. Many Britons thought it was time to give the Tories a go. Thatcher's victory was therefore more a vote against Prime Minister Jim Callaghan's Labour government than a vote for her reform agenda. Indeed, she took care not to distract attention from Labour's failure by producing too many detailed, let alone radical, proposals.

Her victory was a relatively narrow one given the circumstances, yet remarkably she turned it into a mandate to revolutionize Britain. Many would argue that her triumph in the Falklands War and her second election victory really empowered her: like George W. Bush before 9/11, at points in her first term she looked more like an accidental leader than a lasting one.

The Economist, by 1979, was equipped with first-generation word-processing equipment that allowed journalists to directly input copy. But in a clear example of why Britain needed Mrs. Thatcher, restrictive working policies prevented journalists from making proper use of the equipment. We would input, then print out the copy, which would then be re-inputted on identical machines by members of the printers' union. This kind of costly, uncompetitive behavior desperately needed to be stripped out of the British economy.

In 1979 Election Day, a Thursday, was as usual press day for *The Economist*. We needed to prepare two advance versions of our lead article for the Britain section of the magazine, as the laborious double print-setting process would not allow us to wait for the results. One version, written by the political editor, praised her victory; the other long-shot insurance option, assigned to me as the junior reporter, described why she had lost.

She was too suburban, too tart, too intolerant, and too narrow, ran my thesis. For good measure I added that she did not like foreigners much, when Britain needed to find its place in the world again.

Other, more emollient internationalist types would surely pick up on her prescriptions and implement them in a softer style. Britain was not ready for her.

But Britain was in danger of not working anymore, as the Tory campaign advertising cleverly warned. That previous winter Britain had looked failure in the face, and Margaret Thatcher's time had come. My boss's article was the one that ran.

Watching her come to power gave me an abiding respect for conviction in politics. I was almost as uncomfortable with conviction as my fellow lobby journalists were, but I saw that it enabled Margaret Thatcher to end a failing system of economic management and governance that had allowed Britain to fall steadily behind. She taught me, and many others, a very un-Conservative lesson: you do not enter politics just to govern—you go into it to make fundamental changes. She was a revolutionary, and Britain needed her. I concluded that many other countries also needed leaders like her.

My second conclusion was much less Thatcherite. Domestic reform, admirable as it was, was not enough to recapture Britain's former prosperity. Events had cast the country from the center of the global trading system that was essential to its economic strength. Britain's ambitions and values had also narrowed. Thatcher in some ways remained impervious to this second point. She saw the power of global free trade but was impatient with the idea of building the multilateralist system needed to sustain it. To open up to this latter point, Britain would have to wait until Tony Blair, also a conviction politician.

Under her rule Thatcher did, however, allow her Trade and Industry secretary, Leon Brittan, to break up the clubbish old-boy network (a target for her whether it was in the law or any of the professions) in the City of London. But the consequences went way beyond domestic liberation. As Brittan, a favorite lunch companion of mine when I was a lobby journalist, had anticipated, his "Big Bang" reforms of 1986 made London over the next twenty years once more the financial capital of the world. His program was a dramatic liberalization and deregulation of the rules under which London operated as a financial center. Out went all the restrictive practices that favored the old City cartel, as well as the bowler hats and the long, lazy, soporific lunches that London's City establishment was known for. Soon cohorts of thrusting young American bankers, followed by those of many other nationalities, invaded its sleepy, protected environs. Before long London became the preferred global home for international financial services.

Reform might be painful, but if it led to getting a foot into a global market, the rewards were obvious. Margaret Thatcher showed the country it could come back.

My British childhood before that was an education in equally how quickly a country can lose its way. I learned early on that national success can be ephemeral and that in many ways the relative fortunes of states are played out on a great global Chutes and Ladders game board. When I was a child, Ghana and Bangladesh were richer than South Korea, and Britain was precariously perched astride an empire. The extent of Britain's relative economic decline remained largely hidden. Then during my adolescence in the late 1960s its economic and political failure was graphically exposed, even as a new popular cultural anglo empire of the Beatles and Rolling Stones was established. Then in my late twenties, Margaret Thatcher led Britain to a remarkable comeback, demonstrating that countries and leaders do not have to give up. There are second chances.

I was nine in 1962 when Dean Acheson, a former U.S. secretary of state and an admirer of Britain, famously observed that "Great Britain has lost an empire and not yet found a role." Needless to say I missed this rebuke at the time although a postwar British childhood was in its own way a lesson in national decline. In the school library and in the history classroom, Britain's empire still seemed very present. Kipling, Henty, and Buchan, enthusiastic scribes of empire, were still on the library shelves, and boarding school culture was still deeply imbued with the values that sent generations of schoolboys before me off to run corners of the empire.

But the England in which I grew up was one of self-consciously diminished circumstances. By the mid-1960s, it had precious little empire left to run: a few dejected islands here and there. Born in 1953, I got one of the last postwar ration cards. The early 1950s were followed by a period of recovering affluence that with Labor in power touched more lives than in the past but it was accompanied by eroding international standing and economic competitiveness. Britain's fabled manufacturing sector, which had once made Manchester as central to global manufacturing as Shanghai is today, had lost its way. Harold Macmillan, the Tory prime minister from 1957 to 1963, complacently claimed, "You've never had it so good," words that became an ironic epitaph for the period. Maybe he was right, if you looked in the larder or garage once rationing was behind us, but not if you looked at the world. You've never got it so wrong, the Labour opposition of the day essentially replied.

The ration card, still in existence a full eight years after the war was over, said it all. Britain had been economically exhausted by the war, and as I grew up, it had to watch its defeated rival West Germany sprint past. By 1950 Western Europe was back to prewar levels of output and grew strongly from there. But Britain's share of global trade and manufacturing approximately halved over my childhood. By the 1970s both West Germany and France had higher per capita incomes.

At the time it seemed a British problem. The extraordinary contraction of the U.K.'s role began with India's and Pakistan's postwar independence and in the 1960s moved to an equally rapid exit from

African and other colonies. That would have left any society rattled, preoccupied with adjustment to newly reduced circumstances, and engaged in an obsessive discussion of its role and status in the world.

As the Second World War came to an end, Churchill had shaken his major allies by insisting that he did not mean to live to see an end of the British Empire. His American and Soviet partners thought dismantling the British and French colonies, to create a stable world, was an important postwar objective. Colonies had provoked enough crises and were a dangerous out-of-date construction. I recall the British public broadly accepting the inevitability of decolonization and being relieved that Britain had been able to extricate itself from empire relatively painlessly. Rebellions against colonial rule in Malaya (now Malaysia) and Kenya had brought home how badly the process might still go if Britain hung on. Instead, the political argument was not over whether to leave the colonies, but rather over two opposing visions of Britain's future. The progressive vision hoped that, through participation in the United Nations and multilateralism more generally, the U.K. could become a force for nuclear disarmament and world peace. The other, more defensive vision perceived that Britain, stripped of empire, was now more exposed in a dangerous bipolar world where the forces of international Communism were on the offensive. The threat of succumbing to Soviet domination must be offset by putting the country as directly as possible under American protection.

Would joining Europe be a useful supplement to multilateralism or a way of balancing dependence on America? Many felt that to go back as supplicants into a Europe that we had left as conquerors in 1945 would be humiliating. Joining would mean becoming a junior member of a Europe whose leadership was now in French and German hands. It became a debate about island pride and history.

At the time this predicament seemed to me peculiarly British. Who else, after all, had ever won a war and lost an empire in quite such a spectacularly compressed time frame? Only later did I understand a more universal truth. Not just Britain but the world was to be roiled by changes in comparative status between countries. Within countries, economic change would be more rapid and produce more instability than ever in human history. This has been the global condition during my lifetime. Everything changes. Countries rise and fall. A seemingly formidable ideology, Communism, crumbled from within. Social and gender mobility reached revolutionary rates as old class systems withered and women entered the workforce, politics, the priesthood, and the boardroom at unprecedented levels. Population size in many parts of the world exploded. Some of these changes were heralded, but others crept up on us. Many of them got a dress rehearsal in the Britain of my youth.

Traditional life often seems unaffected, even as beneath the surface things are moving dramatically. Every morning, as Britain was falling behind its peers, my mother and I would drop my father at a local train station, where he took his place among the bowler-hatted men in dark suits and overcoats awaiting their commuter trains to London. As a South African in a status-conscious U.K., my father could never personally, I was relieved to see, bring himself to wear a bowler hat.

The local grocery store Evershed and Cripps still had my mother's account, as it had her mother's before her. Mr. Cripps presided over a busy staff that laboriously filled our orders individually as we stood at the counter. Supermarket aisles and checkouts were still something I was familiar with only from American movies, not that I got to see many of them, as the small black and white television that crouched in a corner of our living room was, until I was about twelve, forbidden territory except for the weekly episode of *The Lone Ranger*, an American western. My grandparents still had their own pew in church.

And then in the 1960s change raced through British life. The bowler hat, many of the train stations, and the local full-service grocery store disappeared. Churches were emptying. Dramatic changes in the social order and in every aspect of people's lifeways, from sex to consumerism, faith, and work, swept Britain. As the teenaged son of a now-widowed mother dividing my time between boarding school and home, I was both excited and a little unnerved by the changed world I would be entering.

Whatever else one might say about the process, it was cathartic. Britain has gotten over empire. During the Battle of Britain in 1940, as waves of German bombers lacerated the capital night after night, Londoners, mostly white and London-born, had descended companionably into the bomb shelters. When the terrorists struck London in 2005, politicians and commentators were quick to invoke the spirit of the Battle of Britain and recall the city's phlegmatic response. Londoners just carry on, they said, however great the adversity. In 2005 the city's demographics had changed: almost a third of Londoners were not originally from Britain. But the values remained, as again Londoners behaved with great calm and decency amid violence and tragedy. New arrivals were among the victims. Perhaps it takes an expat Brit who has spent much of his working life abroad to appreciate fully one of Britain's most significant assets—the liberal tolerance that allows such cohesion. Yet unlike America, however, Britain's terrorists were home-grown. This was the dark side of British tolerance in the name of multiculturalism; spurning the melting pot sometimes allowed differences to metastasize into deadly grievance.

In the continuous up-and-down of global fortunes, exiles and refugees from failed countries like dictator Idi Amin's Uganda or apartheid-ruled South Africa contributed their talents and energies to Britain's revival. London, declining in my early childhood, is now the wealthy, booming center of much of the global private equity and hedge fund industry. Its shops and restaurants have few equals—perhaps the most remarkable change, given British gastronomic history. And even faith is making a comeback of sorts, not perhaps in Anglican churches, which are still linked to state and empire in their structure, hymns, and ceremonies, but in new, less-established, less-hierarchical congregations as well as in temples, mosques, and synagogues. And Britain's leadership of popular culture continues. In the cultural hierarchy it has moved up from a hub for music and style and design to the home of museums like the Tate Modern and live complexes like the South Bank with its rich mixture of theater, classical music, and the visual arts.

Growing up in Britain, I was exposed to the stresses and strains of modernization—the sudden swings of the political pendulum, the agony of those dislocated by economic reform, and the sometimes-obscene financial rewards of those who benefited. I watched my grandfather's small shipping company, which had plied the seas for years, be bought by a speculator off the cheap credit of a boom-and-bust era of the 1970s, then be quickly broken up and destroyed. Like my whole generation, I watched British coal miners struggle to weather change and "city slickers" enrich themselves in a 1970s financial sector boom of unsustainably cheap credit. Economic progress seemed to bring winners and losers, with little social justice.

From the first postwar Labour government onward, Britons had been concerned that, in throwing out its past, Britain might also be throwing out more abiding values. Aneurin Bevan, one of the great twentieth-century Labour leaders, grumbled to his last Labour Party conference in 1959: "It is a vulgar society. It is a meretricious society. It is a society in which priorities have gone all wrong . . . Consumerism is rapidly dissolving traditional community ties: self-assertion, both by individuals and by groups, is coming to replace collective solidarity and class loyalty." Labour politicians must have thought the electorate unappreciative, as Labour's postwar government had established the modern welfare state. It had established the National Health Service and had also addressed public pensions and education. The state's role in the economy expanded dramatically with the nationalization of coal, iron, steel, electricity, gas, railways, canals, road transportation, and aviation. Whitehall's wartime planners had a last hurrah as they placed a large part of the civilian economy in state hands.

With the welfare state Labour had responded to long-standing past social needs, but once it met them it was missing the future. People wanted more. Time and again I was to watch governments around the world bravely respond to a first reform agenda, only to be tripped up by the consequences of their success—a new middle class that wanted still more.

The other warning that postwar Britain equipped me with was the limits of state or central capacity. Taking a first-class school or hospital from a Whitehall planner's mind and successfully implementing it seems almost as hard as taking a plan from a World Bank or UN's program officer's mind and making it a functioning success on the ground thousands of miles away.

From my early teens I read as much as I could about economic and political change in Africa and Asia. Economic historians and political scientists replaced Buchan and Henty on my reading list. Britain had exported its model of high taxes and high public spending to fund ambitious public services, together with a big state role in the economy, to its former colonies. It was Britain's last and near-fatal gift, as many of those countries struggled through the same economic quagmire as a consequence. Vast and creaky public sectors grew up, financed increasingly, as tax systems failed, by debt and aid. These programs were an exhausting burden on national economies and yet proved utterly unable to deliver decent services. Seeing this economic model's impact later, I became so allergic to it that the author of a recent history of UNDP entitled the chapter about my time as its chief: "Fabian Socialists Need Not Apply." In Tanzania I saw how this kind of advice led the first postcolonial president, Julius Nyerere, down a path of economic ruin. Heavily influenced by Britain to introduce the welfare state, Tanzanians had a utopian expectation that

that system could be replicated in a poor country lacking the necessary financial and human capital.

To be sure, the difficulties that Tanzania faced were not due solely to the failure of a particular brand of economics. By the 1970s, as center-left governments in Latin America failed to produce the incomes, services, and lifestyles that people wanted, new governments were taking an often violent step to the authoritarian right. In Africa, the breakdown of postcolonial governments was caused by much more than the bad advice of some British Fabians: pro-market African governments did no better. Kenya had avoided the socialism of its Tanzanian neighbor and instead allowed a chaotic and corrupt market economy of sorts to operate. Tanzanian socialists criticized Kenya as a man-eat-man society; Kenyans responded that Tanzania had become a man-eat-dog society. Kenya, despite its economic advantages such as skilled African and white Kenyan manpower, did little better by its people than its Tanzanian neighbor.

Both countries, as I discovered in 1971, had fallen far in the few short years since decolonization. In that year a school friend named Peter Carey and I, both eighteen, traveled together from the Cape to Cairo over some six months, hitchhiking or in speeding overcrowded taxis or ramshackle buses. For an English schoolboy, after this trip there was no looking back. It was the world's problems, not Britain's, that fascinated me now. In Tanzania, I saw the dilemma: a fine president, Julius Nyerere, aimed to put the country's assets in its people's hands, but the country needed economic growth, which was less likely to come, in the short term at least, from African smallholders than from large white-owned commercial farms.

In his eagerness to control the commanding heights of the economy, Nyerere quite literally seized a mountain. He repossessed the astonishingly fertile white farms in the foothills of Mount Kilimanjaro and redistributed the land to African farmers. We tagged along with a white farmer to an angry town meeting where the farmers warned of the likely damage to the land's productivity. Many of the white farmers had come to Tanzania after the Second World War and built farming paradises of breathtaking views and astonishing agricultural productivity from what they remembered as uncultivated scrub; for them, the redistribution was a terrible end to their dreams. But for local African families it meant the recovery of a smallholder subsistence-farming idyll that the invasion of big white farms had pushed aside. For both groups, futures and precious ways of life were at stake.

Then as now, I was torn between the white farmer's prediction that much less would be grown and my strong conviction that returning the farms to African hands, while giving proper compensation to the former owners, would ultimately serve justice and political stability. The white farmers may have been right on the productivity point, but it was hard to sympathize with their angry condemnation of the aspirations of newly independent African governments and their blind belief that nobody had farmed the land before them. Today in Tanzania, thirty years later, the smallholders have failed to overcome hurdles of product transportation, investment, and land management, but the story has taken a further twist. A progressive but pro-market government is now in power; a developer has bought part of the Mount Kilimanjaro land and is apparently planning to build a polo club to attract rich Westerners to build vacation homes on the ruins of Tanzania's grain basket.

On a roadside in Zambia the chairman of the national grain marketing board picked Peter and myself up. As we raced along in his Peugeot, he explained that the government purchased grain and stored it in warehouses. His job was to protect it, but it was a losing battle. Thieves were continuously stealing the grain to supply an active black market because government prices were artificially low. The warehouses were infested and damp, and he did not have government funding to fix it. He was on his way to inspect another warehouse in hopes of preserving its contents. He gripped the steering wheel as he drove, his shoulders tense, and we bucked our way across unmaintained pot-holed roads. The situation epitomized the African dilemma, the postcolonial lack of capacity and capital, and certainly put Britain's adjustment difficulties in context. Countries everywhere were having difficulty making things work.

Back from Africa, I immersed myself in the study of history, economics, and politics, first at Cambridge University and then at the University of Michigan. Two things were becoming clearer to me. First, in order to prosper, countries, whatever their political complexion, had to focus on improving their flexibility and competitiveness against others. Having found a niche or a comparative advantage, they had to attend to labor flexibility and productivity and the cost of capital; they had to find ways to build and hold an edge in innovation. That was the lesson from parts of Europe and Asia. The second truth that dawned on me was that some regions were hopelessly handicapped in global competition, given the way the world was organized. These nations were either too far away from transportation, lacked sources of capital, or were crippled by disease and geography. To be landlocked and in a malarial belt of Africa was a poor hand to be played.

To study history for an undergraduate degree at Cambridge is to be cured of easy assumptions about the causes and consequences of anything. We did mental gymnastics to answer questions such as: Did Chinese peasants know who Mao was? Did they really understand that he was a Communist committed to change, or did they just assume he was another emperor in far-off Beijing? In the 1970s Cambridge's heroes of economic history that we studied were not just illustrious public figures and Cambridge men themselves like John Maynard Keynes but were also entrepreneurs like the eighteenth-century Josiah Wedgwood, who by predicting coming trends in manufacturing, transportation, marketing, and consumer fashion was able to build a global pottery empire. Britain's industrial revolution rested on the shoulders of entrepreneurs and their interplaying efforts to build steam engines and railways, seek out new markets, and create a modern consumer. Broad economic changes, such as the shift of population from the land to the cities and into a cash economy, mattered. In my three years of studying British and world history, I started to understand how long-term trends interacted with personal vision and leadership. And as I immersed myself in Africa's past through a lingering fascination with imperial history, I constantly hankered after Africa's present. During my months of trekking around the continent, I had hesitated to go home to university. There seemed so much to do.

After Cambridge, I went off to the University of Michigan to pursue a M.A. in political science. There I began my lifelong love affair with America, the country where later I met my wife, Trish, and where we have for the most part raised our four children. As a young graduate student, I found, after the cramped life of the U.K., that everything seemed bigger in the United States. My first surprise was the enormous car a fellow British scholar, who was a year ahead of me, came to meet me in. This was the good life.

I also discovered the puckish Ali Mazrui, a former professor at Makerere University in Uganda. Forced to leave during the Idi Amin dictatorship, he now lived in rather ill-fitting exile amid the winter snows of Michigan, with only a limited African-studies program around him. But he was a celebrity academic, opining mischievously that ethnicity counted more than class, and that women should run Africa because they were better at keeping the peace, would reduce defense spending, and already ran the farms and markets. The still heavily Marxist American academics took offense, but since then his views have worn rather better than their orthodoxies. I relished Ali's heresies; so did another student who would turn up thirty years later as a talented head of policy planning at the State Department; so did another who later became a bishop in Tanzania.

My university years provided me with a compass of sorts for what lay ahead. Some things did seem pretty much beyond dispute. How people moved from rural to urban employment was important, and so was whether they left behind a viable agricultural sector that could efficiently feed a growing urban workforce while freeing labor and capital for the latter. Similarly, free trade seemed a sound idea: it had played a dynamic role in British imperial history, and wherever I looked, economic success appeared to be export-led.

By contrast, the countries that sheltered behind import barriers cut sorry figures. The Soviet Union had made a great leap in output in the 1950s but had slowed dramatically when nobody wanted to buy its shoddy consumer goods. What was worse for most failing countries, change in the global economic league was no longer an incremental affair: rapid overall rates of economic growth and decline made the stakes very high. And as the Cold War receded and newly independent countries demanded a say in the world economy, the track records of success and failure were exposed for all to see.

The Cold War was a dangerous time of nuclear confrontation and political repression, and political tragedy was never more than a step away. Another lesson I learned in these years overshadowed my intellectual development: In the name of national security, governments lied and covered up. The Westerners excused their support for bad governments by saying they were a necessary front against Communism; the Communists excused their fat military budgets by saying that weapons mattered more than their people's standard of living. Both excuses looked increasingly thin. Students on both sides were asking persistently: What are we fighting or sacrificing for? Surely government must be about offering people opportunities for a better, freer life. East and West, governments could not postpone this question indefinitely, while they pursued a deadly global competition. It cost too much, both at home and abroad.

One day during my school years a grim-faced schoolmaster came into a classroom, where we all sat at rows of wooden desks that bore the carved initials of children generations before us, and announced that President John F. Kennedy had been assassinated. It shook our little world. What else lay beneath America's glamorous surface? Then we learned about the murders of Martin Luther King and Robert Kennedy. Nor was prosperous Western Europe, intent on making itself into a comfortable middle class, at peace. The student protests of 1968 seemed an innocent, almost frivolous, affair, but small terrorist groups in Germany and Italy spoke to something darker and more dangerous, seeming to threaten the bourgeois order that had so successfully reestablished itself in postwar continental Europe.

We were also becoming aware of the brutal toll that the arms race was taking on the living standards of Soviet citizens. Friends who had visited the USSR as students or as journalists painted a very different picture from the official one. Soviet rulers and Western official spokesmen seemed to have a convenient common interest in pumping up their accounts of a formidable Soviet war machine; on both sides, military budgets depended on it. The Soviets had to persuade a skeptical public that even if their civilian economy did not work, they were at least masters of military performance, able to send a man to the moon or hold their own in combat with the United States. The United States, and Western governments generally, seem to have been guilty of allowing tales of Soviet prowess to remain unchallenged so as to justify their own defense budgets.

During the Cold War years governments lied a lot—about missiles, spies, economics, human rights, each other's actions. We grew up fearing war but also suspecting governments' claims. Whose side you were on seemed to matter more than what you did. Claims about allies' economic prowess were mostly unqualified by concerns about poverty and human rights violations. President Mobutu Sese Seko in Zaire and other long-running African dictators were praised as patriots and reformers while their corruption and government failure were overlooked.

Coming of age in this era left me with a sense of a governmental order that was artificially propped up by the Cold War's threat of conflict. When the Cold War finally came to an end, sure enough the pieces came tumbling down. The state everywhere suddenly seemed not all it was cracked up to be.

CHAPTER TWO

UNITED NATIONS DREAMS

W hat balanced system of international economic cooperation would fill the space left by the end of colonialism? In this new world, how were trading links to be governed and economic relations between countries to be fairly managed? I wish I could say those questions were racing through my head when I left graduate school in Michigan to take a job at the United Nations, but in truth I was just excited to be moving to New York.

It was January 1977, and the Cold War still had twelve long years to run. I had hoped the UN would boldly step in where countries hidebound by the U.S.-Soviet standoff could not, but the same super-power standoff froze it too. Hopes that it might launch a new era of collaborative endeavor to fight poverty remained just that, hopes. The UN had settled into its own long winter.

At that time the United Nations was still digesting one of its more significant decisions. On May 1, 1974, the General Assembly had adopted a Declaration on the Establishment of a New International Economic Order (NIEO). The NIEO was the culmination of years of debate following the dramatic period of decolonization in the 1960s. It was intended as a step toward establishing a whole new sys-tem of international economic relations, one that would reserve a fairer share of the pie for the newly independent states of the global South. In less than a decade, membership in the UN had more than tripled from its forty-eight founders. The new majority sought to shift the debate in the General Assembly from concerns of northern security to those of southern development.

First, the NIEO would do for other commodities what the 1973 Middle East Crisis had done for oil, that is, push prices up and keep them there to ensure that poor economies, dependent on a single commodity export like coffee or sugar, gained a decent assured income. Second, the NIEO attempted to regulate the behavior of multinational companies to prevent them from exploiting poor, weak developing countries. Which aspect most offended Western boardrooms and governments was not clear.

Arriving at the UN three years after it adopted the NIEO, I saw that the details of the original proposal had already been lost as each side sought to interpret it in its own way. Some saw the passage of the NIEO as the moment when the UN had finally gathered the courage of its convictions, whereas many others viewed it as a misguided power grab by developing countries in league with a few earnest Scandinavians. Still others railed that the NIEO was a conspiracy to put the world into the hands of some vast Gosplan-style Soviet state-planning system. In those days, almost every diplomatic act was seen as a plot by either the Americans or Soviets. Something proposed by developing countries for developing countries was, within this narrative, not plausible. There must be a hidden superpower agenda.

Far from changing the course of things, the NIEO proved to be more a footnote than a foot in the door. The wrongs of decolonization and the romance of international socialist solidarity were acrimoniously debated. But the NIEO soon collapsed under the weight of Western suspicions and its own pretensions. Too many considered it an antimarket, indeed anti-economic mugging to make the West disgorge part of its wealth as reparation to the countries of the South for the sins of colonization.

Behind the rhetoric, however, this botched agenda was a first response to a shifting global economy. First, it reflected the needs of new states for some kind of framework that would enable them to participate in the world economy. Second, the issue of predictable commodity price income was important to successful development strategy. In the late 1970s commodity and agricultural exports were worth more than 15 percent of world trade; today they are less than 10 percent.

When I first arrived at the UN, the NIEO was not yet dead, and I thought the General Assembly would shoehorn in some regulatory framework regardless of Western objections. The smell of gunpowder still lingered in the air, and the sound of tumbrels, being readied for the Western capitalists, hummed.

The controversy over the NIEO left me with the abiding impression that economic class warfare between the countries of South and North was here to stay. Under colonialism, metropolitan trading centers had dictated trade and investment terms to their dependent colonies; its end had created a vacuum in international economic relations; surely that vacuum must somehow be filled by new, more equitable arrangements.

To my surprise, however, this economic logic fell victim both to East-West hostilities and to an arid bureaucratic debate that closed off the whole subject to all but a dedicated few. The venues where the debate took place—the UN's Economic and Social Council (ECOSOC), the UN Center for Trade and Development (UNCTAD), and the UN Center for Transnational Corporations—were as inaccessible to the general public as their names might suggest.

My excitement at having arrived at the center of world power was quickly tempered as I sat through meetings where officials of different countries droned on. Even though they spoke in any one of the UN's five official languages, they always used a universal idiom that combined acronyms, pet ideologies, conviction, and obfuscation in a thick wooden monotone that transcended conventional language.

The keen graduate student exploring his palace of dreams risked disillusion. UN debates were not going to set the world on fire.

A further surprise were the spies, who were at least a relief from the debates. The UN building has plenty of pillars for spies to hide behind, but here they used less theatrical means. They did extensive phone-tapping; governments put spies into staff jobs at the UN as well as their own embassies. For countries whose diplomatic presence in Washington was limited because they were ideological enemies, New York was a spies' playground. Years later one of my neighbors claimed he had bugged the premises of what was then a Middle East diplomatic mission but was now my office when he was a young FBI agent. He wondered who was listening in now.

Back then, however, my entertainment was confined to encounters with Russians eager for new friends. Was their motive recruitment or simple loneliness? I found it hard to tell. Most of the Westerners studiously avoided the Russians. I struck up a cautious friendship with a Russian who, as far as I could tell, was anxious to protract his New York assignment as long as possible. He spoke fondly of his earlier spells in New York as the UN was setting up and seemed as proud of those memories as any of the Western "Mohicans," the original UN staff. He was also the victim of a career-long joke: his surname was Forshin, but sniggering colleagues insisted that the correct Russian pronunciation was "Fuckin." Friendships are hard to develop when colleagues dare not refer to you by name.

We know now that in those days the UN in New York was the center of some very serious spying by all sides, so the caution toward Mr. Forshin was perhaps merited. Still, it added to my impression of the UN's dysfunction and malaise.

Britain and America had provided many of the UN's officials at the start, and the instinct of the Westerners was to establish an ascendancy of Anglo-Saxon officials. Through a Michigan contact, I was drawn into this informal network. These dedicated people chose to believe the UN could not function without them. The UN certainly thought they could not write without them. Britain was heavily overrepresented, and for reasons of geographical balance, the lower ranks of the secretary-general's office were filled with people who could not write well in English, the main working language. The UN could not hire an extra paid native English speaker—the system already had too many of us. But once I was let in as an unpaid intern, I could later be hired for other duties.

That was UN personnel practice in a nutshell: a set of impractical rules, bypassed by people with contacts and a foot in the door, and another Briton enters. In fact, the secretary-general's office had a very good Brit within the allowed quota (he would go on to become a Tory MP), and a Dane, later killed with his wife in a UN plane crash, who had no trouble with English. Both turned out the letters, memos, and directives that were the staple outputs of a secretary-general. They did not need me, so I was installed at the other end of the corridor.

From this prime location, I quickly learned the workings of the UN, at that time just over three decades old. My chief, Bill Buffum, was a former American ambassador to Lebanon, one of the most dangerous jobs in the world for an American diplomat. For his reward, the U.S. State Department had assigned him to this plum secretariat position, in which he handled various political matters. The job was quite literally more sedentary than Beirut as he had to sit beside the president of the General Assembly on the podium when the secretary-general could not. As Buffum listened to delegates railing against American imperialism from the floor of the assembly, his lugubrious face seemed to droop even further. I'm not sure he found it much less stressful than dodging bombs and bullets in Lebanon.

Those who think George W. Bush and the Iraq War dragged the United States to a historic low in its relationship with the rest of the world should revisit the 1970s at the UN. They would get a salutary reminder that America has been there before. During the Vietnam War and in the aftermath of the 1973 coup against President Salvador Allende in Chile, which appeared to have had CIA and American business involvement, many in the UN considered the United States and its allies to be on the losing side of history.

Daniel Patrick Moynihan argued robustly that the UN was filled with America's enemies who needed to be reminded where their real interests lay. Interestingly, Moynihan (who was then U.S. ambassador to India and soon would become the U.S. ambassador to the UN) was inclined to fault the intellectual legacy of British socialism, not just Soviet troublemaking in the third world, for American isolation at the UN. He had the same difficulties with the British Fabian types that I had.

The UN building was noticeably threadbare. Despite the ambitious postwar architecture, a sense of dowdiness and tiredness pervaded both the structure and its people. To a young graduate student, this slump confirmed how far the UN had fallen from its initial ideals. Debates in the General Assembly were jaded and stereotypical, and officials only went through the motions of writing reports. States asked for the same report year after year as proof of their inalienable commitment to the rights of some group or other, but the reports were just for appearances' sake. Roosevelt and Churchill's dream had settled into a rut where process was king. In 2006 we were to count up these annual mandates and found more than ten thousand for which the General Assembly was still owed annual answers.

Still, a willing young listener could easily be cheered by the war stories of the organization's great early leaders. Just down the corridor from where I sat, the finest of their number presided. Brian Urquhart had been there quite literally from the start and was one of the last of the "Mohicans." A former British Army officer who had reputedly lost a couple of inches in a bad parachute landing, he had been assistant to the British diplomat Gladwyn Jebb, the acting UN secretary-general before the first permanent appointment was made. Scarred by war, he was part of that deeply idealistic group who saw the UN as the vital antidote to the proclivity of individual states to pick fights with one another, but he was impatient with those who expected too much of the organization. Urquhart had been on the inside of every UN crisis to date. During the Suez Crisis he had helped set up the peacekeeping force that separated the British, French, and Israelis from the Egyptians, and he had been called on to do many encores. When the UN's mission to the Congo was coming to a bitter recriminatory end, Urquhart was dispatched. And he had subsequently written the biography of Dag Hammarskjöld, the legendary secretary-general who had lost his life in a 1961 plane crash as he shuttled between sides in the Congolese civil war. To a young intern, Urquhart was a hero.

Another hero was Sir Robert Jackson, known as Jacko, who during the Second World War as a very young Australian naval commander had defended Malta. He had thereafter bounded into leadership of the first UN relief effort in Palestine, then had been involved in a number of controversial massive engineering and infrastructure development projects in West Africa and Indochina.

These men had pioneered a UN that pushed ambitiously into the traditional territory of governments; they were not afraid to grasp the nettles of security or development and go where angels, or at least bureaucrats, feared to tread. Whether they were injecting blue-helmeted peacekeepers between combatants in Gaza or the Golan Heights or building mega-dams, these men seemed giants: not just because of their outsize ambition in the field but because of their outsize ability to buck the New York bureaucracy.

For in New York, timidity stalked the corridors. Shirley Hazzard, the writer who had worked there as an interpreter, published ten years earlier a coruscating account of bureaucratic lassitude. In her 1967 short-story collection *People in Glass Houses* she described bored, demoralized officials longing for the weekend and, beyond that, for retirement. Gone already was the reforming spark that had ignited the UN's founders and first officials.

My first impression of the United Nations, then, was that the early luster had vanished and that bureaucrats ruled. Member states, through their constant politicking, held the organization in check. To some extent creative and ambitious innovators, their sense of mission hardened by the experience of combat in the Second World War, kept the place going. But my overall verdict had to be that the UN was laboring under its bureaucratic load. Urquhart and Jacko, working through their informal networks of young followers, were the exceptions, not the rule.

One of my early tasks was to help draft the terms of reference for an investigation into the suspicious death in a 1977 car crash of Uganda's Anglican leader, Archbishop Janani Luwum. This was new territory for the UN, reflecting the first stirrings of a modestly more assertive approach to human rights. After the drama of its establishment under Eleanor Roosevelt's leadership, the UN's human rights role had slumped into rolling out conventions and statutes that governments chose largely to ignore. The UN had not yet awakened to the thought that it might have a prosecutorial role—challenging governments on their human rights performance. During this era, it merely set standards that governments could follow if they chose.

Uganda's volatile and ruthless president Idi Amin (ruled 1971-79) was widely suspected of being behind Archbishop Luwum's murder. Hollywood portrayed him in the 2006 movie *The Last King of Scotland* as a terrifying and violent ruler, a grinning villain. Ugandans have told me he was even worse. On my 1972 African road trip my friend and I had hitched a ride with a nervous Ugandan-Asian businessman, who told us hair-raising stories of the pressures that he and his family were living under because of Amin. A little later the entire Asian community in Uganda fled the country—many to the U.K.

The West despised Amin for destroying Uganda's economy and for the ridiculous pretension reflected in his title (which he had awarded himself): "President for Life, Field Marshal, and Conqueror of the British Empire in Africa in General and Uganda in Particular." But some African quarters accorded him a certain grudging respect for standing up to the British and the Asians, whose dominant role in the economy seemed to exclude Africans from their rightful heritage. Robert Mugabe in Zimbabwe was to win some of the same status many years later. But both dictators destroyed their nation's economy, threw millions into poverty, and replaced democracy with police states.

President Jimmy Carter and his UN ambassador Andrew Young, an African American, pushed hard for a human rights investigation into the archbishop's death. Others stuck to the more usual circumspection; a *New York Times* headline just after the car crash read: "Black Africa is expected to remain largely silent on rights in Uganda." Africans saw the investigation as undue interference in Uganda's national sovereignty, a line the UN was not supposed to cross, while Western public opinion was outraged that a loutish dictator could get away with so brazen an assassination of a church critic, a man of peace.

As the secretary-general's staff picked its way through this minefield, I saw that progress at the UN depended on the individual officials involved. The UN was still new enough that an energetic official could set precedents. Those who dared could quite literally lead the UN into new areas; meanwhile those who put caution first and went with the flow would do no harm to their careers.

In the Luwum case, the UN had reason to be timid: Africa would be incensed by an investigation into one of its own, whatever Amin's shortcomings, however horrible the killing. But Carter, the first American president to appoint an assistant secretary of state for human rights, was ready to champion an investigation. The UN had to show some courage and expose the mass murderer that Amin had become, reigning through terror in a Uganda now semi-closed to the world.

Seeking precedents, I enthusiastically sought from the UN archives long-hidden files describing the UN's investigation into the assassination of its envoy Count Folke Bernadotte in the Middle East in 1948 by a Jewish terrorist group. The files were not to be found. A registrar suggested they had been checked out to a senior British official years earlier. Those secrets, it seemed, were not to be shared.

The investigation was ordered, and senior secretariat officials who sensed the possibility and horror of the moment showed some interest. But it turned out to be an empty gesture. A Somali UN political officer and his colleague were dispatched—and Idi Amin himself picked them up in an open Land Rover and took them on, by all accounts, a hair-raising ride to the accident scene. Their report arrived at no significant conclusions. The cause of Luwum's death remained undetermined. Peace was kept among governments, but the people of Uganda would have to wait for justice. The cautious UN found the case simply too hot a potato and for all intents and purposes dropped it.

One of my jobs for Buffum was to maintain daily contact with the Human Rights Center in Geneva. The center was headed by a frustrated mid-level official, a Dutchman named Theo van Boven who was well known in international human rights circles but, lacking rank, had little clout inside the United Nations. That was the way governments wanted it, and Buffum's thankless task was to make sure that no outbreaks of human rights activism disrupted their comfort.

Thereafter human rights languished at the UN. In 1993 I went to Geneva to lobby the organization to do more to address the terrible human rights crisis in Bosnia. My friend Aryeh Neier accompanied me. Neier in one way or another had had a hand in founding much of America's nongovernmental human rights capacity. He had worked at the American Civil Liberties Union and then founded Helsinki Watch and Human Rights Watch. Now he was president of George Soros's Open Society Institute. As we drove into town, I noticed he was showing a keen interest in Geneva, the UN's human rights capital. To my surprise, he said he had never felt it worth visiting before. From his perspective, nothing interesting in the human rights area happened at the UN.

Human rights were part of the flawed design of the UN's founders, who in the absence of governments' agreement left the matter to the energies of individual officials. The Americans had wished to establish a strong Human Rights Declaration to guide behavior between states and those they governed; that drive was much imbued by America's own experience of freedoms protected under the law, of citizens' rights defended against the risk of an overbearing state. In this vaulting American ambition lay also the flaw. Americans had fled from Europe and beyond in search of freedom and then fought Britain to win their independence and secure those freedoms. Much of the world for which Eleanor Roosevelt, as head of the American delegation, sought the same privileges still lived under the heel of authoritarian rule. Such governments had no interest in this agenda; nor for quite a while did their people. In the 1970s Russians, for example, were often thought to be more interested in jeans and the Beatles than in freedom.

Certainly Eleanor Roosevelt's words and those of the Universal Declaration of Human Rights, the result of her labors, excited oppressed peoples around the world. Then came the intergovernmental negotiations, held amid a mangle of Soviet-U.S. mutual suspicion in 1947. By the time the proposed enforcement mechanisms emerged, the new international human rights machinery was a shadow of what had been hoped for. Since then the officials who might have been guardians of its flame and rescued the original ambition have too often opted for the safe life. Far from being risk-takers, willing to use the UN platform to defend the human rights of individuals, they lost themselves in a world of platitudinous reporting. Perhaps during the Cold War they had little choice.

In the 1970s, to the extent a human rights "debate" took place at the UN, rather than a conspiracy of silence, it was an extension of the arguments that had brought about the NIEO. The world's great economic inequalities mattered more than political rights. After all, two human rights covenants supplemented the Declaration of Human Rights: one covered political and civil rights, but the other economic and social.

This latter set of rights neatly aligned the Soviets with much developing country opinion and allowed them to blunt any Western attacks on their own shortcomings in the areas of political freedom. The exchanges between Western and Eastern bloc delegates occurred in conference rooms in a dark basement. The show had become a well-established ritual, with rules and lines that barely changed from year to year. If the USSR supported Cuba, the West supported apartheid South Africa. If the USSR lacked free speech, the West lacked free housing. And so it went on in a ritualized block-and-tackle that both sides probably intended to prevent the UN from gaining any independent authority in the field of human rights. Neither Soviet dissidents nor nonunionized Western workers would have had any idea that their rights were being fought over in a windowless UN basement by "the Third Committee." The delegates spoke that impersonal and abstract language, in the acronymic monotones far removed from what someone brought up on the rhetoric of Gladstone or Lincoln might have hoped to hear in this prospective world senate.

At its creation the UN had looked much more promising. During the 1945-46 victors' honeymoon, it was possible to envisage a world co-policed by the United States and the Soviet Union, with help on the side from Britain, France, and China. During this small window an extraordinary bout of euphoria and optimism poured forth for a UN-centered future. The momentum of the Allies' victory over fascism seemed that it might carry through into an alliance for world peace, self-determination, and prosperity.

The moment was short-lived, but its giddy expectations might have prevailed if (and it is a mighty *if*) the United States and the Soviet Union had been able to preserve their alliance. Roosevelt had first used the term *United Nations* early in the war. He meant not today's gaggle of 192 members but rather the wartime alliance fighting not only to defeat Nazism but for a larger and more enduring cause. He had had staff quietly working on the concept throughout the war years.

At one level, the plan was a way for Roosevelt to build and sustain an American constituency for the war. It was neither a war of presidential choice nor one to be entered lightly. The country must be brought behind it and kept there. Roosevelt had no option but to build a case: much of America was resolutely set against involvement in the Old World's war. So he had to cast its causes in broader and more ambitious terms than just another European power struggle.

At another level, the plan represented his vision of a progressive world, remade more or less in America's liberal image, and a very practical hope that Stalin's Soviet Union might be steered into joining this project. The sweetener was the Yalta understanding (or betrayal, in the eyes of many) of a world divided into spheres of influence. Perhaps "Uncle Joe," as the American public had affectionately called Stalin during the war, could be turned into a reliable partner. Perhaps a U.S.-Soviet alliance could become the backbone of a stable world order that would resist being thrown off-track by Europe's ancient and volcanic disputes. The origin of the term *United Nations* matters: it was the wartime allies' name for their own alliance, not a mass membership organization where everybody enjoyed equal voting rights. They were going to combine to sort out problems and keep the postwar peace. It was to be a system of enlightened collaborative hegemony, not a universal debating club.

Roosevelt was not naïve. He recognized that a United Nations must be a practical structure that could contain and resolve deep differences of interest between the United States and the Soviet Union. The struggles would be titanic, but he hoped they could be kept to the conference table rather than unleashed on the battlefield.

Both countries shared a hope that their allies Britain and France would give up their colonial possessions, which increasingly seemed anachronistic and an impediment to stability. Both were also deeply suspicious of the devious European diplomatic machinations that had delivered the 1919 Treaty of Versailles, triggering a further war rather than laying the foundations of a stable peace. No American or Soviet leader wanted to allow the Europeans to weave an artful and dangerous web around postwar issues; both wanted to avoid old Europe's cynical re-entrapment. The United Nations could be the platform for escaping it.

Held during the victory lap, the San Francisco conference establishing the United Nations produced ambitious hopes and designs. The new organization would be nothing like the League of Nations, which had stood futilely on the sidelines as the world descended into war in 1939. It would have authority and enforcement powers. Its principally American designers stage-managed its launch in San Francisco with a novel eye to presentation and public relations. The charter, once concluded and signed, was flown back to the East Coast with a parachute attached, so precious was the document considered. It was the Beijing Olympics of its day, intended to showcase both America and America's hopes for the world.

In his State of the Union address in 1941, Roosevelt had first spoken of four freedoms—of speech and expression, of religion, from want, and from fear; now the promise of implementing them and of removing the scourge of war resonated with an exhausted world that was ripe for this message of hope. The initial reception to the UN in America and in much of the world was euphoric.

Indeed, the words endure. In 2005, when Kofi Annan called for a major reform of the UN to meet the world's new challenges, we borrowed the charter's words for the report's title: "In Larger Freedom." The full quote from the charter reads:

> We the peoples of the United Nations, determined to save succeeding generations from the scourge of war, which twice in our lifetime has brought untold sorrow to mankind, and to reaffirm faith in fundamental human rights, in the dignity and worth of the human person, in the equal rights of men and women and of nations large and small, and to establish conditions under which justice and respect for the obligations arising from treaties and other sources of international law can be maintained, and to promote social progress and better standards of life in larger freedom.[1]

The nascent world body enjoyed great bipartisan support in the United States. In 1940 a Republican internationalist, Wendell Willkie, had won his party's presidential nomination; after he lost the election, he became an ally of Roosevelt in campaigning for the UN, arguing for such international cooperation in his 1943 book *One World*. The book, the result of a tour of the war fronts made at the request of the president, was a best seller, topping the *New York Times* list for seventeen weeks. Two million copies were printed, and it was serialized in more than a hundred newspapers. Reading it now, one is struck again by Willkie's grounded vision. The UN was not a pipe dream; it was the best shot by the ablest politicians of the day to create a flexible and durable system for managing world affairs. They recognized that there would be different ideologies and different interests, but they imagined competition could be managed by diplomatic means rather than by war. "Jaw, jaw not war, war," as Winston Churchill famously asserted.

In 1944 the Republican candidate Thomas Dewey refused to support the creation of a successor to the League of Nations, which led to a loss of key newspaper endorsements and public support for his presidential bid. The international engagement tide was running strong.

But it was short-lived. Strobe Talbott, a former U.S. deputy secretary of state and now historian of multilateralism, points out that already in March 1946, three years after Willkie's book, the Federation of American Scientists published a cautionary retort with the title *One World or None*. Their concern was the new nuclear dimension. The honeymoon was over. U.S.-Soviet relations were plunging. The Allies, original bearers of the name *United Nations*, were united no more.

Its creation during the honeymoon gave the UN an oddly contorted design and setup. Some big ideas got through in that short period; others did not. But those that did fell foul of the subsequent Cold War confrontations. Essentially, it left the UN a confusion of ambitious concepts, broken hopes, and limited follow-through.

Still enthusiasts, through thick and thin, have held on to the 1945 charter for fear that, if the world let go, there might not be another moment when, however briefly, big powers put aside their short-term interests and dared to dream and plan a better way of running the world. The question now is whether, after more than sixty years of low-intensity conflict among delegates in conference rooms and corridors, the model has been so degraded that it cannot be recovered, or if a foundation remains on which a more effective UN can be rebuilt.

At the organization's halfway point thirty years ago, when I joined as an intern, the question was as relevant as it is today, except that the level of Cold War confrontation and postcolonial recrimination made the likelihood of improvement even harder. And certainly one could imagine little political basis on which countries might come together. Back then, I thought the UN's leaders had no choice but to do the best with what they had. Even thirty years later, when we sought to implement Kofi Annan's reforms, we were at pains to find ways to do so without opening up the Charter to revisions, fearful that any such review would end up weakening it. In 2005 no Roosevelts or Trumans, and indeed precious few statesmen, were around to defend the UN.

During the reform debate in 2005 the Russian delegation called for a revival of something called the Military Staff Committee. Called for under the charter's Article 47, the committee had not met since 1948—I had had no idea the provision even existed. It presupposed, according to an essential Rooseveltian concept, that the wartime allies would be the UN's peacekeepers, furnishing troops to keep order in the postwar world. They would seek local support as appropriate but not at the expense of the ultimate big stick. Any miscreant who broke the peace would provoke the full wrath of the war's victors. In fact, today India, Pakistan, Bangladesh, Nigeria, and Jordan are the biggest troop providers. The former allies have disengaged as significant troop contributors and have become largely financial contributors; they are increasingly unwilling to put their own troops in harm's way. Their replacements are often savvy peacekeepers. But imagine how different the UN's peacekeeping record might have been if it had been able to deploy the world's best-equipped troops backed by the full political force of the United States and its fellow permanent members of the Security Council.

Cold War circumstances forced UN peacekeeping in a very different direction. Indeed, the UN did no peacekeeping at all until the Korean War, when the Security Council approved a U.S. force under a UN flag at a brief moment when the Soviets were boycotting the institution. Not till the 1956 Suez crisis did the UN, through Brian Urquhart's ingenuity, stumble into what has become the long-term peacekeeping model: begging and borrowing troops from wherever they could be found to serve under UN command. This approach has worked as a light way to keep apart warring, but willing, parties that needed a third party on the spot to prevent disputes flaring up. But UN peacekeeping has lacked the equipment, will, and means to stop real troublemakers.

Currently eighteen UN peacekeeping and observer operations are under way, with more than one hundred thousand borrowed troops. That makes the UN the second-biggest deployer of troops in the world after the United States—way ahead of NATO, the African Union, Britain, Russia, or China. But it is still an underfinanced, undermanaged affair.

How can it be fixed to deliver something closer to what the charter envisaged? By the 1970s, peacekeeping was not only weak but also distrusted. In retrospect the first success, Suez, looked like beginner's luck. In the UN peacekeeping mission in the Congo, divisions in the Security Council had destroyed Dag Hammarskjöld politically before a plane crash while there took his life.

When I arrived at the UN in 1977, Lebanon's civil war was under way, and it was not UN peacekeepers that moved in to keep the peace. As I sat down for work, someone shoveled the Lebanon file onto my desk. Bill Buffum, as a former American ambassador to Lebanon, had been handed the task of coordinating the UN's response. I had spent a summer there before the war erupted and was deeply curious why this prosperous little Switzerland-like country had blown up in the way it had. I remembered cheerful evenings in a British-style pub, the Toby Jug, with cosmopolitan, Western-minded young Lebanese. My encounters with Syrian students in Aleppo, over chess and coffee, had been altogether darker. The latter, fearful and distrustful of the government, were whispering tales of massive human rights violations. Syria seemed much riper for ferment.

Maybe the beer-drinking had clouded my judgment: I did not meet enough Muslim Lebanese, who tended not to frequent the Toby Jug but whose aggrieved sense of disenfranchisement would trigger what was to happen. I had gone to the Bekaa Valley, later the home of Shi'a terrorism in Lebanon, but all I saw was a French flautist, Jean-Pierre Rampal, play classical music amid the ruins of the Baalbek temple for an audience of cosmopolitan Beiruti concertgoers. Unknown to me, small Shi'a communities in the valley were seething at the Christian dominance of Lebanese life. When the war erupted, it put an end to the Baalbek festival for many years.

In 1977, military power in Lebanon rested in the hands of its ambitious expansionary neighbor Syria, which saw its role more as occupier than as keeper of the peace. The UN struggled to gain some political purchase on the situation. The conflict had already cost something like forty thousand lives; we tried to deliver humanitarian assistance to the victims fairly across divided communities and neighborhoods. But we did not succeed, and the war in Lebanon was to descend through many more phases. A catastrophic deployment of American and French troops outside a UN mandate in 1983 led to 241 American and 58 French soldiers being killed when their barracks were blown up. The UN failed to get on top of the situation, sowing the seeds of later failures in Bosnia, Rwanda, and Somalia. The UN lacked the clout and the means to direct events toward peace. As a young intern, I saw the organization's impotence very clearly.

As on many other occasions, the UN effort in Lebanon was a cobbled-together affair. A long-serving official of the United Nations Development Program (UNDP) directed an overworked humanitarian operation there; a political brief was quickly added to it. As usual, the UN had neither the budget nor the will to do the job properly. We could not dispatch a real team of Middle East political operatives to take on the job. It was peace on the cheap, which meant no peace. The UN troops were situated uncomfortably between the warring Lebanese factions and thirty thousand Syrian troops. The Syrians quickly moved from liberators to oppressors.

At the humanitarian level, though, the UN seemed to be doing good things. Representatives of the UN Children's Fund (UNICEF), the UNDP, and the Office of the High Commissioner for Refugees (UNHCR), gave us accounts of field adventures they'd had and food and water they'd distributed and health services they'd provided—stories of lives they'd saved. Sitting at the side of the room taking notes, I longed to be in the field rather than in New York. Managing the political side of things in New York, I was quickly concluding, was mostly a dull, thankless business.

Late in the morning I'd often pick up the phone and take a call from one of our people in Beirut, hearing what sounded like shelling in the background. The caller would usually be seeking political advice on how to deal with one faction or another. I'd race off in search of the office director, who handled these day-to-day matters. As it was lunchtime in New York, I went to the Delegates' Lounge to find the director, who survived on a liquid diet. He'd come to the phone and give advice that was composed and seemingly coherent. But it hewed close to the prevailing UN operating principle: do as little as possible. That wasn't easy in the midst of a civil war, but during the Cold War caution was the modus operandi. Taking action would inevitably upset somebody.

The UN, I saw, had been crushed by competing government demands; it lived permanently under the shadow of Security Council vetoes; it was run by civil servants, far from the real lives of real people in the field; and it was kept on a financial shoestring. Process reigned.

One day when I was having dinner in Greenwich Village, the power went out and stayed out all over New York for several days. I fumbled my way home, then showed up the next morning at the UN building. On the ground floor my harassed colleagues were stymied: the overnight code cables and papers were up in the secretary-general's office, but the elevator was still out. As the youngest member of the thirty-eighth-floor team, I volunteered to walk upstairs to get them.

Even by that day's standards, the UN communication capacity was primitive. The telephone switchboard on my floor looked as though it had come off a 1930s film set. I would not see its like until the 1990s, when I was advising an Eastern European telephone company on privatization. On a normal day the young switchboard operators would shout down the line to presidents and foreign ministers to ensure that they had made contact before triumphantly plugging in the secretary-general. The mad machine had wires and plugs going in all directions, much like the UN I was getting to know. A chaotic, poorly constructed place that was occasionally brought to a successful outcome by the ingenuity and enterprise of a few dedicated staff—like the young telephone operators.

"If you want anything to be read in this house," Jacko had told his young admirers, "stamp it confidential." The cable operation, like so much else at the UN, seemed to have been designed for the grand ambitions of San Francisco, in the expectation that busy, talented men and women would pore through rich analyses from the battlefronts and design ambitious plans to end wars and build the peace. The cable messages were coded at the point of dispatch and then decoded at the other end. But surely those codes posed little challenge to any intelligence service set on reading them. Astonishingly, that tradition continues even today, in our era of easily available electronic e-mail security systems.

The UN was headed, it seemed to me, toward a League of Nations grave. Trapped in Cold War politics and saddled with a cautious, demoralized bureaucracy, it could rarely rise to occasions. Kurt Waldheim had been chosen secretary-general in 1972 and would later be reelected because he epitomized the governments' caution and determination that the UN rock no boats, even when lives and justice were at stake. Younger UN idealists like me feared palpably that strong leadership had died with Dag Hammarskjöld, the simple Swedish tax collector and amateur poet who had been plucked from obscurity in 1953 and put in front of the world. A man of conscience in an age of caution, he symbolized the independence and vision that we UN watchers yearned for. Waldheim would be found, after his retirement in 1981, to have hidden an association in his earlier life with the Nazis.

If Hammarskjöld's flame was still alive, it burned far from head-quarters. In politics, security, and human rights, the UN of the 1970s was performing way below what its founders had hoped for, but in development and humanitarian assistance it was holding its own. The reason, I came to learn, was that that staff kept a physical distance from the intergovernmental gridlock of New York. As long as UN officials were in the field, emulating my risk-taking UN heroes Jacko and Brian Urquhart, they could still find useful things to do.

Disappointed with my years at UN headquarters, I might have fallen into despair. But my view hardened that somehow the UN must be made to work better. Its failures did not mean it should be abandoned; rather, it had to be made to work.

CHAPTER THREE

GLIMPSES OF SUCCESS

In late 1977, instead of pursuing a field job at the UN, however, I went to the U.K. to become a journalist for *The Economist*. Two years later I was in the Midlands covering a particularly dismal local political story: two hard-left factions of the Labour Party were competing for control of city government; charges of gay sex and misused allowances were being hurled. Labour had begun its eighteen-year descent into unelectability, and Margaret Thatcher was ascendant.

In my hotel room I received an intriguing phone call from a personnel officer for UNHCR, who offered me a job helping the Boat People in Southeast Asia. Now that America's long war in the region was over and the local Communists had won, refugees were flooding out from Vietnam, Laos, and Cambodia by land and by sea. I jumped at the opportunity to help. In fact, I had lobbied my editors at *The Economist* to send me to cover the story, but to no avail. Now I could be part of the story and, better still, back in the UN, for which I still harbored hopes.

Some months later I found myself at the Thai-Cambodian border, facing a Khmer Rouge functionary who was dressed in the black-pajama uniforms of Pol Pot's men. I had sought this meeting. I'd made it clear who I was—my car's roof and sides were painted with

"UN" in big blue letters. A few yards away on the Cambodian side, my driver flew a UN flag on the hood of his car.

I was urging the Khmer Rouge officer to allow me to evacuate the wounded and the women and children from the battle zone inside Cambodia. During the Vietnam War, the Khmer Rouge had cooperated with the North Vietnamese in a common socialist front against the United States. But after America's military withdrawal from Vietnam, ancient rivalries over territory that had gone back through many dynasties on both sides undermined that unity. Starting in 1975 the Khmer Rouge under Pol Pot had ruled Cambodia through a genocidal reign of terror, but now in early 1979 their erstwhile allies, the Vietnamese, had pushed them from power. With their backs to the Thai border, the Khmer Rouge appeared to be staging their last stand. The death toll was likely to be appalling; hence my rendezvous. I was there on a humanitarian mission to offer food, medicine, shelter, and protection to noncombatants who wished to follow me back into Thailand.

Once the Khmer Rouge commissar was convinced of my bonafides, he whistled a signal. What I saw next astonished me: the field stood up. The overgrown greenery had camouflaged hundreds of women and children and some men, all of whom had silently squatted beneath the cover. At his sign they rose—a great silent, attentive organized regiment of people. What should have been a defeated demoralized rout was highly disciplined.

They had certainly never heard of the Geneva Conventions, let alone the international refugee covenants that governed humanitarian access to conflict zones or the rights of noncombatants. Nevertheless, as foot soldiers in the world's most ruthless military zone, they understood my role, wished me no harm, and appeared grateful though unmoved by my offer.

The most their leader would allow was that I could return the next day with a medical team, and we would be taken farther into Cambodia where there was a field hospital that had only a few local herbal medicines available to it. We could treat people and perhaps arrange the evacuation of some wounded civilians.

The next day we went in as agreed, and at the hospital we were able to give a little immediate relief, leaving some penicillin and pain-killers to supplement the berry and tree-bark remedies that were being administered to people with smashed limbs and heads. But properly stocking a military field hospital would breach international humanitarian law, so in order to treat them properly we insisted on bringing the worst cases back to Thailand. It was agreed we could return the next day with stretchers.

As we slipped back toward Thailand, I remember thinking that this negotiation was taking too much time. I wished we could have prevailed on them to do all this on the first day. After we had gone about two hundred yards, a massive bombardment began. Vietnam-ese troops had evidently waited for our departure before destroying the field hospital and the surrounding military unit. It had no Red Cross or other hospital symbol on it and was situated in a Khmer Rouge position. The Vietnamese were probably within their rights and had after all chosen to wait until the man from the UN and his medical team had gone. While the fighting between Cambodians and Vietnamese was bloody, genocidal, and ignored anybody's rights, they granted the humanitarian outsider a perverse respect and secu-rity. We were not part of their quarrel.

America had certainly taken a terrible knock in Vietnam: some 58,000 American lives were lost. While the peace agreement briefly saved some face, a renewed northern assault on Saigon came quickly. By 1975 Communists ruled in Vietnam, Laos, and Cambo-dia. The dominoes, as the American architects of the war had insisted on describing these countries, had fallen.

The Indochinese who had collaborated with the Americans were marked men. They and their families had little choice but to flee. The result was a massive exodus by boat and land. At its peak in 1978 and 1979, up to sixty thousand people a month were boarding boats from Vietnam in a desperate search for asylum. Nor was the displacement limited to the middle class: whole hill tribes from Laos joined the middle-class pro-America exodus. It was a straightforward humanitarian crisis.

These refugees were victims of a war that America had lost, and a lesser country might have preferred to save itself the memories and the embarrassment, rather than lead the world in assisting them. But decent Americans sought to pick up the pieces and do what was right. Empire, with its curious burdens of conflict and conscience, had fallen on America's reluctant shoulders. The United States, as well as France, Canada, and Australia, stepped forward with generous refugee-resettlement programs, by which they all reaped an injection of enterprise and industry. The prospect of resettlement also gave the so-called countries of first asylum—Cambodia's neighbors, including Thailand and Malaysia—an incentive to stop callously turning away boats and refugees.

Humid Bangkok, when I arrived, felt like the set of *The Deer Hunter*. Indeed, Maurice, the proprietor of a French restaurant next to my hotel, had been a prominent extra in that film. Bangkok was still a postwar town: its stripper district Patpong popularized pole-dancing years before it reached America; its crew-cut American military clientele propped up the bars; and foreign correspondents, in search of the next war, mingled with them.

In 1979, after the Vietnamese invasion overthrew the brutal Khmer Rouge regime, the first Cambodian survivors crossed the land border into Thailand. The Khmer Rouge, intent on reengineering the country in their own image, had perpetrated an indescribable genocide. It had convulsed a whole nation and cost upward of a million lives. Yet it had happened silently and invisibly because no Western reporters had been allowed in to cover it. In 1980 Sidney

Schanberg, a reporter for *The New York Times* who had been stationed in Phnom Penh, and his translator, Dith Pran, were able to tell the story of the "killing fields" to the world. Many journalist friends found it a terrible rebuke to discover that right next door to the world's most intensively covered and reported war, this cataclysm had gone unnoticed.

For all of us involved in humanitarian work, the Cambodian genocide taught an enduring lesson: our presence counts as much as the food and medicine we deliver. It became an axiom of the expanding UN humanitarian world that we had to be physically present in conflict zones. By bearing witness, we could head off some of the uglier human rights abuses. Just to the north of the location where Laotian and Cambodian refugees came over on Thailand's eastern border stood Burmese refugee encampments, from which the Thai authorities succeeded in keeping us away. Their plight similarly went largely unnoticed for many more years.

Western responsibility for the failed war and its bitter consequences led to a deep sense of collective guilt. Few of us aid workers had had any direct connection with the war; we were too young, though some of our American colleagues had elder brothers or even fathers who had served. But all felt a connection with this epic spasm of political violence and misjudgment that had harmed everyone it had touched: Vietnamese, Cambodian, Laotian, American, and others. My colleagues and I headed for the Thai border on a clean and simple humanitarian impulse. It was not complicated; we just had to help.

When I got to Thailand, I found Americans, wrestling with conscience and realpolitik. They both wanted to help victims of a situation that they acknowledged having helped create and that their government's departure had only made worse. They saw how they could use an independent agency like UNHCR to manage some of the fallout of empire. UNHCR was undergoing a dramatic transformation, as the United States responded to those fleeing assertive

Communist assaults from Indochina to Afghanistan. Only recently the U.S. annual contribution to UNHCR had been $400,000; it leaped at one point to more than half of the budget, as the budget went from $76 million in 1975 to $580 million at the end of the 1980s.[1]

UNHCR's origins lay in the business of reunifying and resettling European families after the Second World War. Its small staff of diplomats and lawyers essentially did casework, occupied with Europe's diminishing refugee population. Then in 1966 Prince Sadruddin Aga Khan became high commissioner. The State Department opposed his election; an internal memo admonished that he was likely to have "an Afro-Asiatic orientation" rather than caring for the traditional European caseload. Luckily, their fears were correct.

A member of the cosmopolitan ruling family of the Ismaili sect— South Asian Muslims who had spread across the world as traders and businessmen—Sadruddin was an effortlessly charismatic leader. In many ways unlike Jacko and Brian Urquhart, he was a natural aristocrat, who arrived at the same kind of leadership. He was willing to take risks and make big bets in the cause of a long-term vision. He rarely deviated from the strategic direction that he had set himself.

Sadruddin moved UNHCR away from Europe to focus on the megarefugee movements of Asia and Africa, placing different kinds of demands on the organization. The new locations were not equipped with the infrastructure or social services of a modern state. Nor were the host governments as able, or willing, to help as those of Western Europe had been. It was useless for lawyers to lobby governments to provide services to refugees that they did not even provide for their own people. Now the governments would rely on UNHCR to provide direct support. Lawyers and diplomats found themselves called on to run massive feeding operations and to determine the sites and construction of camps for hundreds of thousands of people. These staff, however, lacked the skills to carry out these tasks. And they weren't plentiful: until quite late in Prince Sadruddin's tenure only eight international professional staff were assigned to the whole of sub-Saharan Africa. Like so many of the first generation of the UN staff, some had served in their governments' colonial administrations.

In 1978, in the early stages of the Asian Boat People crisis, Sadruddin stepped down, but he had laid the groundwork. For a time in Thailand itself we had a British chief, whose passion was amateur dramatics. He was a decent, thoughtful man, but I wearily concluded that offstage he was stuck in one role: the English colonial administrator. His immediate chief, the UNHCR coordinator for Southeast Asia, was a brilliant, wily Pakistani, Zia Rizvi, who conspired to find "political" solutions to "humanitarian" problems. We had to persuade refugees to go home to their countries of origin, he would silkily whisper; the West would not support them forever. Neutrality bored him and, he believed, left refugees in indecisive limbo. He was widely distrusted inside the organization because he had been Sadruddin's chief of staff and was viewed as a scheming gatekeeper.

I frequently opposed Rizvi's solutions, which too often in my view merely shifted refugees back into the hellholes from which they had escaped. But I was utterly taken by his ability to think strategically about refugees and seek a solution for them that cleverly took account of the geopolitical context rather than rigidly, but often unrealistically, insisting on doing it by the book and claiming for refugees all the rights proscribed for them in the postwar-European-inspired refugee conventions. This was not the world where refugees and migrants seeking a better life were clearly separate. Mixed in with the flow of officials who had collaborated with the Americans were farmers and others who wanted to escape the grinding poverty of a failed communist system. Was it really right to demand a new life in America for them, too?

His subsequent career was a series of disappointments, as he offered clever but cynical solutions and bumped up against a ceiling of distrust within the UN's higher command. He cared for the UN as much as any—perhaps even putting the UN's interests before those we were trying to help—but the Western networks that still dominated the organization's administrative culture deemed him too slick and too political. Above all he exhibited little of the milk of human-kindness that was the stock-in-trade of humanitarianism.

In Southeast Asia, our source of local knowledge consisted of Americans who had come to the region because of the war or as part of the Peace Corps, and European volunteers who had previously done grassroots development work or taught in village schools. They understood from the bottom up what the war had done. But even this group did not know much about trucks and latrines and clean water. Dumping tens of thousands of people on an empty piece of land puts an immediate strain on basic life-support systems. Unless UNHCR had as a partner an efficient European state to take care of its refugees, we had little practical experience in getting things done ourselves.

The surrounding Asian nations were unable and unwilling to share the load. An uncontainable human flood of people were pressed up against the Thai border; but Thailand was reluctant to admit refugees into the country for fear they would become permanent fixtures and because of a concern that impoverished local Thais would resent government or international money spent on refugees and not on them. Undoubtedly such local jealousy did exist. The Thai government decided that if international public opinion was going to force them to admit refugees, then the international community would pay for them and take care of them. This would be a UN operation.

At an army base I met the Thai prime minister, General Kriangsak Chomanan, while he cooked a meal for the troops—it was the signature skill of this peacetime general who had been lured into politics. His battlefield skills were unproven, but his culinary expertise was legendary, and he gave me an exposition of Thai-Vietnamese relations as he stirred. I wondered whether I had been summoned to hear that or because he was curious to see the only other man in the country, or so it was claimed, with his own helicopter. Earlier in the day the Swedish pilot of our white UN helicopter had cheerfully nipped in ahead of the prime minister's, to seize a landing spot at a refugee camp. I had feared this might count as a unique insult and loss of face, but apparently not.

The prime minister explained that he feared that the Vietnamese might pursue the Khmer Rouge into Thailand. In order to avoid any direct clash between Vietnamese and Thai soldiers, he wanted a UN demilitarized zone. At the time Thailand appeared chaotic and corrupt, no match for the disciplined Vietnamese. A common joke suggested that it would take the Vietnamese only a day to get from the border to Bangkok, but then they would be stopped by the traffic. That point hinted at a commercial dynamism in Thailand that was at odds with the perception of the country as the next corrupt, failed domino likely to fall to Communism.

Kriangsak did not formally get his UN zone, but the humanitarian infrastructure of refugee camps, workers, and food convoys became the de facto neutral space. In late 1979, a handful of us built refugee camps to house hundreds of thousands of Cambodians. My colleagues and I found a local contractor, and we commandeered bulldozers and water trucks. Armed with the example of Brian Urquhart and Jacko, I had decided, "Nothing ventured, nothing gained." We would build camps with whatever means we had and usher in refugees until somebody made us stop. Over time a host of volunteers turned some fairly unpromising sites into refugee camps. Kriangsak had his buffer zone. Our presence would keep some kind of peace and deter atrocities. The international community had been absent from the Khmer Rouge's Cambodia, but at least we were there now on the border bearing witness and bringing succor.

The Thai authorities finally admitted the mass of Cambodians pushed up against the border.[2] And in the refugees came, by bus or by foot, gaunt but walking. Others were too sick to make it on their own. Malaria, hunger, and dysenterylike symptoms took a terrible toll. On one painful day I saw an emaciated newborn abandoned under a tree. I picked him up and got into my car, where we were driven to a clinic. A rather solitary only child, I had never held a baby before. He died on my lap—a moment I remembered as I held each of my four healthy children for the first time.

My Thai deputy Kasidis Rochanakorn had been a student activist who viewed his own government and expatriate do-gooders with equal skepticism. With barely concealed irritation, he put up with translating for me to Thai officials. However, we came to recognize that we shared a view of the world and of our own incongruous roles—inexperienced young men suddenly charged with the safety and welfare of hundreds of thousands of lives. A strong friendship quickly blossomed. Kasidis has gone on to be a leading light in UN humanitarian work.

Hundreds of relief workers turned our border camp into an international metropolis of sorts. Swaggering Italian doctors in tailored surgical fatigues sat down at noodle tables and sipped Singha beer beside unshaven T-shirted Americans and eager young Japanese volunteers. Aranyaprathet, the local town, became the humanitarian equivalent of a gold rush community. One Japanese aid worker was gunned down in the market square by local gangsters for his NGO's weekly payroll; he died in the back seat of my car as I rushed him to hospital.

At its peak, the operation covered hundreds of thousands of refugees, settled in camps inside Thailand or in border encampments under the control of various anti-Vietnamese Cambodian military commanders. The operational costs ran into the hundreds of millions of dollars. Modern humanitarian relief operations, which had begun with crises in Bangladesh and the secessionist Biafra region of Nigeria, were now fully up and running.

Through the early weeks of the Cambodian drama, the world press had excitedly followed us each day, trailing Rosalynn Carter as she brought her husband's U.S. presidential reelection campaign to the bewildered refugees on the Cambodian border or tracking our attempts to build camps in time for new waves of arrivals. Then suddenly the media moved on, first to Afghanistan (when the Russians invaded in 1980 and drove millions of refugees into Pakistan and Iran) and then to Central America and the Horn of Africa (where similar Soviet-American proxy wars were tearing up people's lives).

Relief workers were on the move too. As Zia Rizvi had correctly predicted, we left no solutions behind us. In Thailand the refugee camps would not be closed for many years. Almost ten years after I left Thailand, I took my wife Trish to Khao-I-Dang on our honeymoon. A rumor swept through the camp that I had come with a plan for finding them a permanent home. Only after many more years would slow resettlement in the United States for some and repatriation for others finally close this chapter.

In my case, I left Thailand to help write the emergency handbook for UNHCR on the wisdom of keeping the latrines away from the water supply and of measuring rations to make sure that people were not falling below nutritional minimums. There was a lot to learn, and I was understandably anxious to prevent future generations of young workers from repeating our mistakes. This was no business for gifted amateurs. The book, in a blue plastic cover to protect it from floods and war, is still something of a staple of disaster response. I am rather proud of it.

Later I went to Central America and the Horn of Africa. As I crisscrossed the world's trouble spots in the company of other footloose young humanitarians, my thoughts would sometimes go back to the UN of New York. It seemed a million miles away.

Refugee work thrived as a by-product of the Cold War. Operationally, the two superpowers stood aside and let the UN and their NGO partners address their refugee problems. It was an easy way to tidy up the human flotsam after their proxy wars were over. The other side's victims were automatically your friends and properly beneficiaries of your compassion. For each major refugee crisis, we had a sponsor, sometimes the Soviet Union but more usually the United States. But of course the motive for that support was not simply unalloyed compassion. It was politics.

The humanitarian momentum has never really been broken since. In general, relief workers do not stay in the work very long, as marriage and family responsibilities soon pull them back to a desk somewhere. But new cohorts always follow, as natural disasters, famine, and politics fuel fresh movements of victims. These UN offices and programs with their NGO partners have become the eyes, ears, and conscience of a troubled world.

O n a trip back to New York in 1980, I sought out Brian Urquhart to tell him what I had done in Thailand. He listened, intrigued but skeptical, as I spun out my simple theory that UN humanitarian activities could grow and succeed as long as they could be kept well away from the UN's political side. UN politics, I thought, was a dead end. The humanitarian work needed to be branded as separate and neutral, like the Red Cross. It should be governed by clear principles of humanitarian action and be designed to help civilians but not soldiers. It would provide assistance on both sides of a war zone, and its administrators would deal with the local leaders whatever their politics.

Twenty-five years later, as deputy secretary-general, I heard similar lectures from the then-head of humanitarian affairs at the UN, Jan Egeland. He and his colleagues needed humanitarian space to do their job, he argued. They and their NGO partners could not risk being mistaken for UN political operatives. The association jeopardized their personal safety and their mission, but above all it tied them back to a politicized, cautious, slow-moving bureaucracy in New York. They wanted their freedom.

The UN today raises and spends billions of dollars on humanitarian work. The World Food Program alone has a budget of almost $3 billion. UNHCR itself has actually declined in relative importance as refugees have become a smaller subset of overall humanitarian crises. More people than ever get displaced by war or natural disaster, but they either don't cross a border or don't suffer from the direct political persecution that would qualify them as refugees. But humanitarian activity turns the original purpose of the UN on its head, boosting relief operations without tackling the root political and economic causes of conflict. It is cleaning up after wars but not stopping them.

Nothing at the UN is as simple or straightforward as it looks. A quarter-century of growth of the UN's humanitarian work has taught me how complicated its motivation always is. An angry quarrel that broke out in Thailand back in 1980 between UN and U.S. embassy staff illustrates the point. At its peak, the United States' generous resettlement policy was bringing large numbers of Indochinese to that country. Some of my UN colleagues thought this was a seditious brain drain: attracting people to a better life in America depleted the skills and human capital of countries that needed these skills to rebuild after a devastating war. Would these strangers really even settle into this world of concrete high rises, highways, and fast food? asked some of my colleagues. Or were they just pawns in a U.S. effort to stifle Communist reconstruction of these nations? The United States was outraged that its motives and its generous provision of asylum were questioned in this way. Zia Rizvi and a brilliant ex-British volunteer in Laos, Martin Barber, were the chief protagonists of this argument against open-ended resettlement in the United States. Americans who had fought long and hard in Washington to win generous refugee quotas, as the means of discharging the moral debt they felt to all those who had sided with them in this bitter conflict, felt their efforts were being thrown back in their faces.

Rizvi and Barber were, in my view, wrong about America's intentions. Barber, I sometimes thought, had seen too closely the terrible military and human consequences of the indiscriminate American war in Laos to realize that the United States was seeking its own redemption—not still prosecuting the war by other means. Neither had spent time in the United States watching Americans in both government and NGOs struggling to make sense of their default role as modern empire and to reconcile it with a progressive, compassionate humanitarianism. The results may not always have been straightforward, but their motives were for the most part honorable. Nor should one ever underestimate the remarkable capacity of the United States to absorb fresh generations of refugees and immigrants or the ability of those newcomers to adapt and succeed.

But at a less specific level, Rizvi and Barber had a point: refugee operations could not just go on dealing with victims for as long as they were around, like some kind of global emergency service. The sheer size of modern displacement meant that we had to start finding other answers. People who were not offered Western resettlement places could not be left in camps for decades, as was starting to happen. We had to find ways to get people out of camps and into homes, either their old ones or new ones.

In July 2005, ten years after the massacre of Muslim Bosnians at Srebrenica, I stood in a Bosnian graveyard and on behalf of Kofi Annan sought to atone for the UN's failure to take sides and stop the killing. The graveyard was a natural amphitheater. Reaching high up the terraced hill in front of me were mounds of earth, and beside them rows of green child-sized coffins. Each had its small clutch of silent grieving relatives. Many had come back from abroad for the ceremony, having chosen to escape living daily with the terrible memories of ten years earlier. An American NGO that had begun its life trying to identify the remains of lost servicemen in Vietnam had painstakingly reassembled the scattered body parts of victims from mass graves, but there was not much left to fill even such small caskets. I was just one of a number of dignitaries whose words of regret echoed emptily on that hillside that day. We expressed regret and promised that it would never happen again, but our words were thrown back at us by the hills above us and by the numbed, uncomprehending faces of the grieving relatives watching us. We were men, mostly, in suits with excuses.

Back in Sarajevo, I sat late into the night in a hotel bar as Samantha Power, who won the Pulitzer Prize for her writing on modern genocide, explained to me again the UN betrayal and desertion of Srebrenica. She recounted the story of Dutch UN peacekeepers handing over their weapons to the besieging Bosnian Serb forces in return for a worthless promise that those in the town would be safe. The massacre began far away from international eyes while Power and other journalists holed up in Sarajevo desperately trying from a distance to confirm reports of the killings. UN officials seemed frozen by events, stuck in routines in New York and their Bosnian field headquarters. They took no news to be no news rather than a cover-up for genocide. By the time the alarm was rung, eight to ten thousand had died.

Many of us thought this lopsided UN, where we could bring food and medicine when given permission but would be locked out when a government wanted to massacre people, was just too much to bear. What good is providing Band-Aids of international relief if political conflict continues unabated? Yes, Bosnians in Sarajevo and Srebrenica needed food and water, but even more they needed the lifting of the violent siege of their cities. They needed a truce, not just bread.

Long before that sad Srebrenica hillside, I had come to see this need for a more muscular humanitarianism. During the Bosnia conflict, I had squatted in the back of a Hercules aircraft with Morton Abramowitz, both of us bursting out of flak jackets, with ill-fitting helmets perched on our heads. We must have both looked rather like the hapless presidential candidate Michael Dukakis peering out of a tank in a helmet. As we left Sarajevo under siege, we were plotting how we might turbo-charge traditional humanitarianism with an aggressive political advocacy intended to take on the causes of conflicts and thereby find solutions.

I had first met Abramowitz when I was on the Cambodian border—he was the U.S. ambassador to Thailand. He and his wife Sheppie were committed to the cause of refugees in a way that exceeded all bounds of usual diplomatic decorum. He had a rather unusual ambassadorial trait: he cared passionately and let you know it. Some in Washington, predictably, believed his furious interventions with the Thais on behalf of the unpopular refugees had compromised America's other bilateral interests. After Bangkok he spent a period in limbo before his career was rehabilitated. He was one of the operators I was getting to know who insisted on making a difference and were indifferent to just getting along.

In Thailand Mort and I had pleaded first for assistance and then for resettlement places abroad for the Vietnamese. In the aftermath a group of Americans who had watched us recognized we needed an advocacy arm. Their efforts led to the creation of a small Washington-based lobbying operation called Refugees International. For many years first I, and then my wife Trish, served as its vice-chairman. For most of this time Lionel Rosenblatt, who had been the refugee counselor in Abramowitz's embassy, functioned as its executive director. His wife Ann, a nurse, had gone to the Thai-Cambodian border even before me. The Rosenblatts had a habit of getting places first. Trish and I noticed how many of the people we admired in this work were husband-and-wife teams. Perhaps work that demanded that a person spend so much time away from home and that put so much strain on families required an especially understanding partner who was in the same line of work. Better still if home could move with you both.

Lionel, who had been the leading defender of the U.S. against Zia

Rizvi and Martin Barber, understood more viscerally than perhaps anyone the responsibility the United States bore toward those who had worked with the Americans in Indochina. When Saigon was on the verge of falling, he convened in the State Department cafeteria a group who had all worked in Vietnam; several of them, led by Lionel, dashed off leave requests to their supervisors and went to Vietnam on an unauthorized freelance basis to get their former staff out. Based on that State Department cafeteria model, whenever a new crisis breaks, young Refugees International advocates would quickly arrive, eyes and ears feeding back breathless firsthand reports to Congress and the media.

But Mort and I, on board the Hercules, had something bigger in mind. We wanted to stitch together advocacy of the kind that Lionel had again done brilliantly for Bosnia, but also undertake a more sustained promotion of solutions through the media and through lobbying governments and legislatures. We needed to back this effort with a credible analysis of situations, their causes, and possible solutions so that governments could not brush us off as well-intentioned amateurs, guilty of raising problems but offering no solutions.

We had seen too much of the phenomenon of good men doing nothing in the face of evil. It is no good leaving people in camps or sending them somewhere where they will not fit in. We did not want to empty Sarajevo into camps; we wanted to find a way for Muslims to live in peace with their neighbors. We had to put the politics—or at least solutions and persistence in the face of government pushback—back into humanitarianism. Caring was not enough; we had to matter where it counted: at the political level. And we had to make it harder for regimes to slam the door on us.

Bosnia had given Mort and me a working example of what our International Crisis Group (ICG) might look like. I got a Saturday-morning phone call from George Soros, already the most political of philanthropists for his work seeding freedom in Eastern Europe before 1989. Having seen the media coverage of the siege, he wanted to help. He wanted my advice on which humanitarian organization should receive his check for Sarajevo relief.

I explained the evolution in my own thinking, from simply wanting to help and keeping the politics out, to recognizing that to be effective, one had to do more than provide relief. He immediately understood and quickly agreed that his money should not just target critical relief needs but should be put through the UN with the goal of getting the UN more politically engaged. He would also fund a separate international advocacy effort aimed at stopping the slaughter by getting the international community to step up to its responsibilities. The obstacles were clear: the Clinton administration felt that Europe, rather than the United States, should be taking the lead in any intervention to lift the siege of Sarajevo. After Somalia, where American UN troops had been humiliated in 1993, the United States had little taste for intervention. The Europeans were divided and weakened by their different historical associations with Serbs, Croatians, and Bosnian-Muslims. The Russians wanted no creeping eastward expansion of Western and NATO influence via intervention in Bosnia.

This was going to take some exceptional lobbying. We assembled quite a cast of characters. Soros himself played a lead role, as did Sadruddin Aga Khan, the former UN high commissioner for refugees in Europe. In the United States, Paul Wolfowitz (later a neoconservative architect of the Iraq War) was a leading agitator for action, as was Richard Holbrooke (who later would go back into the Clinton administration as its Balkan negotiator and browbeat the parties into peace at Dayton). Initially we confronted foot-dragging and excuses in Washington, New York, and across Europe.

To protest weakness in the face of violence, and to lobby the United States and Europe to engage, we deployed the tools of mass marketing as well as old-fashioned access. We took out advertisements in the media, distributed talking points, and built networks of academics, out-of-office policymakers, and citizens.

Nor did we leave the relief operation alone. With the help of

Refugees International (RI) and the International Rescue Committee (IRC), we placed Fred Cuny into Sarajevo. A six-foot-three Texan who flew his own Cessna plane and was never, it was claimed, without his boots, Cuny fondly told tall stories but also educated generations of young relief workers around campfires across the world. As my adviser on the Thai-Cambodian border, he and a colleague had taught me most of what I knew about water pressure and other key points of relief logistics.

Dismayed by the slow, limited relief operation in Sarajevo, Cuny smuggled a whole water system into the city and set it up in a road tunnel in the hills above the town. He flamboyantly challenged the official relief agencies to match his ingenuity and flair while chiding the United States to get involved. As a visiting American general ruefully noted, Fred flew a Texan, not an American, flag outside his Sarajevo home—a pointed reminder that the United States had no official presence in the town. Shortly after Sarajevo, he was to be murdered in mysterious circumstances in Chechnya on another such mission for George Soros. When Lionel Rosenblatt went in search of him, he found open by his bedside a John le Carré novel about spies and relief workers, in a modern version of Central Asia's Great Game for influence among competing powers. Fiction imitated life.

From those beginnings the ICG has grown into a real force as a kind of unofficial alternative State Department or Foreign Office for the world's victims. Still chiding governments and UN agencies for their shortcomings, it now maintains a considerable international staff and is a forceful analyst of most of the world's crises. Its last president, Gareth Evans, was formerly Australia's foreign minister and most famously negotiated the settlement to the Cambodian War. The ICG gave this energetic, peripatetic man a global canvas. Mort Abramowitz and George Soros remain on his board, joined by me when I am out of government. Its new head is Louise Arbour, a former UN high commissioner for human rights who helped rescue human rights at the UN from the doldrums described earlier. At the official level, spurred on by Evans, there was after Yugoslavia and Rwanda a move to end the optional character of humanitarian intervention. In the last years of the twentieth century, the idea that governments could still hide behind claims of national sovereignty even when they were bombing or murdering their citizens on a wide scale, and that neighboring countries and the Security Council could ignore these crises out of convenience, seemed increasingly implausible. Surely, after Cambodia, Yugoslavia, and Rwanda, let alone lesser-noticed killing fields in Africa, we were better than that.

Kofi Annan, as the new UN secretary-general in 1997, talked of a responsibility to intervene. The world could no longer ignore out of deference to national sovereignty, he argued, mass crimes committed against peoples by their own governments. In some situations this inviolate principle of the UN charter should be overridden. For some years dismayed ambassadors disparaged such presumption. But their criticism has slowly subsided as Canada, France, Japan, and several others nudged the idea forward. In 2005, toward the end of Annan's term of office, the General Assembly unanimously adopted the content of the Responsibility to Protect doctrine. It was a tentative victory, grudgingly acknowledging that in extreme circumstances, if states abused their citizens on a mass and systematic basis, outside intervention might be necessary, but it was short on detail. It contained no agreement on when and how such a doctrine might be triggered. But at least wheels were turning. Humanitarian intervention, it seemed, was gaining political traction.

The Responsibility to Protect was a high point for principled humanitarian intervention at the UN, but the early years of this new century also carried a different and discordant message. The Iraq War and the related War on Terror prosecuted by the Bush administration cut across humanitarian neutrality everywhere. The shrill refrain to choose sides drove UN humanitarian operations into a deadly, unsought embrace with Western security interests. Suddenly the UN was a target in Baghdad and Algiers. The blue flag, like the Red Cross symbol, was no longer above conflict but rather became a soft target because it carried less protective security than its alleged Western sponsors. Humanitarian workers, after all, cannot do their job from inside a tank or a fortified building.

But as UN officials became targets, inevitably security had to increase, and their freedom to reach those they are there to help has decreased. Parts of southern Afghanistan and of the Darfur region of Sudan have become inaccessible because they are too dangerous. When the Taliban last sought power in Afghanistan, UN staff routinely discussed operational matters with them, as I had done with the Khmer Rouge. Now, whether it is the Taliban in Afghanistan or Hamas in Palestine, if the United States and its allies consider the group a terrorist organization, even humanitarian negotiation becomes impossible. When in 2006 Kofi Annan was considering allowing middle-level UN officials to have contact with Hamas to discuss humanitarian issues, I was warned the individuals concerned might lose their American visas. No wonder groups like Hamas have come to see the United Nations as an arm of their Western enemies.

Worse still, deteriorating international relations after Iraq brought further challenge to Responsibility to Protect. For some, Iraq demonstrated that the whole enterprise of intervention was riddled with double standards. The acceptance of the doctrine in 2005, in very general terms with little of the specific detail around which international case law could be built up, began to look like a high-water mark.

The limits of the concept were clearest in Darfur. Sudan's central government had armed Janjaweed militias, nomadic herders, and encouraged them to burn and sack the villages of the settled farmer-cultivators there because the latter were thought to provide sanctuary for antigovernment rebels. Sudan's army was a sorry mess, lacking the mobility or training to deal with a rural insurgency, so the country's president Omar al-Bashir relied on these rural allies, who had been fighting with their farmer neighbors for years. In a region where environmental deterioration had already created intense competition for usable land, all-out conflict was soon under way, with massive human displacement.

The international community had been distracted by its preoccupation with bringing to a negotiated end Sudan's other civil war between north and south. But in 2003 it noticed what was happening but could not agree on what should be done. It was an egregiously unambiguous example of government-sponsored violence against its own people. The U.S. secretary of state Colin Powell called it genocide. President George W. Bush and Prime Minister Tony Blair threatened retribution. Others were more cautious. Sudan's African neighbors were not willing to accept the precedent of intervention in its messy internal affairs. The Chinese had become Sudan's major oil exporter and so had their own interests to protect. Others perhaps saw similar opportunities of trading their vote for oil. Still others, including some of us in the United Nations, swallowed hard at the scale of the UN military operation that would be needed to control Darfur and doubted that, for all their brave words, the United States and Britain would, after Iraq, do it themselves. Throughout the Darfur crisis, as a UN official and then as British minister, I have struggled to manage some diplomatic containment of Sudanese repression with the dubious backing of an underresourced peacekeeping operation and lots of bluster by Western leaders.

Long years of growing international outrage initially did little to stop the killing. International Criminal Court indictments were brought against Sudan's leadership. First an African and then a small UN and African joint peacekeeping force emerged. But the killing and displacement continued, albeit at much reduced levels. The political will to stop them seems absent. The competitive two-bloc world that was willing to see victims of its wars helped is gone today, and the system underpinning such norms has broken down. In a world of rapidly devolving power, prickly local players jealous of their sovereignty and authority often command the action. The United Nations is in truth less Western than it has ever been; the Jackos and Urquharts have long since been replaced by a much more fully multinational staff, but after Iraq, it is viewed as more Western than ever. As a consequence humanitarian neutrality has come crashing down.

In Darfur international pressure and broader internal political issues have eventually led the government and rebels alike to ease up, producing an unstable peace. It was achieved when a number of us tried to break away from the finger-wagging diplomacy of Bush and Blair and engage the Sudanese in a fuller political dialogue. But there was no bold assertion of the Responsibility to Protect. We tiptoed into Darfur, rather than march in behind the new doctrine, and the results remain precarious.

CHAPTER FOUR

GREAT EXPECTATIONS

The Darfur crisis began as a failure of politics. The regime's support came from the army and urban Islamic groups, and the rural farmers and herdsmen hundreds of miles from the capital had no adequate political mechanisms to air or redress their grievances. The desert was creeping in on both farmers and herders even as their numbers were growing sharply, forcing groups into confrontation with each other over land and water.

What had come to worry me about humanitarianism was that it dealt with consequences, not causes. In the 1980s I already understood that that was not good enough. Long before Darfur I had concluded that politics did not start after the crisis; it should start before. People had to be helped to find peaceful ways to solve their disputes. And the best form of peaceful conflict resolution seemed to be democracy. In Latin America, Asia, and Africa, in the 1980s and 1990s, general international approval of democracy sent generals, or at least their titles and uniforms, back to the barracks and put elected presidents and prime ministers back in charge. After 1989 the former Soviet Union countries adopted the vote imperfectly but formally as the way of choosing leaders. Between 1985 and 2000 the number of democracies on the planet doubled from fewer than 60 to about 120—about

60 percent of the UN's membership. Even Sudan has held nationwide elections to be followed by a referendum to resolve the continuing tension between the country's north and south as well as Darfur.

When I was in Khao-I-Dang, I spent many evenings sitting in my bamboo and rush-mat office as Cambodians stopped by to reminisce about their former lives. Some told me how the Khmer Rouge had lured them home from exile, appealing to them to lend their skills and talents to building a new Cambodia. Then the nightmare had soon overtaken their dreams of nation-building; they had been bundled off to villages, sometimes with their families and sometimes separately, to be reeducated. Books were taken away from them and schools closed. Parents and children alike were assigned to work in the fields during the day and be trained in party ideology in the evenings.

Those who hesitated were brutally killed as an example to other waverers. Many others, unready for village life, died of hunger and disease. Nawi, a young Cambodian woman who would later find asylum in Australia, helped keep my little office clean and the cups of coffee and sweet tea flowing for visitors. She had lost most of her immediate relatives and seemed to gather courage just from being near foreigners. She had become afraid of her own fellow Cambodians and would hang around the office for security. Her apparently placid brown eyes, like so many others in the camps, had seen more than any young person should. She waited and hoped for news of her family.

As the camp formed, a group of teachers and other middle-class professionals who had had to hide their learning for nearly five years of Khmer Rouge rule came forward. Could they start a school so their children could begin to make up for the lost years? they asked. Classrooms were quickly set up and teachers recruited, but they recreated their own Cambodian textbooks. A culture was being recovered in front of my eyes. The project brought intergenerational therapy beyond my imagining.

The pain and loss, and the subsequent healing, made me an ever more confirmed democrat. Democracy, I became convinced, might have saved the million or more lives lost in little Cambodia. But the political struggle had been between a royalist middle class and a radicalized peasantry. Democracy was viewed as a distraction. My friend William Shawcross had just told the story of Cambodia's descent into genocide in his brilliant 1979 book *Sideshow: Kissinger, Nixon and the Destruction of Cambodia*. All of us in Cambodian refugee work must have read it; what I had taken out of it, even more than the machinations of Kissinger and Nixon on the one side and of the Vietcong on the other to draw Cambodia into their war, was the Cambodians' lack of political choice. A weak king had been replaced by Communist butchers because the country lacked a democratic stage on which any other ending might have been played out.

If Cambodia had held elections, it might have produced alternatives. The corrupt administration of King Sihanouk that favored the francophone bourgeoisie of Phnom Penh over the peasantry might have been booted out at the ballot box, not at the barrel of a gun. Reformers might then have satisfactorily shifted things around without resort to violent, senseless revolution. But democratic elections are not summoned up with the wave of a pen or a wand. They have to be worked for and sometimes fought for.

The rise and fall of hopes for democracy tracks the rise and fall of hopes for humanitarianism. After the Cold War we hoped that there would be no more Soviet gulags or Cambodian killing fields, and we expected that the wider adoption of democracy would be an inevitable step to better government. Freedoms would be respected, and we would be moving firmly along the road toward rights and opportunities.

Democracy came back in grand style. I witnessed its return in the

Philippines in 1986. My search to do something about the roots of conflict, not just its symptoms, had taken me there as a political adviser to the long-shot protest candidate who was running against the country's authoritarian patriarch, Ferdinand Marcos.

Just after the vote, I was squeezed with Teddyboy Locsin, the candidate's speechwriter and press aide, onto the end of a cathedral pew. Manila's cardinal, Jaime Sin, was offering up prayers for a successful resolution of the political crisis that gripped the country. Sitting in the front was our candidate, Corazon Aquino. To the amazement of many in the congregation, Aquino appeared to have just won the election, but less surprisingly Marcos was clearly not going to give up without a fight. As we strained to see, the country's grandees stopped by her pew at the front of the cathedral to pay their respects. The old president, however, was holed up in his palace, refusing to concede defeat.

A well-known judge paused at Aquino's pew a moment longer than others to whisper something that was evidently more than the standard greeting. Back at her campaign headquarters, she called us in. The whispered message had been that the vote count was being manipulated by Marcos; a group of the young technicians who were computing it were going to walk out and declare it fraudulent. Aquino told us that we should be watching for this act of defiance and try to get the technicians in front of the press, as this event seemed likely to be the smoking gun, the proof that Marcos was trying to steal the election.

The seesaw election season had been full of such moments. The international face of the campaign was a small widow in yellow, Cory Aquino, defying a dictator and risking her life for democracy. Behind an almost fairy-tale clash of good and evil lay some complexity. The self-made elite that had formed around Marcos and lived off his largesse was keen to hold on; the riches that came from association with him were not easily put aside. On the other side, old families, whose traditional power and wealth had been pushed to the sidelines during the Marcos years, had combined with social reformers, human rights activists, old politicians, churchmen, and clean government advocates to create an unlikely political coalition that now stood on the verge of power.

The old man in his Malacañang palace was playing his last cards. Everybody, except perhaps he and his family, saw that. The cathedral mass was to pray that the election results be respected, but it was also an expression of solidarity with Aquino, a celebration of impending opposition victory.

Later in the evening, Teddyboy and I waited outside the election commission building. Suddenly a commotion developed inside as a small group of vote-counters made for the door—surely the ones the whisperer had meant. They were still dressed in the white lab coats that Marcos had made them wear for public relations purposes, to represent the claimed scientific neutrality of the vote count. Outside the building several station wagons bowled up to the door, and out jumped athletic-looking men dressed in civilian clothes. Teddyboy recognized them as part of a group of young army officers who had called for national renewal and the purging of corrupt officials, including Marcos, but who had feared that elections would give power to weak civilians. They were suspected of preferring a new military strongman to Aquino.

The men hurried the election workers into the station wagons and raced off into the night. Surprised by this evidently well-planned abduction, we waved down a taxi and followed them into the night. Where would they hold the press conference? Gradually it dawned on us that, in a moment of Filipino theater, they were going to a church. There, at a high altar lit by candles, the officers allowed us to help prepare the disaffected vote-counters for a late-night press conference.

I knew that some American election observers were still in town, staying at the old colonial Manila hotel, where General Douglas MacArthur had once based himself. I raced to the hotel lobby and called upstairs to Senator John Kerry, the prominent publisher Mort Zuckerman, and several others and urged them to come and see for themselves this moment of truth and melodrama amid the candles and incense.

I have had a hand in a lot of press conferences, but this one remains my favorite. Still in his lab coat, flanked by nervous colleagues, the leader of the vote-counters started talking in a low hesitant voice. President Marcos had directly ordered them first to delay the counting, he explained, and then to change the results. From their places in the nave journalists, observers, and Filipinos strained to catch every word. Given the time difference, the story landed in that evening's American news broadcasts. Marcos was duly humiliated in front of the American public, the audience he seemed to principally care about. The rest was history. As peaceful Filipino demonstrators surrounded the palace, an American helicopter airlifted Marcos out, to carry him to an unhappy exile in Hawaii.

This scene concluded a drama that had begun in August 1983, when Cory's husband, Benigno Aquino, upon returning from exile to challenge Marcos, was assassinated on the tarmac of the Manila airport. Three years later Cory's campaign had been rich in the melodrama that the Filipinos celebrate in their local Tagalog-language film industry. Indeed, one of Cory's senior communications advisers (and her sister-in-law), when not involved in politics, was a prominent local film director.

But behind the theatricality was the false promise of a new democratic start. In the Philippines population growth was racing ahead of the economy's ability to support it, and the relatively anemic economic growth benefited mainly the high-living, well-connected business class. Could democracy fundamentally resolve these inequalities? Or would democracy became a vehicle for similar special interests:

for some to get back into power after long years on the outside; for the generals and other assorted strongmen to exit while preserving their new ill-gotten fortunes?

President Aquino appointed as finance minister Jimmy Ongpin, a chief policy adviser and a real modernizer in the Philippines' otherwise very nontransparent business world. He pushed an orthodox plan of financial stabilization and debt management. But the president's cabinet secretary, Joker Arroyo, and others who represented a new cause-oriented civil society, wanted a much more radical break with traditional economics. They talked of a government debt default to force creditors to write down what was owed and of major social spending using the savings from debt service. A few years later debt reduction and cancellation would become respectable, but then it was thought to scare off foreign investors.

This particular clash ended tragically; Ongpin resigned and then took his own life, deeply dejected at the government's failure, as he saw it, to move forward in a unified economic direction. And certainly Cory Aquino was no Margaret Thatcher. But she understood, better than either of the rival factions vying for control of economic policy, that she had no mandate for either course. She had been elected to restore decency and honesty to government and to allow Filipinos to choose who governed them. Mandates for particular policies would have to wait till later. Her elected successor, Fidel Ramos, a retired army commander, gave the country six years of a decisive direction in government, then tried to change the constitution so he could stand for another six years; Aquino led demonstrations to stop him. For the widow of a man who had been gunned down for his democratic beliefs, democracy, and respect for its rules, was everything.

Aquino and the Filipinos were not alone in investing so much hope in democracy. Americans and Europeans watched this campaign with as much intensity as if it were one of their own; they became protectors of the process. For a democratic opposition candidate, international interest has become the best guarantor of a fair election. At most elections since that one in the Philippines, international observers have become a ubiquitous presence. The world likes the electoral story to be dramatic and straightforward. It needs a hero, or heroine, and a villain. Preferably the lead players will have pronounceable names and speak English. And in a touch that Aquino pioneered, we like our favored candidate to give the electoral revolution a color or a symbol. Her People Power Revolution colored itself yellow. Since then revolutions have been orange and blue, cedar and velvet, to name a few. The Russians, whose sphere of influence has lost a number of countries this way, have a warning term for it: "the color revolutions."

The Philippines was the first of many elections I was involved in from 1986 to 1994. I had left the United Nations because my work there seemed mainly to involve cleaning up after political failure. The logic of humanitarian work at that stage led me to conclude: if only people got to choose their governments, surely these terrible refugee crises would not happen.

British politics seemed like little more than a sort of breed of municipal politics, rather grandly dressed up but dealing mainly with small changes in public spending. One party might tax a little less and the other spend a little more. But democratic revolutions—now, those were a grand canvas. Across the developing world the future was up for grabs. To preserve their rule, dictators invoked the Cold War: Marcos argued that if he fell, the Communist insurgency would quickly overcome the Philippines; against such an enemy, the weak, untested Cory Aquino could never prevail. But his own corrupt rule became a principal recruiting agent for the Communists. Many thought that if a democratic alternative restored integrity to government, got the economy started again, and restored basic services such as health and education, the Communist threat would fall away.

In Manila in the mid-1980s, then, big ideas were on trial, and I was determined to be there. A vocation for my thirties, I had to play whatever small part I could to stop another Cambodia. Filipino violence was unlikely to degenerate to that point, but I was eager to tip Filipino politics in as peaceful a direction as I could.

In subsequent years the Filipino campaign would be replayed across Latin America and then the former Soviet Union: economic failure would trigger an election. In the Philippines the World Bank, the IMF, and the U.S. government had finally pushed Marcos into economic reform, or "structural adjustment," as it was known. That brought to an abrupt halt years of runaway patronage spending by which he maintained his political machine. The consequence was a recession and rising unemployment.

For a veteran political survivor like Marcos, high public spending was a vital prop to his rule, and economic reform a dangerous business. The costs of reforming the Philippine economy hit hardest the poor urban and rural voters who had been the mainstay of his populist regime. The World Bank and others were slow to understand that for such rulers, good economics was not good politics. Hence Marcos in the Philippines, Mobutu in Zaire, and Alan García in Peru would resist the bank until they had exhausted all other options. They understood that the bank's reform program of reduced public spending was a suicide note. When later I joined the World Bank, I solemnly thanked the official who had been in charge of the Philippine program for his contribution to our election victory. He was gracious enough, although a little perplexed, to laugh along with me.

Against this backdrop, Marcos emphasized a strongman's platform. At a time of crisis, he argued, he was best placed to maintain order. He would right the economy, beat the Communist guerillas, and maintain law and order. Initially Cory Aquino, a political neophyte, seemed easy for such a campaign to beat. She had a weak grasp on policy and was a hesitant public speaker. Marcos's domination of the official media allowed him to control how she was portrayed.

Then the editor and publisher of *The New York Times* came to interview her. At the time of their visit she was sitting in the family kitchen, distracted by a grandchild on her knee. She had thought it would be a social call. But the paper described her as an overwhelmed amateur, and regardless of the paper's misgivings about Marcos, the critique of a woman apparently unfit to rule was devastating.

I wanted to help her as a political consultant. I was thinking about joining the Sawyer-Miller Group, which might allow me to work with her. One of the principals, David Sawyer, was a Democratic Party political consultant. Through him, I met Robert Trent-Jones Jr., a golf course designer who was itching for a change from fairways and bunkers. Trent-Jones had built Cory Aquino's family a golf course on their Tarlac sugar plantation and was also an activist in Democratic Party politics.

Trent-Jones and I traveled to the Philippines, where we found Aquino on the stage of a provincial rally far from Manila. He introduced me as somebody who would fix her problems. She was understandably skeptical: what could a tall foreigner who had never been to the Philippines before usefully tell her? And beyond that, wouldn't involving American political consultants in her enterprise strip it of all sanctity? She did allow, however, that I might be able to do something about *The New York Times*. She hired me. Later, this apparently saintly woman (who literally hid in a nunnery for security reasons on election night) would deny that she had American consultants helping her: after all, I was British.

I quickly realized that Filipinos had the same difficulty with her candidacy that *The New York Times* did. Was she up to the job at a time of national crisis, they wondered, and was this really the time to jettison an experienced leader?

First we set about demolishing Marcos's credentials. We pumped up rumors about his health, that he had lupus, and we taunted him that he could not stay away from his dialysis machine. We promoted an Australian scholar's research that cast doubt on Marcos's war record. We played up the extensive corruption allegations and questioned his economic management. That was not difficult, given the World Bank–induced recession.

Correspondingly, we built up Cory's reputation. Integrity and courage were what her devastated country needed, we said, and she had both in abundance, together with the skills of a conciliator and healer. She zealously pressed the flesh amid growing crowds at considerable personal risk, in contrast to the old man who was unable to stray far from his kidney machine.

We made use of the international media, which were all over this campaign. In 1986 newspapers and television came in force to cover the story of the democracy campaigner, the widow dressed in yellow taking on the old fox cornered in his lair. Marcos kept a tight rein on the domestic media, but the international media turned against him. How did Filipinos see that coverage? American military bases in the Philippines had their own television channel that carried the American networks. Filipinos quickly tapped into it to watch the astonishing stories of Marcos's failing health and his falsely won war medals. Then those stories seeped into the domestic coverage. This bouncing of international news coverage into the local press set a powerful precedent. From now on dictators would have fewer places to hide. It helped provide a new lever of power that, in popular hands, could confound the leader who held all the old levers.

Cory Aquino had taken up the fight against Marcos—and won. But the old man did not go easily: he had to be bundled out by the American ambassador. Teddyboy broke from the crowd milling outside the palace and climbed the gates; he was one of the first into the presidential bathroom. He brought me a souvenir towel decorated with Imelda Marcos's initials. That night Cory's irrepressible spokesman came up with the legend of ten thousand pairs of shoes in the fallen first lady's closet. It was the confirming image of a presidency that had lost touch with the people.

Working for Cory seemed to confirm my Cambodian insight: democracy allowed people a nonviolent way of changing a government.

Further, people were willing to take risks to stand up and vote. The vote mattered.

But then came the actual business of governing. As the Philippines quickly showed, the path of democracy is rock-strewn and twisting. The political change seemed more seismic than it turned out to be in fact. Old elites rode democracy back into office. Marcos cronies had controlled illegal gambling, beer, and coke, as well as customs and excise revenues. Democracy did not dissolve these networks instantly. As the old crowd shuffled out, new ones tried to push their way in. Aquino did her personal best to keep them out, but the system was too entrenched.

So Aquino's victory initiated—but no more than that—the transition to a more liberal, competitive, and transparent economy. The old groups battle on to this day for control of the presidential ear, now that of Cory's son, viewing democracy as a new, more expensive way of buying power than in the past, but considering power to still be for sale. The behind-the-scenes cynicism of some Filipino power brokers was utterly at odds with the euphoria and hope of the hundreds of thousands of Filipinos in yellow T-shirts who greeted Cory's rise as a simple uncomplicated victory of democratic good over authoritarian evil.

Despite the exuberance of the huge peaceful expressions of "People Power," real power did not yet lie with the people. Marcos lost because he was deserted by the business sector and then by the military. Yet the sheer tenacity of the old power centers was remarkable. What surprised me more than old power's ability to co-opt the democratic process, or at least survive it, was its ability to endure in the face of demographic change.

From the 1960s to the 1980s, authoritarian rulers had taken power in newly independent states around the world, and weak democratic institutions could not check them. But those years of political oppression and dull, featureless regimes were also years of demographic transformation. Between 1960 and 1985 the world population grew by more than half. In Africa it nearly doubled. Latin Americans increased by 80 percent and Asians by 70 percent. So whenever democracy returned, voters would be much more numerous. In the Philippines the total population had almost doubled. Voters were younger as the population bulge reached voting age, but they were also older as life expectancy lengthened. Globally, between 1960 and 1980, life expectancy for women grew from 53 to 63 years and for men from 51 to 59 years.

The other dramatic change was that people everywhere were on the move. They were leaving stable, quasi-feudal village life, where a landlord or headman could control political life, to seek a better life in the cities. Fortune smiled unevenly on the new urbanites, mostly living in shantytowns. Some eke out a living recycling garbage or selling cigarettes and matches on street corners. Others have become the labor force of an industrial revolution in China and Southeast Asia.

One might have expected this demographic revolution to smash the pattern of old political loyalties. But as I plied my political wares across the developing world, the resilience of old political parties astonished me. They should have been gone, I thought, victims of demography if not democracy; but time after time they clung on or came back when democracy was restored.

Political machines, it seemed, could still deliver votes even in transformed demographic contexts, even when party leaders were blithely unaware of the degree of social change that had occurred during their country's nondemocratic years. They fell back into their old, habitual practices—rallies in distant small market towns, long motorcades snaking through the countryside, the candidates waving to the occasional curious peasant in a field—while paying insufficient attention to the dirty, chaotic, new urban voting concentrations that showed little deference to or respect for the visiting candidates.

But nobody could ignore one change: the mass media. Radio and television had spread out across slums as well as the more prosperous parts of towns and cities. In previous decades, military officials had painstakingly pored over the daily newspapers before censoring them even though only a small middle class read them. The censors, like the rest of the capital city establishment, failed to notice the profusion of local radio and television stations that were transforming the mass media.

A most striking demonstration came in 1990, when Alberto Fujimori ran against Mario Vargas Llosa, the novelist, for the presidency of Peru. Fujimori ostensibly won "from nowhere," but he had actually been broadcasting for years on agricultural issues over the radio to the poor as they bused to work or toiled in the fields. He did it very early in the morning, when the politicians and the middle class were still in their beds. He thereby built a huge constituency that they had never noticed.

I had courted and won his opponent Vargas Llosa as a client. The country was under threat from a Maoist insurgency; its democracy was barely functioning; and its populist president, Alan Garcia, had driven it into bankruptcy while the generals watched nervously from their barracks. Vargas Llosa had started as a maverick outsider, an intellectual dismayed by corruption and bad government. But then the traditional parties threw their support to him, and whatever limited organizational advantage he gained was more than offset by his association with these largely white upper-class organizations. It lost him any connection with the Indian and mestizo poor. Suddenly the outsider had become the spokesman for the old insiders. And this political machine could not deliver.

Our polling and focus groups exposed this dramatic vulnerability, and I unsuccessfully pleaded with Vargas Llosa to break with the old parties. An opponent needed only to exploit this weakness to turn a liability into a defeat. Fortunately most of the other candidates were even more tarnished by traditional political ties or else were too much on the fringe to gather support. One candidate, campaigning under the single name Ezekiel, was a great bearded figure who seemed to have popped up out of the Old Testament. He achieved a brief flurry of interest when he predicted that his election would lead to a modern equivalent of Jesus feeding the five thousand. The next day a huge cohort of dead fish was promptly washed ashore near Lima, the capital.

Vargas Llosa was unflinchingly realist in his account of what the country needed. Like Cory Aquino's filmmaker relative, his brother-in-law was also a campaign aide and a maker of low budget Hollywood horror movies. Lucho Llosa ran soft television advertisements for him. But Vargas Llosa would have nothing to do with an election narrative coated in sweet melodrama; he chose to tell it as it was. He promised austerity and painful reforms. It was splendidly honest but also a political suicide note in a country where economic failure had left many on the breadline. Vargas Llosa likes to say with some pride that I told him he was the worst candidate I ever worked for. He was also the most intellectually honest, and that of course was no coincidence.

Our polls and focus groups quickly picked up on the popularity of Fujimori, the mystery candidate, although Vargas Llosa did not want to believe it. On the night before the first round of voting, I had dinner with a complacent vice chairman of one of the parties supporting Vargas Llosa. This man did not know Fujimori's name; believed he was of Chinese, not Japanese, origin; and tried to bet me that in the next day's vote the little *chinito*, as he disparagingly referred to him, would be crushed.

The next day Fujimori came in a strong second and then went on to win in a run-off. Once in office, like so many other reformers, he soon fell back on old habits of control, corruption, a military intelligence network, and deals with powerful business interests, all publicity-coated with a strong streak of populism. He did initially introduce radical, tough economic reforms intended to reduce public spending, similar to what Vargas Llosa had championed during the campaign, but then quickly gave in to a populist recipe of high spending. His tough, authoritarian tendencies, combined with his democratic mandate, gave him a dramatic and vital victory over the Maoist insurgency, Sendero Luminoso, or Shining Path. But Peru paid a price, as Fujimori's presidency did terrible damage to the country's political culture, human rights, and economy.

Over almost a decade international elections never got simpler. Democracy, I reflected, had more continuity with the previous political order than anyone, especially those who euphorically voted, expected. Revolutionary economic and social change might have swept interests and parties away, but the old power brokers somehow clung on. Democracy did not necessarily encourage truth-telling during the election or, once leaders were elected, making hard choices.

The elections in the Philippines, Peru, and elsewhere helped me understand the limits of instant democracy. I saw no better way of government, yet the elusive project of a better world was evidently not going to be found through the national ballot box alone.

In fact, democracy was a bit of a tease. At a time of astonishing global change, it was sometimes the snake-oil salesman offering remedies that raised hopes often only to disappoint. The democratic governments I worked with were overwhelmed by the scale of the demands placed on them. The demographic changes of population growth, longer life expectancy, and urbanization were creating pressing demands for health, education, and pensions as well as jobs. Democracy alone could not oil the economic machine to create these things.

Nor was democracy a panacea for human rights. Too often one elite replaced another, or one ethnic group pushed out a rival, within a winner-takes-all system. Losers found themselves locked up or exiled, as they had been under the generals. These young democracies lacked the software of a democratic society. The media too often were not free; simple rights such as freedom of expression were curtailed. Too often the society was missing an enforceable framework of laws to allow citizens protection.

The British democratic model that had looked rather dull when I fled it now seemed rather respectable. Perhaps the real human capital or software of democracy was built up over centuries, not in an election or two. In an apocryphal story, a tourist asks a college gardener at Oxford for the secret of the immaculate lawn he is tending. "Five hundred years," came the reply. I was beginning to fear that democracy too takes time to grow.

Now I sit in Britain's parliamentary upper chamber, the House of Lords, and watch the careful minutiae of legislative scrutiny, the stout defense of civil liberties, and the occasionally fierce cross-examination of ministers. This is grass-blade-by-grass-blade democracy even though this British upper chamber is anomalously not currently elected. The rules, and the culture that sustains them, were built up over time. By contrast, too many of the new democracies are, in practice, elected dictatorships. The vote may or may not be relatively free, but the conditions for freedom and participation between elections are not present. The press, the parliament, the judiciary, and the market too often remain in the iron grip of those in power.

In 1988 a New York human rights organization introduced me to members of Chile's "No" campaign, the referendum on General Augusto Pinochet's rule, and I came on board. I persuaded George Soros, who was establishing his network of Open Society institutions, to finance opinion research that showed the opposition that they could win. It was a further step in my growing association with international human rights and democracy groups that sought to oust authoritarian rulers at the ballot box.

Once again a strongman apparently toyed with aborting an election or trying to change the vote count, then pulled back because the international spotlight fell on him. Following their success in the Philippines, international election observers were everywhere in Chile. The U.S. National Democratic Institute and its Republican counterpart; former President Jimmy Carter's Carter Center; and similar foundations in London and Stockholm have all become part of the election industry, providing observers, training, and materials such as ballot papers and vote count software. UNDP, when I became its head, was to join this active group. Initially, I never thought observers were terribly good at catching actual fraud. Their arrival at particular polling stations was usually well known in advance; some officials were willing to hide any scam; the visitors often did not know the country or the language; and they seemed to lack the mathematical skills to follow the votes from the polling booth to the national tabulation. There seemed to be too many opportunities for cheating along the way.

But in impressive recent cases their statistical modeling arguments have made me revise even this point. And the organizations that sponsor this work have become cannier in their methodologies. Some of them, as old political operatives from Chicago, the American South, or Florida, might even wryly acknowledge that no one is better suited to catch misdeeds than the poacher-turned-gamekeeper.

A further lesson I learned in these years as a democratic mercenary was that the millions who bravely massed on streets in Moscow and Tbilisi, Manila and Seoul, Nairobi and Soweto, Lima and La Paz wanted not only the vote but economic liberation too. They were marching for a wider range of choices and opportunities. Their aspirations were down to earth: jobs, health care, education, and a better standard of living. They viewed democracy as a means to get there, not the end in itself. They hoped their governments would provide them with honest, noncorrupt support as they sought to better their families' lives.

But when democratic governments, once in place, proved little better than their authoritarian predecessors at running the economy and reducing poverty and inequality, people started to hanker for the old days. A controversial poll that UNDP commissioned in Latin America in 2004 showed that years of low growth and worsening inequality had taken its toll. People were losing faith in democracy.

I came to understand that democracy does not stand alone but must be attached to economic reform that delivers results for the poor; absent that reform, no glib campaign strategy or media message can save it. Building a democracy takes patience and time, and it must improve the lives of those in poverty.

Good economics is the precondition for good politics. Just as the search for better, fairer elections had once drawn me closer to international vote-watching activities, I realized now that the real challenge was how to modernize a country's economy. Economic growth became the platform for sustainable democracy.

Economics too was becoming an international affair. Domestic agendas were being globalized. As the increasing integration of trade, investment, and communications drew countries into the global economy, globalization seeped into the political debate. More and more political discussions were looping back to global change, that disruptive force that stranded mineworkers, steel workers, and small farmers but showered others with opportunities to take advantage of a country's competitive position in the global economy.

Globalization affects the political debate even in countries that it has left behind. A Bolivian client of mine, Goni Sanchez de Lozada, had been brought up in the United States and set out to become a Hollywood scriptwriter. Decades later, when he ran for president, we surprisingly turned his heavily American-accented Spanish to his electoral advantage. In the campaign's advertising, my team linked his ease with English to his ability to steer Bolivia out of its backwater and into the global economy. His foreignness qualified him to be president. Later it would be his undoing. He won the 1993 election and proved to be a real reformer. But when the backlash against globalizers came, it brought him down. He was easily cast as an elitist businessman with no sympathy for the indigenous poor. The last time I visited him in his presidential palace, he pointed to the bullet marks above his desk where an angry crowd had taken pot shots at him. A year later in 2003, during his second term in office, Goni had to hop onto a plane to Miami and exile when an indigenous political leader whipped up populist class and ethnic anger against his leadership.

The quest for democracy has increasingly been dogged by disappointment, not just for the Filipinos, Peruvians, and Bolivians who voted for change but also for their legions of supporters abroad; those who made financial contributions to human rights and democracy-building groups, and the television viewers and newspaper readers who cheered Cory Aquino and Boris Yeltsin as they went against the odds and appeared to deliver fairy-tale endings.

From town hall balconies across Latin America, candidates inveighed against the past and promised a brighter future. The old Spanish-style squares would rock with anticipation as stoic-faced peasants gave in to the four-year itch and believed again that this leader, this *caudillo*, might change things. Like others in the town square, I hoped that this time the candidate might be proved right. But the next morning, before the campaign posters were even taken down, the shift at the mines or the back-breaking work in the fields would begin again, and kids would miss school to help their parents bring in the sparse harvest. Meals would be skipped to pay for medicine for a sick baby. Poverty is relentless. And the answer to it is to be found in a combination of domestic and international economic reform that democracy can support but not replace.

My personal crusade for national democracy as the cure for a country's backwardness had run up against its limits. It was a vital but not sufficient condition for development. The country's economic constraints had to be tackled, and that could not just be done at home. It meant drawing a country into the globalizing economic mainstream and helping it find its most useful place in the international trading system. Democratic countries are no more islands than dictatorships. The world, and each country's relationship to it, matters because therein lies the real route to national freedom and emancipation.

CHAPTER FIVE

THE MONEY CRISIS

Over the New Year 1995 holidays, Lew Preston, the World Bank's tall but stooped patrician president, was disconsolately striding through his otherwise deserted offices. "Don't they realize the peso is going to hell in a hand basket?" he demanded of me, his new head of external affairs. He supposed his senior staff's holidays were too precious to be broken for a mere financial crisis, he said, even for one of the bank's major borrowers, Mexico.

The sluggish response from his staff was revealing. As Mexico's iron-cool new president Ernesto Zedillo and the formidable U.S. Treasury secretary Robert Rubin assembled an $18 billion rescue package, the bank, to Preston's frustration, ambled along on the sidelines. Whereas its sister institution the IMF had a mandate to preserve global financial stability and the ability to extend very large short-term credit lines to governments, the World Bank's main function was long-term development. This apparently meant that in a crisis its senior managers need not interrupt their holidays. Nevertheless, as Preston knew all too well, precisely this sort of crisis jeopardized the bank's development mission. Mexican banks had committed the classic error: they had borrowed in dollars and then lent in pesos. In the wake of a presidential election they were caught in an exchange rate squeeze as both Mexico's public and private debt veered toward the cliff.

For similar reasons I shared Preston's frustration. A critical difference between democrats and dictators is that the first are in a hurry. They have fixed terms of office before retirement or reelection, and to make an impact they must move fast. Investment made early in a presidential term on new services and infrastructure may, just may, make a difference to people by the end of that term and the next election, when they will need to be able to show results. Spending and investment decisions that are made the middle of, say, a four-year governmental term will bring popularity for the next government, not the current one.

The World Bank just did not seem to get that. My clients at my political consultancy, often first-time democrats after years of authoritarian rule, should have been able to find the World Bank their indispensable partner; it should have got quickly behind their reform agenda and helped make their governments a success. Instead, time after time, to my clients' frustration, the bank had delayed. Bank procedures were painstakingly long, and its officials seemed both self-important and cautious, imposing endlessly on ministers' time but dragging out the lending process interminably. A few months earlier my own impatience with the bank's procedures, had brought me to its doors. I hoped that from my new perch I could light a few fires.

The World Bank version of economics did not distinguish between democrats and authoritarians. Given that many of the democrats had found their way to power as a result of an economic crisis, the first thing the World Bank and the IMF usually demanded of them was drastic belt-tightening, or "structural adjustment." This action hit most of these new leaders' own supporters the hardest: the structural adjustment programs infamously put the main burden on the poor. Usually the new democratic government had to eliminate subsidies for basic necessities like bread and fuel, impose education and health user fees, or increase consumer taxes. These measures might have helped balance the budget, but they were sheer hell for a new president. Many knew all too well that exactly these belt-tightening policies had brought their predecessors down.

So when the baffled World Bank, besieged by public relations problems relating to this perception of being out of touch with the needs of the poor, asked me to head up its global communications efforts, the offer was an irresistible challenge. Bank president Lew Preston, a former head of JPMorgan, had taken on the job at the behest of his old friend President George H. W. Bush. For an old marine in his late sixties, it was a career afterthought, one I suspect that at times he regretted. Far from being a quiet victory lap for a distinguished and hugely well-regarded New York banker, the job unceremoniously dropped him into the middle of globalization's culture wars. NGO critics complained the Bank was a heartless champion of the expansion of international capitalism rather than a protector of the poor. Dams, highways, school fees, and radical cuts in public spending were, in their view, imposed ruthlessly on powerless people in developing countries.

The bank staff found the criticism perplexing and hurtful. Yes, they were a development elite able to live well in Washington's suburbs on generous tax-free salaries with near-permanent tenure. Nevertheless, they had in many cases come into development via NGOs, and many had also turned down more remunerative careers in banking, law, or accounting to be there. Most felt a strong sense of vocation. Others would have made illustrious careers as academics.

Therefore when NGOs targeted them as agents of evil, World Bank staffers felt a strong sense of bewilderment and unfairness. Some got defensive, but others became so self-righteous that they became the institution's worst defenders. They would not hear out the critics, and their response—essentially "trust us, we know best"—struck many as arrogant and condescending.

I was rushed into the job in 1994 to combat the critics. The bank was about to convene its annual meeting in Madrid and feared something close to a pitched battle. The meeting lived up to its billing. Antibank campaigners clambered through the steel rafters of the exhibition hall where the plenary was being held. As Preston tried to speak, they showered fake dollar bills bearing environmental and antidebt slogans down on the listening finance ministers. As the journalist Sebastian Mallaby wrote of this incident: "Preston, in fact, had lost more than the audience; he had lost the bigger game as well."[1]

The bank and its president had run into forces larger than the noisy NGO agitators. The more fundamental truth that fueled the complaints was that as countries struggled with democracy and accountability at home, they found themselves butting up against an institution that had loaned billions of dollars to their nondemocratic, usually corrupt predecessors, and for which they now were responsible. Little new infrastructure or development had resulted from the loans; the funds had no doubt partly ended up in hidden foreign bank accounts. The bank was notorious for having turned a blind eye to this problem. Now the new leaders found that the bank gave them no breaks. It expected repayment in full, and new loans carried onerous conditions and delays.

Impatient new democratic leaders quickly wondered whether the bank was really on their side. As a political consultant, I was accustomed to large bank delegations arriving in town soon after my clients had taken office. With no sense of apology, they would immediately begin telling my clients that the electoral promises they had made were impractical and must be dropped if the bank were to help. The education and health plans were too expensive; the commitment to job creation was unrealistic. And before you do any of it, by the way, went the message, you owe us a regular payment on the old loans each month. It reminded me of the 1980s British television sitcom *Yes Minister*, in which Whitehall civil servants would gently direct ministers from their foolishly overheated promises to voters and redirect them toward a more palatable status quo. The World Bank seemed to be a global Whitehall, frustrating everyone from its own president to these struggling new national leaders.

The World Bank had not yet caught up with the way democracy had remade expectations. First, its technocratic long-term development planning process made no concessions for the urgency of results in a democracy. Second, the Bank had a bias for growth over reducing inequality. Although the bank sometimes argued otherwise, they are not the same thing. It too often assumed that a healthy rate of growth in a country would benefit everybody, but growth in an unequal society often really benefits only the rich.

Plenty of individual bank specialists in education and health warned that in a country where wealth is very unevenly distributed, the rich are likely to go on getting the lion's share of future growth. But those in charge of operations remained largely blind to this charge and unenthusiastic about targeting the poor if it risked slowing overall growth. So the dominant agenda emphasized growth, which in turn meant focusing on privatizing loss-making government enterprises, balancing the books by reducing public spending unless offset by tax increases, and radically liberalizing a country's trade by cutting tariffs on imports.

All these steps hurt the immediate interests of those now enfranchised to vote, who had not voted for their governments to do any of them. They saw privatization as transferring a state monopoly in electricity or water to a crony private monopoly, a combination of powerful national owners with international partners who were even less accountable for quality and service than the government had been. In places like Cochabamba in Bolivia, huge protests would develop when municipal water, viewed as a national patrimony, was no longer free for the poor. When a candidate like Mario Vargas Llosa in Peru did run on an explicit economic program of privatization and liberalization, it typically led to electoral failure.

The liberalizing of trade did destroy millions of jobs in developing countries as national companies producing processed foods, clothing, or other basic consumer items could no longer compete with enterprises in China and Southeast Asia. People who had worked at jobs making these exports in Africa and Latin America lost them. Adding to the unfairness was that the World Bank and the IMF had steamrollered over domestic lobbies to impose much lower import protection in these regions than it did in the United States or Europe, where farmers and other domestic producers were protected.

The choice of cutting spending or increasing taxes was not easy. Government spending provided not just the basic services of education and health for the poor but often the public sector jobs together with bread and fuel price subsidies that made life bearable. New taxes largely fell on spending, not on wealth, since income tax was often hard to raise, so increases hit the poor while the income of the rich remained untouched.

In my view, much of the bank's policies were intellectually defensible. The bank was, after all, run by the smartest minds in development. The status quo economic policies they were attacking had to go. Countries could not afford them. Jobs propped up by subsidies were not sustainable. Broadly, at least at the macro level, the bank's recipe was the right one: these policies are essential to long-term growth, which is indispensable to development and poverty reduction. Still, it needed a lighter, more sensitive touch in implementation, rather than an unintended attack on the new democracies and particularly their majority, the poor.

During my years at the bank that institution's mission slowly bent toward accommodating the demands of the poor. It was a remarkable conversion, but even as individual World Bankers got it, the bank as a whole was slow to move. The tramlines of orthodox economics seemed just too deeply laid for the bank to change direction quickly.

Preston fell ill with cancer in 1995 and, sadly, died very quickly.

His death accelerated the contest to succeed him. By tradition, the White House nominated an American for the job, and the rest of the World Bank's board went along. Because that process was traditional rather than a formal requirement, the White House was expected to come up with a good name that enjoyed international support. Larry Summers, the brilliant, iconoclastic economist then at the U.S. Treasury, seemed the principal contender. He had earlier served as the World Bank's chief economist. But Vice President Al Gore, the administration's environmental conscience, was thought to oppose a candidate who had appeared to support a World Bank research paper that provocatively argued that a good thing about poor people was that because of their low level of economic activity they could not pollute. (Much later, Larry's tenure as president of Harvard would be brought short by a similarly dismissive comment about the scientific aptitude of women scholars.)

Then Jim Wolfensohn, who ran his own investment banking boutique in New York, emerged from the White House as its nominee. I had met him through the ABC news anchor Peter Jennings. I was very much in Summers's corner at the time, and Jennings had mischievously relayed to Wolfensohn my feeling that the bank did not need another elderly investment banker at its helm. Wolfensohn telephoned me to challenge this view. Initially I thought the caller was Jennings, a Canadian, doing a poor impersonation of Wolfensohn, an Australian. I soon discovered that it was the real man and that he was as mad as hell that the bank's head of external affairs viewed him in this light.

He was soon in Washington to lobby the White House, and he asked me to go out to Washington National Airport to ride in with him. His short rounded physique exuded a bustling energy. The pockets of his overcoat were stuffed with several NGO-authored diatribes against the bank. I saw almost immediately that he had that purest of pure investment banking skills: salesmanship. He focused relentlessly on understanding what clients and partners wanted and how to meet those needs. He was clever and creative but above all a salesman. He was also driven by a real passion to make a difference in the world. He and his wife Elaine adopted poverty as their cause, in her case supplemented by a lifelong interest in education.

For the World Bank, Wolfensohn's arrival as president was a painful shot in the arm. He was zealous for the bank's basic mission but immediately acknowledged that much of the NGO criticism was correct. His agreement that the bank had indeed got it wrong won him space and the institution a short reprieve. It also made him many enemies among the bank's older managers.

Refashioning the bank was a herculean task. In the face of Wolfensohn's peremptory demands to do things his way, some of the best senior managers mounted an exodus. And while he was a great salesman, he was no manager. The senior managers could not tolerate that a development novice could so precipitately accept most of the critics' case. Mallaby, in his account of Wolfensohn, describes a titanic struggle of wills between president and institution.[2]

But a third comer to the contest was the growing demands of developing countries. The new democracies needed better and faster help than they were getting. They were impatient. The heads of government that Wolfensohn hobnobbed with used milder, less public language than the NGOs but were just as frustrated. The bank was not helping them with their people, their voters, and was utterly lacking in the skills of listening to them and then responding quickly and effectively. Wolfensohn, the ex-banker, became the hinge between anxious new democracies and a bank that could not, or would not, listen.

Very quickly, low disbursement rates picked up, new priorities such as health and education jostled aside older ones such as infrastructure, and Wolfensohn's bank plunged into an issue that fainter hearts had avoided: debt relief. A precious orthodoxy held that the

Bank, which borrowed in the markets for most of its loans, could never allow developing countries to default. That would undermine the bank's own creditworthiness and sow moral hazard among the borrowers, who would stop taking their World Bank and IMF debt seriously. Wolfensohn challenged it all.

The new priorities spawned new departments and new kinds of bank staff and consultants. Wolfensohn's bank became more diverse and colorful as the new recruits mingled with the gray suits. The staff, deeply socialized into a culture that valued cold sober analysis, discovered that it was okay to care, that they could wear their emotions more openly, and that they could be passionate about development without anyone questioning their judgment and objectivity.

Meanwhile Wolfensohn wept, hugged, and backslapped his way around the world. He was a Bill Clinton of development—emoting, feeling the grief of the poor, angry for them when they were locked out of village schools by fees they could not afford or when their natural habitat of forest and field, on which they depended for their livelihood, was unable to sustain them anymore. As with Clinton, empathy became Wolfensohn's trademark.

But the hardest leap of imagination to make was to understand that even after he had added all the ameliorative social and other development dimensions, the basic bank prescription remained unkind to the poor. Tight public spending inevitably hits the poor most.

Despite the eruption of new initiatives at the top, in other ways the bank was slow to change. The basic economic model that bore down so heavily on the poor remained largely untouched. Sometimes the changes seemed like bells and whistles to distract from an unchanged core institution. But finally events nudged the bank toward real change even as economic orthodoxy remained deep in its veins.

The Asian financial crisis in 1997 was the catalyst. In the preceding years Southeast Asian growth had been known as "The Asian Economic Miracle." It had transformed the agricultural economies of Southeast Asia into low-cost manufacturing dynamos, workshops to the world, in the way the U.K.'s Manchester had been in the nineteenth century or that their neighbors, Shanghai and southern China are today.

Starting in the middle of 1997, however, the miracle began to look more like a bubble. Panic grew as foreign investors started pulling their funds, first out of Thailand and South Korea and then out of Indonesia, Malaysia, and the Philippines. By pure coincidence, it started the day after the British flag was lowered over Hong Kong for the last time and the Chinese flag was raised. Journalists covering that exuberant all-night party recall being rudely awakened to news of a meltdown. But the loss of a British imperial possession could no longer trigger an international financial collapse; the fault lay elsewhere. Over the coming months, billions of dollars were withdrawn from the region, leading to a rapid economic contraction.

In the previous two years some $65 billion in short-term loans and investments had rushed into these economies in a fashionable swarm. Now those billions turned and fled. Just as the original influx of funds had shown the markets to be exuberant lemmings, so the withdrawal was an equal overreaction. But overreaction or not, nobody wants to be the last in or out of a market. Being left holding the plate, so to speak, is a very expensive place to be. So a panicked rush to divest is a market contagion that, once under way, is hard to stop.

Asia's vulnerability was even worse, for even as the economic boom had pumped up Asian confidence and put the region on economic steroids, its businessmen and bankers had drawn in foreign capital in the form of short-term dollar-denominated borrowings. When the tables turned and money started to leave, local currencies depreciated against the dollar, making the loans too expensive to service because the businesses all operated in local currency. Worse still, the lenders, desperate to get their money back, would not roll the loans over and wanted their principal back, as well as interest, in now impossibly expensive dollars.

Once a country enters this vortex of financial crisis, the effects on the real economy quickly follow. Businesses contract or close, jobs are lost, and inflation rises as the cost of imports increases. Per capita GDP in the affected Southeast Asian countries was reduced by 8 to 20 percent during and after the crisis. And again the poor bore the greatest brunt. Poverty rates in Indonesia increased particularly sharply.

The consequences for the World Bank and the international financial system generally were various. First, again, the World Bank was on the sidelines. Jim Wolfensohn was even more aggrieved to be on the margins of the financial crisis negotiations than Lew Preston had been two and a half years earlier. Bob Rubin's U.S. Treasury—supported by the IMF, whose chief Michel Camdessus and principal deputy Stan Fischer were at the heart of the negotiations—sought to calm the markets by offering rescue packages in the form of credit lines big enough to awe them into suspending their retreat. He promised tough stabilization programs in each country and fresh development finance to correct the structural shortcomings in the financial systems.

Jim Wolfensohn, however, was reluctant to write a check to finance someone else's emergency pool and let others make the running. He bombarded the White House and others with demands to be included. But he was not, and the exclusion began to be reflected in policy, not just in personalities.

The IMF and the United States were imposing a real contraction on the Asian economies to squeeze out weaker businesses and force a restructuring of the banking sector. Wolfensohn realized that the consequences of the economic slowdown were falling on the poor; his instincts told him that the remedy for falling demand should be more, not less, public spending, and that it should target the poor to ensure that even as jobs fell away, health and education remained in place. He ordered the bank to finance public works schemes, at least to provide some temporary work for those who had lost their manufacturing jobs.

It was Keynes versus Friedman. The two institutions—the Keynesian bank and the Friedmanite IMF—glowered at each other across Washington's Nineteenth Street. Each side drew its own lessons from the earlier Mexican crisis, in which a short contraction turned, a year later, into a growth rate of more than 5 percent. Each side thought Mexico made its case.

The two main spokesmen were both highly distinguished economists who had, at that time, little regard for each other's point of view. Speaking for the bank was Joseph Stiglitz, a refugee from the Clinton administration, whose big-spending views as chairman of the Council on Economic Advisors had put him at odds with Robert Rubin and the Treasury. He was delighted to offer intellectual heft to Wolfensohn's suspicions that cutting spending and thereby forcing a recession were the wrong prescription. (Stiglitz would later win a Nobel Prize in economics for his academic work on information economics.) Speaking for the IMF was Stan Fischer. Born in what is now Zambia and later a naturalized American, Fischer had come from MIT and a spell as chief economist of the World Bank. Today, he is the chief of Israel's Central Bank.

Stiglitz and Fischer are two of the smartest, most decent men in international economics, sharing progressive instincts. But they could not abide each other. Like many dueling economists, they both in my view had the wrong end of the stick. What distinguished Mexico from Asia was not narrow economic policy but, first and foremost, good leadership.

Mexico's new president, Ernesto Zedillo, a former technocrat who was to usher Mexico to a full democratic transition and an opposition presidential victory at the end of his term, was a deft statesman with strong economic skills who quickly understood what mattered if Mexico was to navigate the storm successfully. He had to project confidence that the problem was short term, and he had to quickly draw back international lending and investment into Mexico. Mexico's problem, like Asia's, was short-term dollar-denominated liabilities, in this case a central-bank-issued debt note called a *tesobono*. He needed a rescue package to stabilize markets, including a means of restructuring and paying down the *tesobono* debt in an orderly way, and he had to convince Mexicans and the markets that he could quickly get the country back to growth. A Yale-trained economist, he projected exactly the calm authority the country needed, and he prevailed. Stabilization measures (the IMF-Fischer-Friedman medicine) were quickly followed by a more expansionary growth-oriented approach coupled with increased social spending (the World Bank-Stiglitz-Keynes-Galbraith tonic).

The lesson of the Mexican crisis was that strong domestic political leadership by Zedillo, the right sequence of squeeze and expansion in economics, and bold international support were what saved the day. In the United States President Clinton and Secretary Rubin bypassed congressional authorization for the package because they knew that approval would come too slowly and be too restrictive to stop the crisis. They also guessed that a Republican Congress would secretly be relieved to be off the hook of having to either approve a big bailout or be responsible for chaos on America's southern border. While fighting off domestic critics, Clinton and Rubin marshaled Europe and the international financial institutions to support them. Under Rubin's flawless leadership, backed by Larry Summers's bold vision of the way forward, the Treasury seemed almost to replace the State Department as the architect of foreign policy, just as economics seemed to briefly trump politics in this era of globalization. The crowning glory was that Mexico quickly repaid the U.S. financial aid with interest. The treasury made a profit.

Asia was not so lucky. From Washington to its own capitals, its leadership was divided and tremulous. In Washington the World Bank and the IMF were still waging civil war on Nineteenth Street. When you need to stabilize markets, you have no time to blink. Speculators must believe that the government has a single policy and is putting its full weight behind it. Stabilizing markets involves a big element of the gaming tables of *Casino Royale*. In Mexico, the hand was played flawlessly and the markets settled. In Asia, squabbles and prevarication spilled over, and the markets sensed it.

The IMF and the World Bank offered competing alternatives, when they should have offered two steps in a common process. First, markets should have been stabilized with an IMF support and adjustment package to shock and awe the markets at the lowest outlay possible from lenders. Second, the economy should have been reinflated with heavy public works and social spending, as preferred by the World Bank, so as to preserve productive capacity.

Instead, Wolfensohn and Stiglitz made trips to Asia that emphasized their different points of view. Michel Camdessus, the head of the IMF, went to Indonesia and was seen as browbeating the leadership into austerity and devaluation. Wolfensohn, on the other hand, offered empathy and support to ordinary Indonesians. They should have joined forces in a constructive "bad cop, good cop" routine, which might have won them respect. Instead, their behavior exposed the wide, and frankly irresponsible, gap between them. Firefighters should wait to debate tactics until the fire is out.

That said, the real leadership failure was less in Washington than in the Asian countries. The democracy deficit was apparent: the governments had little popular support and therefore little capacity to introduce unpopular reforms. Quality leadership was also missing: the Asian countries had no Ernesto Zedillos. In Indonesia, Thailand, and South Korea the crisis would eventually give a decisive push toward more democratic open government. But before it got there, the weak and corrupt Suharto dictatorship in Indonesia breathed its

last breath only to be succeeded by an even more ineffectual transition government and then a weak first democratic government. In
Thailand, an old-style retired-general politician was bundled out in
favor of a rather competent democratic government that, however,
never fully overcame its legacy of economic crisis and was replaced
by a populist billionaire who did the new democracy immense damage. In South Korea, the government's mismanagement allowed the
longtime opposition leader Kim Dae Jung (an old political client of
mine) finally to win a presidential election and push through market
reforms that were surprising, given his old left-wing connections.
Kim realized that the antidote to South Korea's chronic crony capitalism, reflected in the interlocking chaebol corporate conglomerates,
was more market competition.

The only country where a leader looked the crisis in the eye and
refused to blink was Malaysia. Malaysia's prime minister Mohamad
Mahathir inveighed against speculators, Jews, and the West in appalling terms, but he held his ground. He allowed no devaluation. He
refused to seek the mercy of an international bailout. His relative
success had probably more to do with earlier conservative fiscal policy than with his appeals to nationalist self-reliance. Nevertheless,
this crisis burnished his credentials among some, as did his philosophy of Asian independence from the tentacles of Western finance.
He provided a lot of political impetus for the later tendency to rely
on regional economic self-sufficiency. Countries in the region have
since run up huge reserves and for a while talked of creating an Asian
IMF to ensure they were never again dependent on a Washington
institution. They have certainly contributed hugely to the now widely
held view that the IMF has lost both its way and its role.

As the crisis was building during the summer of 1997, my family
and I spent a weekend at the house of George Soros. While I was
there, my office faxed me an account of a speech by Mahathir attacking my host. Soros was leading the speculators who were breaking

Asia's currency, Mahathir said, just as he had famously broken the British pound. The speech contained a big dose of anti-Semitism. It was also short on facts; notably, Soros had quietly left all those currencies well ahead of the crisis because he had seen how perilous their situation had become. He was not one of those who had later stampeded out and provoked the crisis.

I had first met Soros in 1987 at his Long Island weekend home, where I was soliciting his support for the "No" campaign in Chile. For dinner he sat at one end of an impossibly long baronial dining table, and his then wife at the other; I sat halfway between, and a butler shuffled between us. He asked me about the Thai stock market, since at that time he "inconveniently" found himself owning a lot of it. It was my first introduction to his disconcerting mixture of wry self-deprecation and sheer financial power. I observed that stability in Thailand rested on one factor alone: the health of the king. That silenced even Soros, and when I asked him for money for Chile, I got it.

Ten years later, I knew him well enough to know that Mahathir was railing at the wrong target. George was not the moneylender of Mahathir's anti-Semitic imagination. In his Southampton garden we agreed I would give him the right of reply. At the time I was organizing the annual World Bank meeting in Hong Kong, and as Soros and Mahathir refused to appear on the same platform, I arranged for them to speak back to back at a seminar series there. At Hong Kong two very different views of globalization were on display: Soros touted a liberal internationalist world of laws and transparency, while Mahathir advocated a closed nationalist one of self-reliance. But both made a common point: any economic system that did not protect and support the poor would inevitably fail. Globalization, if left to the markets, would not work. If it was to enjoy popular consent, it had to operate within a strong framework of public policy.

The 1997 crisis shook Asia's faith in globalization. The poor did suffer, as rescue plans protected foreign and domestic business interests rather than the weak, and the political establishment appeared to be in the pocket of those business interests. In Thailand, the government made ridiculously expensive efforts for much too long to support the local currency, the baht, against the dollar: the purpose was to help the businessmen, who had dollar-denominated debts, stay solvent.

Letting international investors escape with something has a logic, as does supporting domestic businesses as they struggle through the crisis. Both would be needed afterward, as parts of globalization's long-term infrastructure and therefore vital to a country's economic future. But that logic had to be balanced against protecting the poor. Their voices were not heard, as they were outside the rooms where the decisions were made. Many in the region developed an abiding distrust of international institutions as part of an antipoor conspiracy.

During this period I spent an enormous amount of time being interviewed on TV channels that broadcast to Asia and in Asian newspapers, explaining the logic behind the rescue plans. I would shuttle over to CNN's Washington bureau at daybreak or late at night to calm markets or to talk up the Thai baht or other endangered Asian currencies.

I knew, however, that we were not sufficiently reaching the region's poor, in either words or deeds. They lacked access to the international cable channels; more significantly, they did not see that our money was helping. Before the crisis they had been precariously above the poverty line; now they were dunked back below it.

Incipient democracy may have brought people more accountable governments, but financial crises were a blunt demonstration of how little control they or their governments had over the increasingly volatile global economy. The crises made more certain that national politics would realign around globalization, the primary economic driver in our lives, as ever-present as class had been in my British childhood or imperialism in the colonial heyday. Globalization shaped our opportunities and allocated losses in society. Further, as Asia had shown, when the globalization rodeo throws you, it throws you hard. Asia took a terrible knock, and even when it climbed back, its politics were not the same.

Politics had to respond effectively to the wild ride of globalization, and not only at the national level. A compelling case could be made that global institutions had to become more accountable. Policy toward Asia had been driven to an alarming extent by egos and turf wars in Washington, not by the demands of the region's poor, let alone its leaders. By contrast in 2008 when it was the West's turn to be hit by a financial crisis, the World Bank and IMF leaped to attention, and their policies were very different. Asia had every right to be mad.

CHAPTER SIX

JOINING UP DEMOCRACY AND DEVELOPMENT

In 1999 I was drafted into running the world's second-best-known international development agency, UNDP—Avis to the World Bank's Hertz, as I quipped to my colleagues old and new. My first UNDP project visit took me to a women handloom weavers' project in Lesotho. It was a salutary place to start as it brought me right up against how different UNDP's possibilities were compared to the World Bank's. Funds for the project were short, and only a handful of women were involved yet several UN experts were attached to the project full time. That meant the project had a huge expatriate overhead for almost no developmental return. It was tokenism. I had to think hard about where UNDP's comparative usefulness really lay.

At its simplest UNDP was poor, and the World Bank was rich; UNDP also did not always apply the bank's development rigor to its projects. But it had one undeniable advantage: developing countries considered it to be on their side. It was their development agency, and unlike the heavily Washington-based World Bank staff, most UNDP staff were in the field close to their clients. At its best it lived on development instinct where the Bank lived on intellect. In the future, my hope for the organization was that it could add the professionalism of the World Bank to the trust and strong sense of mission for the poor that it already had.

The World Bank brims over with more development expertise than any other institution—development agency, university, or NGO—in the world, but its borrowers often do not trust it. The bank, I had reluctantly concluded, despite the herculean efforts of Wolfensohn remained disconnected from and unaccountable to those it was working for, be they the poor or their governments. In part that was part of being a bank. Being a borrower is a humbling and disempowering experience at any level, whether as an individual consumer or a country. But still, something was missing.

So when I was offered the job at UNDP, it seemed an opportunity to run an organization that could be an antidote to many of the World Bank's problems. Its board was balanced between donors and developing countries. It was not shy of tackling the political roots of development failure and had a strong sense of itself as a friend to poor governments.

UNDP was, though, an intergovernmental institution whose authority derived from governments. It suffered from the UN's exaggerated respect for the prerogatives of government, but its feet were on the ground. As the Human Development Reports showed, it put the poor first and was willing to name and shame governments that were not performing well.

My predecessors at the helm of UNDP had all been Americans, again much as the World Bank chiefs were nominated by the White House. But this tradition had less impact on UNDP's culture, partly because of the remarkable Americans chosen, but more because the institution's main orientation was toward developing countries. UNDP's culture was self-conscious of being Not-the-World-Bank.

In 1999 Kofi Annan faced a dilemma: his predecessor had agreed that the next UNDP administrator would be a European, but the Europeans' first instinct was to behave like the United States and choose that European from among themselves and present him as a fait accompli. Annan could not accept this process—he wanted greater openness and transparency in such appointments. He had no interest in seeing the Europeans picking up the Americans' bad habits.

Further, the Europeans' way of choosing their candidate made the highly political process of the White House look almost reflective. Before the rest of Europe had even begun thinking about it, the Danes in some low-level Brussels committee that handled international appointments preemptively corralled support for their own development minister. European Union members felt obliged publicly to support their official candidate, but a number left Annan no doubt that they would feel relieved if he chose someone else. Paul Nielson, the Danish minister, was deeply committed to development and UNDP, but his rough divisive style did not become a fundraiser; nor did he have the coaxing skills needed to get things done in the UN. His critics thought he would rub both donors and developing countries the wrong way. As the controversy built, Annan looked for alternative Europeans.

Annan wanted UNDP to become a major force in development. But its resources had been contracting, and with the progressive Jim Wolfensohn at the head of the World Bank and with Brussels's growing aid effort, some wondered whether UNDP was even necessary anymore. Not only did Annan want to put UNDP back at the center of development, he wanted to make the choice competitively and break the bad habit of allocating top international jobs through backroom deals between countries. The White House got to choose the president of the World Bank and, in the past, the administrator of UNDP. The Europeans similarly chose the managing director of the IMF. The rest of the world increasingly resented this closed shop.

Even for jobs that had no long-term national hold, too often intercountry horse-trading settled the selection. A country or region would assert it was its turn for a particular job, then expect to nominate the candidate. Even the position of secretary-general adhered to a strict tradition of regional rotation, although there was a little more international involvement in the selection. Kofi Annan held the job because it was Africa's turn, just as his successor would be chosen because Asia insisted on its turn. In terms of keeping the different regions committed to the UN, the rotation had some logic, in a way that one country "owning" a job did not.

Annan believed that UNDP was going to need someone accustomed to moving easily among Europeans, Americans, and other donors as well as figures from the developing countries. The organization was in crisis. The Americans' financial support had sharply declined. Other donors too were losing confidence in its effectiveness; meanwhile developing countries were resisting reforms.

The British ambassador, Sir Jeremy Greenstock, asked to meet me, and we sat down behind the high-backed white chairs of the UN's Indonesian lounge, where Arabs and Israelis or other bitter enemies would, it was reputed, gather to whisper anonymously to each other. Greenstock, one of the UN's ablest diplomats, assured me with some embarrassment that I had his own good wishes in the contest but that the U.K. government, as part of Europe, was committed to the Danish candidate. He then asked if he might leave first and if I would wait for some minutes before following. He did not want people to realize we had been meeting.

Annan's selection of me, and the General Assembly's endorsement, was certainly a braver and perhaps a more democratic selection than most. For although my own country had not nominated me, the developing world and the Clinton administration were strongly behind me since I was Annan's candidate and had already gathered something of a reputation as a reformer, with progressive views by World Bank standards. I was well known at the UN because it had been part of my brief at the World Bank. (Four years later, when I would stand for reelection, the rift had long since healed, and the Europeans would be my foremost champions.)

When the General Assembly confirmed me, Sweden's Washington ambassador Rolf Ekeus, an old UN hand, opened the first champagne to celebrate. In my early months as head of UNDP, to Denmark's chagrin, Sweden would be the main sponsor of my reform agenda and my most ardent supporter. Germany, however, which had the presidency of the European Union at the time, felt that my election slighted the official European candidate. In the midst of a federal budget crisis, it followed Denmark and cut its contributions to UNDP. Both countries eventually moved past their initial opposition and became my firm allies, but the incident is a naked illustration of how resources for the poor are not immune to the aggrieved politics of the rich.

From the World Bank I had noticed that UNDP had attempted to compete across too many areas of development, stretching its expertise too thin. It had agriculture and education experts, public health and forestry units, urban planning expertise, and much else— even though the UN had other specialized agencies in each of these areas. Over time UNDP, distrusting the competence of these other providers, had built up what amounted to rival expertise.

If the UN was ever to be an efficient instrument of aid, we had to cut the redundancy and make use of the specialized agencies. That way we could concentrate our resources where they made the most difference—in governance, postconflict nation-building, poverty reduction, and sustainable development. Focusing on these activities would also please the donor side of our board.

The donors were demanding greater efficiency. We had gotten stale and rather middle-aged; too many senior staff were stuck in New York rather than in the field. Our greatest asset perhaps was that we were more field-based, much more decentralized than the Washington-centered World Bank, but we were in danger of frittering away this advantage. After years of budget cuts and retrenchment, we needed to get back on our game.

I arrived with a growing conviction that a development model based on economics alone did not work. I was looking to hook up my insights about democracy and development. Government and aid had to become accountable to the poor; otherwise, despite all the experts' best intentions, the poor would not benefit. I wanted to make UNDP a political institution because therein, I had become convinced, lay the key to successful development.

We were an antipoverty agency that had to employ democracy as a way of tying policy-making to the needs of the poor. For us, democracy was not an end in itself but a means to ending poverty. The longtime argument about whether democracy was a necessary precondition for development or whether regimentation and discipline at the early stages contributed more to development than democracy could, missed the point, I thought. The key relationship that drove poverty reduction was accountability to the poor. If policy-makers felt they had to answer to the poor, they would act at least partially in their interests.

My new home at UNDP, by pushing me to a broader, noneconomic vision of development, also nudged me toward remembering that the fight for democracy is more than just better incomes and more investment or even better services. Having the freedom to make choices about one's life is as intrinsically important as earning the daily wage. Each contributes to the quality of life, and they are mutually sustainable. You cannot have political freedom without economic security, I had come to understand, and vice versa.

In 1989 a predecessor of mine as UNDP administrator, Bill Draper, had had the remarkable courage and presence of mind to launch UNDP's Human Development Reports, which championed this broader, more political view of development. A bluff and gregarious Republican venture capitalist from California who had been nominated by George H. W. Bush, he had been my neighbor on P Street in Washington's Georgetown. When I became administrator in 1999, he sent a wry message saying he was sorry the job hadn't gone to an

American but was pleased we had kept it on P Street. The intellectual leadership of the reports from three remarkable development economists—Mahbub ul Haq, Amartya Sen, and Richard Jolly—had created a formidable force. Back when I was at Cambridge, I had heard Jolly lecture on Kenyan wages and poverty. It was one of the most personally influential talks I have ever attended—he cut through the refined history I was studying and reconnected to my passion for Africa. Jolly had followed ul Haq and Sen to UNDP's Human Development Report office, where they had already challenged the purist economic view of development emanating from Washington. Ul Haq essentially challenged measuring development results by income improvements alone. People were surely better off when they had more choice and control over their life and better schools and health care for their families. Income alone did not necessarily achieve this. Sen (who would win a Nobel Prize in economics for his thinking in this area) was the elder statesman of the three, keeping a watchful eye on how the intellectual case for human development grew under the leadership of these remarkable collaborators. The office never had much money but in my view was much more influential than the World Bank's well-funded World Development Reports, which because of the resentment against their parent rarely cut through despite a lot more original research on individual development issues.

Development is more than income, our authors thundered annually to an appreciative and continually growing global audience. The poor, like all of us, want choices, opportunity, and some control over their lives. They do not consider themselves better off when their income precariously nudges up above some arbitrary bar like a dollar a day. They evaluate their lives around whether their kids have affordable schooling and health care to get them through simple childhood diseases. A person born in Russia or most African countries can expect a much shorter lifespan than someone born in Norway or Australia. Richard Jolly developed a telling set of one-liners that compared how much we spent on ice cream or coffee to our development spending.

The reports certainly furthered my development education. I came to understand that democracy in development did not just mean holding government to account. It also meant empowering people with the ability to make life choices. Poverty is surely called grinding, not just because of the absence of material possessions and necessities but because it grinds down the spirit by making people slaves of their situation. They can focus on nothing beyond day-to-day survival.

Beyond their struggle to overcome poverty, the poor grapple with a second ring of choices. What kind of world do they and their children want to live in? Do they prefer the stability of village life to the frenzy of city life? Village life may be threatened by environmental degradation and overfarming as land pressures grow, and incomes are lower. But city life is no picnic. Forced to live in far-off shantytowns and make dangerous long commutes for often-marginal work, the poor urban dweller may enjoy greater material well-being, but is the quality of life better?

When my family and I were driving through a Brazilian slum known as a *favela*, just above Rio's Copacabana Beach, my nine-year-old daughter Isobel asked me why, if the people were so poor, there were so many satellite TV dishes. In every other respect, as she had seen, the lives of the *favela*'s inhabitants were overwhelmingly difficult. The one expensive possession, the TV, must have actually deepened the owners' sense of deprivation by bringing home just how much else was missing in their lives. And the fact that Isobel and her siblings could not walk along Copacabana Beach (except during the middle of the day) because of violent crime introduced her to the costs of extreme poverty. By championing an annual analysis and an index that daringly ranked countries on these human development criteria, UNDP convinced many people that we had to think of development through this broader lens.

As I thought back to campaign rallies in Latin America where hoarse-voiced candidates promised a revolution and an end to poverty, and to the survivors' accounts of genocidal betrayal in the Cambodian refugee camps, it all came together for me. Neither the vote nor a stable income was enough. UNDP had to work, not just to keep power accountable to the poor, but to release them from the broader noneconomic dimensions of poverty by expanding their rights and opportunities.

UNDP's resources doubled during my time there, to more than $4 billion a year, but when shared across more than 160 countries, that still did not go far. And a lot of money was already attached to particular projects in ways that we had a limited ability to change. So our real war chest was about a third of the total. This we could direct heavily at the poorest countries, but if our limited resources were to be transformational, we would have to do so strategically.

The World Bank had money and smarts: its sheer money power had the prospect of impacting the lives of hundreds of millions. But we had the trust of clients. And we understood that the greatest development progress could be made around these more sensitive issues of politics, governance, and accountability.

So as my colleagues and I and our partners analyzed where UNDP's real value in the development chain lay, we realized that our real asset was that, unlike the World Bank and IMF, we could speak truth to developing countries on policies and institutions. They trusted us as their development agency. I remember my astonishment on my first visit to China as UNDP administrator-to-be when I was ushered out to President Jiang Zemin's beach house because he wanted to tell me how much UNDP had helped him personally and China in its opening up. His first trip abroad in 1978 as a vice minister was funded by UNDP. It was a good example of the trust and esteem we were held in by developing country leaders.

Unhappily, I concluded that sometimes we had rather abused that trust, taking issue with World Bank advice just because we could, rather than because we should. We had gained a reputation for contradicting World Bank advice just because of where it came from. The feeling was often mutual. Governments, meanwhile, had to choose between following the bank's advice and getting the big check that came with it, or following their instinct and going with UNDP because it was considered to be on their side.

We had to use our access and trust more constructively. If preserving a government's trust meant never challenging that government, what was the point of having that trust? And if our efforts to one-up the World Bank blinded us to the fact that that organization of very smart people was sometimes right then we were missing out on their expertise.

But without the World Bank's checkbook or its army of experts, what role did UNDP play? We concluded that we must focus "upstream," as I described it, on policies and institution-building rather than on thousands of projects, each of which might help a particular community or set of individuals but whose sum was not greater than the parts. We should find our way to presidents and other decision-makers of real clout and help them fashion a real pro-poor strategy for their country and then help build a national capacity to carry out that ambitious undertaking. For an organization whose donors expected it to do small projects like the handloom weavers, this was a wrenching change. The word went out that when the administrator visited your country, hide the handloom weavers!

I was determined that UNDP would build up its own expertise on governance (particularly to help weak or postconflict governments) and on economics (with a focus on making sure growth benefited the poor). It also needed a new expertise on the environment, because development policy has to live within what is environmentally possible. A country did itself no good by ripping apart rain forests to grow more crops, or by crowding city dwellers onto poor land or letting pollution go unabated. Growth has to be environmentally sustainable.

For UNDP to set aside projects that had tangible bricks and mortar, even if not many of them, in favor of giving policy advice was not easy. South Africa, the land of my father and therefore a country with which I have a great affinity, demonstrated the problem early in my tenure. The South African ambassador Dumisani Kumalo, a former preacher and community activist, was worried that giving policy advice would mean lodging more expensive foreign experts in five-star hotels and providing less money for clean water and schools. How could he explain that to his relatives in Blood River he boomed. Blood River had been the scene of a famous nineteenth-century showdown between our Zulu and white South African forebears; the mischievous rhetorical resonance of the allusion was not wasted on me.

One solution was to find cheaper experts who did not stay in five-star hotels and who had personally experienced development issues. So as we built up regional policy experts, we recruited global southerners and people who had lived through the post-Communist restructuring of Central and Eastern Europe to supplement our Western-derived advice.

South Africa is a country of considerable but unevenly distributed wealth; here more efficient governance could hugely improve internal resource allocation if spending better targeted the poor. Pushing for that reallocation was likely to have a much higher impact than a single small project. So in our Human Development Reports and in our work on the ground, we hammered away at the declining human indicators. We even dared to suggest that in some respects the poor were worse off than they had been under apartheid because democracy had not yet given them a real say in the issues of municipal government and health and education that most affected them. For years the government had remained mute about the AIDS crisis that was ravaging South Africa, which caused life expectancy to fall well below the level of the later apartheid years.

In South Africa, impact is always an issue. Compared to the size of its economy, our resources were small, whether we did handloom projects or followed my preferred direction. And sometimes the right small project catches the attention of government and makes a policy point as well—a powerful combination. For example, South Africa's initial postapartheid vision was heavily industrial and urban. In the apartheid era the tribal homelands where people had lived in poverty were like dustbowls; the rich white people had lush game parks and ranches. But South Africa has astonishing botanical and environmental diversity. I consider it to be South Africa's crown jewel and a source of future income for poor farmers. So UNDP supported a specific project, the extraordinary city botanical gardens at the foot of Table Mountain in Cape Town, that helped keep interest alive in the environment.

UNDP had to place its approach within a set of values and principles that reflected our pro-poor philosophy. Many of my colleagues pressed for a rights-based approach to development, arguing that economic restructuring programs must not cavalierly remove access to school, health, clean water, housing or employment because these were human rights. We were equally obliged to both protect those rights and extend them to those who did not enjoy them.

I was uncomfortable with some elements of this approach because, unlike voting and freedom of speech, which are political rights, clean water and health and the like are essentially benefits of successful economic growth that are steered to the poor through good government. They cannot be legislated or enforced by courts. My view on this issue has annoyed some of my human rights friends for years, because it can seem to be demanding only political and not economic rights. But I believe that while they are different kinds of rights that require different strategies, we must fight for both.

Bill Draper and his Human Development Report team had introduced the notion of *human* into *development*. Then the next administrator, Gus Speth, a cerebral leader, who went on to head the environmental school at Yale, added *sustainable*. A longtime environmentalist, Speth rebelled against a materialist development model. Development, Speth understood before most, was running up against the finite limit of natural resources. Forest cover, topsoil, land, water, and energy were all limited inputs into the human wealth-making machine, more limited than capital and labor because there was no arguing with nature. We had run up against limits, he recognized, that were beyond our control. And human-generated processes like climate change were contributing to the problem.

At UNDP, our challenge was to make the environmental message of sustainable growth a very local, and very human, matter. The poor had a lot of inherited wisdom about the value of rivers and forests as sources of food, water, fuel, and medicine. They also understood the importance of protecting and stabilizing adjacent farming land from loss of topsoil. But population and economic pressures often mean forests and rivers are overused, and a community's only permanent resource is squandered.

One morning in early 2002 in New York I was sitting at a breakfast table at the Harvard Club with former Colorado senator Tim Wirth, a longtime environmentalist. He now headed the UN Foundation, set up by CNN's founder, Ted Turner, charged with channeling private resources, particularly his own, to the UN. That day we came up with an unlikely way of knitting all this local experience together: the Equator Initiative. The equatorial countries are acutely poor but also contain great concentrations of biodiversity; local efforts are being made both to reduce poverty and to conserve biodiversity. The Equator Initiative helps share these efforts with people in different continents who are on the same vulnerable frontline between man and nature.

We came up with the idea of giving Equator Awards to encourage communities to propose sharable sustainability strategies. The first awards were given out at the UN Summit on the Environment and Development in Johannesburg in 2002. Masai warriors who were experimenting with eco-tourism, as a means of making a living out of preservation, mingled with Indians from Latin America and small businessmen and women from Asia. All had found ingenious ways of making a living off local natural resources in ways that conserved rather than depleted them. Before the prize night, they spent a week sharing their experiences in turning conservation into a viable economic strategy for their communities.

Fortunately, this Oscar night for the environment and development, as I rather euphorically described it, did not end with winners and losers. A generous donor, the head of the Nature Conservancy, announced that that night everyone was a winner and that all finalists would get prizes of $20,000 for their communities. After doing the calculations—there were a lot of finalists—Wirth made me follow a donor out to the men's bathroom to make sure he didn't try to escape. After we returned, Tim like the good Senate fundraiser he was quickly announced the new awards before there was any change of heart.

UNDP's ability to gather globally and share knowledge locally is a remarkable asset. It was not usually so colorfully or directly accomplished. We invested heavily in electronic knowledge-management systems so that we could steep ourselves in global best practices and then applied them appropriately in different national contexts. We also organized our experts in each area into globally networked teams to build on one another's learning and expertise.

Even as UNDP gathered force as an advocate and adviser, however, I was continuously reminded of how much of development was beyond our reach. We could give governments good advice on how to help the poor escape their condition, and we could even strategically choose a project to demonstrate what government could do, but at a certain point individuals and their government had to take up the challenge and do it for themselves.

Unless a strong democratic consensus emerged around a good

framework of national policies and their links to the global economy, then providing outside development support amounted to pushing on a piece of string. Countries had to get the support and they had to lead—then enterprising people could use the opportunity to start businesses and create jobs that in turn created a tax base to sustain the growing infrastructure and services. The virtuous circle started at home. A country that depended on foreign aid; whose economic activity consisted of what the state itself got up to; and whose policies were chopped and changed in the hopes of pleasing voters or donors, would remain stuck in the poverty trap. There was simply no substitute for local leadership and enterprise.

During my first few years at UNDP, I came to realize that we had trapped ourselves in a statist vision of development. States matter a lot. They provide the infrastructure and services, the security, and the predictability of policies that entrepreneurs require. But unless a private sector and a civil society start to grow, the state is a stage without a play. I began to push hard on behalf of these two vital actors that could partner with states in the fight against poverty.

The first was the private sector: not only the private sector of the large multinationals, with their earnest and important talk about social responsibility, but small businessmen and women on the ground who did not necessarily speak UN English and would not have even begun to understand the term *sustainable human development*, let alone know how to fill in a funding application form. Yet these businessmen and women were the source of the jobs and prosperity that could change their communities. They operated in a void that might become a space of commercial opportunity, but they lacked the means to transform it. I decided UNDP had to champion this sector, and so with Kofi Annan's support I pulled together a panel of businessmen and political leaders who prepared a report.

One of them, the late C. K. Prahalad, described the business opportunity that the poor offer in his book *The Bottom of the Pyramid*. He argued that two billion people have income growth that is carrying them onto the first rungs of a ladder that will bring them up into a new global middle class. They also have emerging consumer hopes shaped by the mass media. But many are paying more for consumer goods than we do because they can afford to buy only in small units from local corner stores. Prahalad charted consumer price differences of at least 40 percent between middle class and poor neighborhoods in Mumbai, India.

Poor people's labor has to be harnessed, he argues, to make the goods and services for their own class. They earn less so they can pay less. In India, sectors such as medicines, glasses, hotels, consumer goods, and financial services are starting to respond with new business models that can build huge and profitable market share because they are providing affordable goods and services.

In a poor country the private sector doesn't necessarily stop in the same place as it does in a rich one. The development community has considered private involvement in education and health for the poor to be anathema. But school fees have kept a lot of poor children out of class. The truth is that in many developing countries even as people's wealth grows, government cannot collect taxes from them and then provide high-quality health and education, because the government capacity is not there.

The poor are more likely to get better health and education services if they pay a fee as they become able to afford it. So in today's poor countries the relationship between government and NGOs is likely to be different than it was in the past. Given weak government service delivery, civil society, like small businesses, will start to fill the gap. It will seize the role on its own or government will franchise it to do so, but civil society will increasingly step in to provide services such as health and education.

During my tenure at UNDP, I visited a large public hospital in Malawi whose limited services were overwhelmed by AIDS victims. For the sprawling mass of sick and dying humanity in the wards, there was little medicine or other support. The few nurses present—many had left for better-paying and less stressful jobs in South Africa or Britain—were overwhelmed. Yet in a corner of the hospital's rundown grounds was a small beacon of hope: an outpatient clinic for AIDS, run with the support of an international NGO. The patients were on antiretroviral treatments and so were well enough to stay home and work. The facility was clean and orderly. The difference between the clinic and the hospital was that the first had a nongovernmental operator, supported by a small international donor, while the latter was government-supported. Both were staffed by Malawians.

In sum, the democratic gale that is blowing through development is restructuring it. It is not just making national government more accountable; it is reordering the pieces of the development system as well. As the demand for support and services for the poor grows, NGOs and businesses will be drawn in both as efficient providers and as advocates for more radical development policies. At the international level, the pressure to make institutions more accountable to poor countries will over time open up their governance structures and ways of doing business.

CHAPTER SEVEN

ALL CHANGE

During my UN years, from 1999 to the end of 2006, first at UNDP and then with Kofi Annan in the Secretariat, the pace of change in the world picked up dramatically. In that short time hundreds of millions of people continued to be added to the global population, and as Asian economies grew at twice the rates of Western countries, political influence shifted inexorably from the Atlantic to the Pacific. The power shift was visibly accelerated by the 2003 American-led invasion of Iraq. To many observers, this war seemed to be the last in which the United States and the U.K. might presume to act essentially alone as the world's policemen far from their own home regions. Asians I talked to over those years found the war puzzling, irrelevant, and indicative of a dangerous Western obsession with the Middle East—a preoccupation with old problems rather than new opportunities.

In addition to this shift in momentum, Western governments sensed power slipping away from themselves. NGOs were occupying ever more political space, particularly in European countries. Equally, NGOs and the business sector both seemed much more adept at addressing new global issues such as land mines, debt, climate change, and corruption; governments seemed to struggle to keep up. For instance, a powerful new tool in the fight against corruption was

Transparency International, an NGO that polled corporations on which countries were the most corrupt to do business in. Governments increasingly became targets not actors, or followers rather than leaders. When it came to land mines and climate change, NGOs increasingly lead the charge; a few enlightened governments joined in but most brought up the rear.

In another historic shift, before the financial crisis in 2007 the developed economies were growing at around 3 percent, whereas the developing countries as a whole registered an astonishing near 8 percent growth. The Asian developing economies stormed ahead with 9.4 percent, including 10.7 percent for China and 9.2 percent for India. Russia registered 6.7 percent and sub-Saharan Africa 5.7 percent.

The early years of the twenty-first century, it turned out, were something of a golden age for global growth. In 2008 the U.S. housing crisis, its subsequent impact on the international financial sector, and rising energy and food prices slowed the trend. But the developing world is now almost certainly on a much stronger long-term growth path than is the developed world. During the recession, Europe's economy shrank doing much more than most of the world's other economies.

In a much-quoted 2003 research paper, Goldman Sachs claimed that "if things go right, in less than 40 years, the BRICs (Brazil, Russia, India, and China) economies together could be larger than the G-6 (United States, Japan, Germany, France, U.K., Italy) in U.S. dollar terms."[1] By 2041, the authors argued, China may have the world's largest economy. Now analysts are cautioning that the report veered to the conservative side and that China may reach this status by 2027. In 2010 it overtook Japan to become the second-largest economy even if its per capita income remained a tenth of Japan's. Private investment is responding to this seismic change in the global economy. In the first half of 2010 there were for the first time more big corporate acquisitions in the developing world than in Europe. Stock market indices in the developing world raced ahead of those in the mature economies.

Economics is following demography. Population growth is currently adding almost a billion people every fifteen years to the global community and will continue to do so for several decades to come. This growth is taking place, for the most part, in the developing countries. In the northern countries populations are stable, and apart from immigration, some are even seeing declines, particularly in Europe, Japan, and Russia.

Business, NGOs, commentators, and others have recognized that this combination of economic and population growth in the South and stagnation in the North has consequences, even as politicians seem sometimes curiously oblivious. For the business sector, this growth means that companies must build a presence in new markets with a very different business model. Not only is the new location away from home, but the company may well have to overcome nationalist and other suspicions.

Nor is this expansion directed only one way. European steel mills are now in Indian hands, and the iconic British MG sports car brand belongs to a Chinese company, as does Sweden's Volvo. Tata of India bought Jaguar and Land Rover from Ford in 2008. So far this wave of reverse foreign investment has had to overcome at least as much nationalist and protectionist sentiment in developed countries as Western companies have faced going into developing countries. A Dubai company was blocked from buying American ports, and a Chinese company was blocked in its efforts to bid for Unocal, an American oil company. The 2008 financial crisis temporarily made it harder for American politicians to be choosy; little opposition has been raised to the fire sale of slices of the country's most prestigious and powerful banks and investment houses to foreigners.

If anything, this American defensiveness demonstrated how profound the rebalancing of economic power is becoming. But even when China has a bigger economy than the United States, its per capita income will still lag well behind, forcing all companies to seek out lower-cost business models and more suitable products and services to sell in the China market. Almost certainly these new markets will accelerate the move of jobs to lower-labor-cost developing countries because these new consumers will be even more price-conscious than their Western counterparts. So production as well as a growing part of consumption will migrate to the developing world.

Carly Fiorina, at the time CEO of Hewlett-Packard, had plans to build a whole new unit to provide information services to the poor. To find out what kinds of products were needed by the poor in India and Africa, she front-ended her business development with significant amounts of corporate grant-making. She drew me in, as administrator of UNDP. My trips to India and South Africa showed me that large local companies had been practicing this sort of social market-development for years. They understood that the poor were their next market and always sought to get a foot in first, even if profits came later.

Increasingly for UNDP, our task was to facilitate new business development. During my time as administrator, the sheer power of private sector growth to create jobs—and start a virtuous circle wherein new employees spend their incomes on goods and services that generate more jobs—became an abiding idea.

The significance of private sector growth was by no means as obvious at first as it later seemed. One reason was the classic civil service distaste for business and businessmen and a fear that officials might unintentionally appear to be sales agents for particular companies. The bigger difficulty was that great tracts of Africa and southern Asia seemed bereft of any visible private sector. The only discernible economic forces were subsistence farming and government, represented usually by a bloated payroll but idle officials because there were rarely funds left to spend on actual services.

On one of my early visits to rural Senegal in West Africa, locals on both sides of a river where economic activity seemed nonexistent were placing vast hopes on a European-donated small passenger ferry, which was expected to arrive imminently. They hoped its arrival would stimulate growth. It seemed to me a long shot. I have not been back to that particular community and can't say what happened, but subsequently a pro-business president took office in Senegal and focused on building out an infrastructure, not just in the capital, Dakar, but across the country. That effort has added jobs to the national economy and has driven up national growth rates.

In the developing world the private sector grows in a context both recognizable and strange. Powerful government officials, gatekeepers to investment, control contracts and issue regulatory approvals in ways that make corruption almost inevitable. In China, for example, during its private sector explosion, there were almost no separate, independent laws, let alone commercial courts that could adjudicate disputes. At UNDP we tried to address this issue by providing know-how and technical assistance to the legal system. The Chinese were much more willing to accept this assistance from UNDP than from Western governments or foundations. Nevertheless our efforts were a mere drop in the ocean, and it was clear that in the years to come foreign investors would have to continue to rely on their political contacts to protect their investments.

This situation will change only as the Communist Party realizes that ending corruption and establishing transparent rules of contract would strengthen its rule. And indeed China, controversially, on occasion executes corrupt officials. But for now, local officials' opportunities to enrich themselves remains a more powerful political glue than public outrage that well-connected contractors build where they will in substandard ways or that factory-owners hold down wages by preventing rivals from setting up plants. Further, as China becomes a more expensive place to manufacture—energy, labor, and transportation costs are now driving up export prices—other investment locations will appear more attractive and issues of relative investment risk will become more important.

From my perch at UNDP I saw fickle investment embrace and then drop countries. First it settled on Poland and Hungary; then it migrated eastward to Georgia, Ukraine, and the Central Asian republics. Worried Mexican leaders told me of their fears of losing U.S. markets to China. In Asia, the Southeast Asian economies had to paddle frantically upstream in their manufacturing as China pressed them from below and was then in turn pressed by Vietnam and South Asian countries. Capital sought out labor-cost advantages but had little further loyalty to location. A country held on to foreign manufacturing contracts and investment until it was undercut and no longer than that. The balance of power seemed firmly to favor business.

Those of us at UNDP were involved in an unending seminar in business and development strategy. How could we help these countries find their comparative advantage but also, given the speed of change, hold on to it? How could we get them to build up their education and health systems as well as the physical infrastructure that would allow them to compete permanently as economic opportunity shifted? In the late 1960s a Dutch UNDP adviser played a role in Singapore's early economic choices. Early on he advised preserving the statue of Stamford Raffles, who had founded Singapore as a trading post in 1819: it would signal to nervous investors that the new government would respect Singapore's open trading history. Quickly, the expert Albert Winsemius established himself as a strategic adviser to Lee Kwan Yew, Singapore's legendary first leader, who consulted him about the long-term choices that would frame his nation's future.[2]

I wanted UNDP to be able to advise countries on long-term strategy routinely. In many developing countries we understood better than anyone the interplay of local development with cultural factors; environmental and energy limits; and the limits of government itself. The development path simply would not be the same as in the United States or the U.K. Government would not be able to do the same things and would turn for service delivery to the private sector, both the for-profit and the not-for-profit sides.

In power generation and water supply, local private enterprise began to fill the gap, providing local solutions. Increasingly, I sought to align UNDP behind these public-private approaches. Given our resources, we could make a difference only at the margin, but to us at UNDP it made a huge difference, opening us to the scale of change under way.

The rise of the private sector and NGOs to power at the international level was becoming visible to all. In 2006 alone the volume of international trade grew by 9.2 percent. The ways that countries addressed labor rights, migration, public health, education, and national economic policy had real consequences both for businesses and for NGO champions of development. Both corporations and the associations that represented them were increasingly thinking and acting globally. On trade and aid, on the environment, education, and health, the NGO voice remains vital for pushing governments and international organizations to do better by the poor than they otherwise would.

When I was at the World Bank, I was initially alarmed when NGOs like Oxfam set up advocacy offices in Washington. Their sights, I knew all too well, were set on the bank and the other official international development institutions. In 1994, at my first World Bank annual meeting, the one in Madrid, protesters were besieging us, and Oxfam was present distributing a pamphlet on the bank that I felt poured oil on the flames. Furious, I telephoned my old friend David Bryer, Oxfam's U.K. chief, in Oxfordshire, dragging him from his bath to take my call. This was the worst kind of NGO behavior, I told him—by parodying the World Bank's positions on structural adjustment, Oxfam was increasing the hostility and misunderstanding we faced. I suspect he sunk back into his bath a happy man. He must have seen my call as evidence that the strategy was working.

But soon the astuteness of Oxfam's development strategy became evident. They fought and won battles for debt relief and more World

Bank investment in education or health, a far more consequential use of their resources than if they had spent them on direct relief in a poor village. Justin Forsyth, a young Briton who headed Oxfam International's Washington office, established himself as a go-to source for journalists and congressional aides wrestling with the complexities of debt relief and the aftermath of the World Bank's structural adjustment programs. He and I must have been on a lot of the same speed dials in Washington, it seemed, rival sources as we were on the development issues of the day. Whereas the World Bank would largely react, Oxfam used its contacts effectively to campaign for debt relief and other development goals.

In some ways the World Bank's management eventually became closer to Oxfam than we were to our government shareholders. We too wanted more debt relief for the poorest countries, while governments wanted less. Oxfam changed too, learning to come into the tent with the World Bank (as some of its peers bitterly noted). Coming into the tent and engaging in our policy debates became an education for Oxfam people. The organization has since come around to bravely champion the benefits of free trade to the poor, even as other NGOs that did not engage in debates stuck firmly to their side of the barricade and retreated deeper into their antiglobalization opposition. Justin Forsyth moved on from Oxfam to become Tony Blair's and then Gordon Brown's development adviser at No.10 Downing Street. That progression showed how far the NGOs and their policies and tactics had become merged into the policy process. In the run-up to Gleneagles, Blair and his senior colleague spoke at meetings of different NGO pressure groups, encouraging them to press other G8 leaders to do more when they came to Gleneagles. It was the G8 lobbying the G8 via NGOs.

At the British political party conferences in 2006, we development campaigners found ourselves guests not just at the governing Labour Party conference but also at the Tories' gathering. In the genteel seaside town of Bournemouth, those Tories who awakened early enough after an evening of carousing heard the development case from me, an African AIDS campaigner, an Irish nun, and Jasmine Whitbread, an ex-Oxfam policy chief who now leads Save the Children. I am not sure the Tory rank and file knew what had hit them, but the leadership seemed eager to identify itself with these issues as part of a more caring Conservatism. Weeks later the Tory leader was off to Darfur, then the next summer to Rwanda with a large group of his colleagues. A modern British Tory leader's duties are no longer restricted, it seems, to Britain's home counties.

Similarly, President Bush doubled U.S. assistance for development, albeit from an admittedly low base. It seems so against the grain of President Bush's brand of politics that his leadership on HIV/AIDS programs has gone largely unacknowledged. It is one area where his original campaign pledge of compassionate conservatism held up. When I became head of UNDP in 1999, annual AIDS treatment cost well over $10,000 a year. Now it has fallen as low as a few hundred dollars. One reason is certainly pharmaceutical innovation and economies in the delivery system, but the more important reason is aggressive NGO advocacy to allow generic drugs to enter the market, which caused pharmaceutical companies to reconsider how drugs are priced in poor countries.

At first the drug companies, set on protecting their research investment in new AIDS medicines, were deaf to demands that they offer the medicines at a price that poor HIV sufferers in developing countries could afford. From their corporate boardrooms and through their public relations teams, the pharmaceutical chiefs ranted that those who reproduced their drugs at affordable prices but without a license were stealing their copyright. One tall beaky-looking CEO looked as though he had waddled off the pages of a Dr. Seuss story. He ran one of the largest companies and put up a number of angry and threatening performances. He successfully importuned President Bush to insist that American AIDS funds be used to buy only fully priced medicines from Western manufacturers, thereby ensuring that the treatment would reach many fewer sufferers than would otherwise have been the case.

Companies such as his have to retain the incentive to do new research and find fresh drugs—but not at the expense of lives. A group of politicians and international officials led by Kofi Annan at the UN and Bill Clinton at his foundation, along with leaders in India and Brazil, cleverly found a way out. They discovered a small provision in an international trade agreement (TRIPS) that allowed countries to break international copyright and manufacture locally without license, in an emergency situation like war or national disaster. It became a vehicle for allowing the local manufacture of affordable AIDS drugs.

A Belgian doctor who had earlier researched HIV-like diseases in Africa, Peter Piot, led the Joint United Nations Program on HIV/AIDS (UNAIDS) from its establishment in 1994. Along with a combative former New York City politician, Carol Bellamy, who was head of UNICEF, and others, he recognized that AIDS was the single biggest threat to health and life expectancy in some parts of the world. It was an emergency, and they cleared their organizations' decks to take on the fight. Figures like Piot and Bellamy remain unknown beyond immediate development and public health circles. By any stretch, they were engaged on a much more important matter than most national politicians.

These leaders as well as HIV/AIDS advocacy groups and development lobbyists whipped up international public opinion to the point that a number of enlightened CEOs, notably Ray Gilmartin of Merck, were happy to back the Annan-Clinton effort. Gilmartin knew that given public outrage, his more callous competitors would have no choice but to follow. Shame proved more powerful than profit. They recognized they could not use international trade rules or the clout of their home governments to block affordable generic medicines for AIDS and poor people's diseases more generally: shareholders and public opinion would not stand for it. So they were drawn into the discussion of how HIV treatments could be made affordable and available. Instead of fully loading the purchase price with research and development costs, companies employed a marginal model by which the price covers production, marketing, and distribution but not development. Sales in developed countries would cover development. A medicine or vaccine that has application only in poor countries is either written off against profits elsewhere or viewed as building new market share for later, when the country or patients are richer.

It could also be subsidized by a public-private partnership to ensure that public money provides an incentive for continuing research and development. In this example, drug companies essentially subsidize lower prices by not protecting copyrights and by discounting their own pricing, while governments and foundations are subsidizing the companies' research and development costs. The Gates Foundation has experimented with promises of purchasing successful new drugs that meet its specifications for poor patients, thereby restoring a market incentive for research and development of new treatments.

At the level of distribution, NGOs and the companies are combining to reach more poor users with regular, monitored antiretroviral treatment for AIDS, vaccination programs for other diseases, and bed nets and other simple preventive measures for malaria. The companies would be unable to deliver these services on their own to such a large and dispersed market in such a cost-effective way. In Botswana, a partnership of Merck, the Gates Foundation, the Clinton Foundation, and others demonstrates these sorts of approaches at work. It is no accident that these partners chose Botswana, which has the continent's most honest government.

The United Nations did not stand aloof from these broader

changes. Shortly after I got to UNDP, I told Annan that I wanted to start a trust fund for our work on HIV/AIDS. By that time UNAIDS, UNICEF, the World Health Organization, the UN Fund for Population Activities, and the World Bank had already set up their own funds, and Annan rightfully suspected that donors would be confused. He came up with the idea of a single megafund to service the whole AIDS effort: the Global Fund for HIV/AIDS, Tuberculosis, and Malaria.

It had to be ambitious; it had to challenge the world to recognize the gravity of the situation; and it had to provide commensurate funds and support. We talked about putting our efforts on a war footing. I did the early calculations for what it would cost literally on the back of an envelope, while Annan was getting competing but escalating numbers from the agencies and experts. The numbers proved about right, so the fund initially sought around $6 billion a year to support total global spending of about twice that each year. It eventually got annual funding rounds of about $3 billion but has been steadily ratcheting up since.

Even if it fell beneath initial hopes, the fund was a huge leap forward. It introduced several innovations. It partnered with civil society at the country level, as well as with UNDP, to deliver where national governments could not or would not because they either lacked the capacity or were unwilling to admit that their country had a serious HIV/AIDS problem. The private sector played a growing role on the fundraising and marketing side as well as in the drug provision.

Ominously, the United States seized control of the design in its early stages to wrench it away from the UN and establish its independence. Annan, who remained vital to its fundraising, was consigned to the role of honorary president, and Tommy Thompson, the former U.S. health and human services secretary who served as the fund's first chairman, tried to keep the UN at arm's length. Thompson and several of his aides had apparently come into public health policy work as pro-lifers on the abortion issue—always a dividing line between the Bush administration and the United Nations—and bore a deep anti-UN animus. That defeated our principal purpose of forming a single fund to support all the international efforts and allow us to close down other fundraising. Management crises developed as a result of the United States forcing its separation from the UN's management platform. This move was popular with UN haters but led initially to accountability and corruption problems in the program.

The Americans had promised funding for the program once it escaped its unpopular UN association, but that funding was not forthcoming at the anticipated level. As a major funder at the country level, the United States insisted on using its own procedures, which needlessly complicated things for recipient countries. At the behest of the United States, Western consultants and auditors were hired and used in costly and ineffective ways.

Its imperfections apart, the fund was a prototype. On the fundraising side, the fund used big, bold funding strategies that drew on the best private sector marketing advice and that targeted popular concerns, such as AIDS and tropical diseases more generally. The public became involved and interested, and governments responded by finding new resources and committing to a multiyear effort. On the delivery side, NGOs and the private sector were involved in both operations and policy deliberations, with seats on the board.

Finally, the private sector was ready to testify to the importance of the effort. One of the most important conversions on the road to better global AIDS policy was the recognition by corporations operating in Africa that preventive measures to keep experienced employees from contracting HIV, and measures to keep HIV-positive employees well enough to work, made good business sense, even if it meant paying a higher health care bill. The alternative would have been a process of permanent employee recruitment and replacement in the face of high adult infection and mortality rates, which was much more costly and disruptive. Beginning in the South African mining sector—which was notoriously tough about worker benefits—a sea change took place. Antiretroviral drugs were made available, and companies not only improved their employee health care but attended to the broader community as well.

Thus after sharp disagreements among governments, foundations, the private sector, and NGOs about the rights and wrongs of the persistent problem of AIDS, all these parties settled into ambitious programs that have made a real difference. Millions of people are now receiving regular antiretroviral treatment, millions more are getting access to confidential treatment, and still more are benefiting from preventive programs that promote safer behavior. A funded program of research into vaccines or cures is under way. All these results show in the numbers. Infection rates have peaked in many places.

Public-private partnerships began arguably with the NGO- and Canadian-government-led campaign to ban land mines—or with the coalition of activists, business interests, and politicians who lobbied for an end to the slave trade two hundred years ago. Whatever the campaigns' origins they have become a staple of international campaigning today, and governments' inner sanctums seem permanently breached. Whether it is trade liberalization, climate change, limiting or banning the use of the most harmful weapons, or even down-to-earth domestic issues like immigration or schools, new special interests have joined the debate in dynamic ways at the international as well as the national level.

To be sure, these dynamic partnerships make the UN and World Bank look dusty and old-fashioned, but all these organizations need one another. International organizations can offer a platform for discourse to NGOs and business groups, but they are also targets, as it is much easier to pressure a country to change its national environmental practices if the World Bank has already been made to change its standards, especially its lending conditions that set national rules.

Justin Forsyth and I initially were on opposite sides of the barricades as NGOs battled the World Bank on debt and the environment, but we became allies in national government, employing our old networks as well as our battle experience to press the world to change. While national politics often seems stuck in a rut, the degree of change around the world is extraordinary, providing opportunities to fashion powerful new solutions between old adversaries.

CHAPTER EIGHT

THE END OF THE AFFAIR

For me as for so many others, the day the world changed started normally. In the early morning sunshine I had jogged down Manhattan's West Side, using the World Trade Center as a target beacon to spur myself on. A business breakfast brought me late to the UNDP building, where like all arriving staff I was stopped in the lobby. The crowd that was forming spilled out onto First Avenue. Something had happened at the World Trade Center, people said. Leaving the growing crowd in the lobby, I raced up to my office.

Craning to look diagonally across the city to the lower West Side, I could see the smoke. The television news brought grim news of an unfolding attack. A little later, as the scale of what had happened became clearer, I walked through the UNDP building with our security staff to make sure everybody had followed instructions and gone home. The few who had not left were shocked to their core, silently contemplating the enormity of what happened. New Yorkers and people all around the world grieved that day. UNDP's multinational staff was a pretty good proxy for the world.

That universal sympathy offered a path for the United States that the rest of the world seemed willing to follow. The UN Security Council swiftly condemned what had happened and endorsed military action against its perpetrators in Afghanistan. No one flinched from supporting an American war against the causes of the 9/11 terrorism, al Qaeda, and those who had harbored it in Afghanistan.

Later Kofi Annan would commission a panel of eminent persons to look at whether the UN charter allows a country a preemptive right of self-defense when faced with an unpredictable terrorist attack.

The world was leaning over to accommodate American anxieties because it shared them. Those who died on 9/11 were citizens of countries east and west, south and north, who had been drawn to American opportunity. Around the world people mourned the loss of countrymen and -women whose search for the American dream had ended so cruelly. But back home they were also afraid for themselves. After all, this was not the first al Qaeda attack. American military installations had been attacked, resulting in local civilian casualties. And the attack on American embassies in Nairobi and Dar es Salaam had caused many Kenyan and Tanzanian casualties. After 9/11, nobody felt safe. The United States had an opportunity to lead a global effort to defeat al Qaeda.

The first fork in the road was a debate about means. From the start the Bush administration saw the principal tools in this war to be military action, counterintelligence, and security cooperation among countries. That last tool has been an unsung success of the effort. But missing from the Bush list in the early days was any political opening to Muslim moderates. What were we to say to Muslims who did not resort to violence but shared some of the terrorists' sense of marginalisation? Should a dividing line be drawn through the world, and everybody who fell on the terrorists' side become enemies of all civilized states? Or did such a broad-brush approach risk driving civilians into the terrorist ranks by discriminating against, isolating, and excluding them in ways that had made a minority of their hard-line peers terrorists in the first place?

Shortly after 9/11, at the London School of Economics, I called

for a response "that must first and foremost be centered on the democratic governance gap in so much of the developing world that has
left other problems unaddressed. That absence of political voice in so
many of the countries from which the terrorists hailed is the starting
fault-line of our failure in so much of the world today. Go back and
read Joseph Conrad writing about the same issues over a century ago!
It is that lack of political voice and democratic debate at home which
has led us today, as so frequently in the past, to the internationalizing
of terrorism."[1]

Here, I felt, was a plausible post-9/11 strategy that could go hand
in hand with the necessarily toughened defensive security against
terrorism: expand democratic participation and achieve a global en-
franchisement where everybody felt they had some say in the direction of world affairs. Not privy to what was going on in the White
House—where, judging from the accounts of Bob Woodward and
others, the die had already been cast and Saddam Hussein already
targeted—I fancifully hoped the administration might also be enter-
taining this approach.

In November 2001, after the American-led overthrow of the Taliban regime, Kofi Annan asked me as UNDP chief to coordinate
international assistance efforts to Afghanistan. I was the first senior
UN official back in Kabul after the Taliban fell. The United States
and its allies were widely welcomed. The only opposition I discerned
came from an elderly Afghan woman who pressed an egg into my
hands and furiously asserted that it was all that was left of her chicken
farm that a U.S. plane had accidentally hit as it attacked a neighboring gun emplacement. Who was going to pay? she demanded. In
front of the accompanying TV cameras, I mumbled something about
a few lost eggs possibly being not too high a price to pay for freedom.

Barely thirty days into the life of a new interim government in

Kabul, the product of a UN-led negotiation in Bonn, we were able to hold a reconstruction conference in Tokyo with strong international support. This was international action at its best: smart, quick, and collaborative. Neither the political settlement nor the reconstruction conference could have happened without strong American leadership, but the U.S. burden was greatly lessened by its partners— German co-leadership in Bonn, and Japanese, Gulf, and European support in Tokyo. The UN provided the platform and acted as the enabler for the whole undertaking. On a wave of international sympathy, the United States saw the long-term intractable problem of Afghanistan become a strategic opportunity almost overnight. The world was at one in doing something.

Having carried the world on Afghanistan, the United States could have kept that global coalition going. And there were early signs that it might, and that the administration recognized the need for a political as well as a military response to 9/11. That did not mean "negotiating" with terrorists or accepting their poorly articulated aims; rather, it meant recognizing that globalization had reinforced a sense of marginalization in much of the Arab and Muslim world, and that, in order to reduce sympathy for al Qaeda and isolate it from the broader Muslim community, the United States had to reach out.

The first promising sign was a Bush-attended UN conference on financing for development held at Monterrey, Mexico. The meeting's purpose was to develop a financing plan to back up the pledges that countries had made in 2000 to support the Millennium Development Goals. European governments and developing countries were promoting an aid target of 0.7 percent of GDP. The Bush administration was deeply skeptical: State Department officials thought it harkened back to the 1970s New International Economic Order (see Chapter Two) and implied a developing country entitlement.

But President Bush was in no mood to have the United States isolated on development. Throughout his presidency, when it came to providing aid to developing countries, he was generous. He could be reluctant to accept binding international aid commitments but was often willing to come up with help for people and causes that he thought were deserving. In addition to his leadership on AIDS, he set up a whole new program, the Millennium Challenge Corporation, that gave large bloc grants to poor countries that had a good track record on education and health spending, on encouraging their private sector and on combating corruption. I worked closely with its first two chiefs to support what I considered a great innovation. Later in his presidency, Bush frankly showed much greater animation in responding to the victims of the Asian tsunami than he did to the Hurricane Katrina victims at home in New Orleans.

He also wanted to get his relationship with his fellow conservative Vincente Fox, the Mexican president, back on track after the disruption of 9/11. Both had promised to make U.S.-Mexico relations a top priority of their terms of office, and Bush still seemed to grasp the concept of a balanced foreign policy that paid attention to Latin American neighbors. He agreed to go to the Monterrey conference, which Mexico, as the host, wanted to make a success, and he did not want to arrive empty-handed if the Europeans arrived bearing gifts.

For us at the UN, such one-upmanship around summits was a tried and true method of bidding up the resource commitments. And at Monterrey, the Americans seemed genuinely willing to do more. The United States preferred to do things its own way and with its own means, however, so it focused on bilateral action rather than on pooling resources with other countries at the UN or World Bank. To complain about this would have seemed churlish, for the good news was that the United States appeared to have understood that it needed to be a leader again in international development cooperation. President Clinton had never taken on a reluctant Congress with vigor sufficient to significantly raise American overseas assistance, something he has expressed regrets about since leaving office.

But shunning multilateral collaboration, Bush missed the chance to multiply his efforts and hid them from wider recognition. If the Millennium Challenge Corporation had been placed inside the World Bank, for example, many other donors would have come on board, and the grants could have been so significant that the corporation really would have had the impact that the administration sought. But the World Bank was too multilateral for the suspicious and instinctively unilateralist new administration to allow it such a role. And after all, it was still led by a Clinton holdover, Jim Wolfensohn.

President Bush joined the rest of us at an opening dinner in Monterrey, eating under the stars as the disused massive machinery of an old factory dominated the skyline. The vast boilers, wheels, and pistons were illuminated by a lighting display of the kind found at the pyramids or a Greek temple. By showing that Mexican industrial workers had lost out from globalization's remorseless pursuit of lower-cost labor, it was a dramatic backdrop for this international effort to build new jobs and opportunity across the developing world. As Mexico had moved on to export new goods and services, it had left behind an industrial rustbelt. Shedding old industrial sectors was not a phenomenon solely of rich countries.

The second sign that Bush was interested in a cooperative international spirit of engagement was the new security doctrine outlined in a National Security Report, announced with much fanfare. It talked eloquently of the need to combine a hard-power response to terrorism with the development of new tools of soft power and engagement. It acknowledged that environmental deterioration and poverty were threats to peace and stressed international cooperation to address them. One of the report's principal authors was David Gordon, an old University of Michigan fellow graduate student of mine and a fellow admirer of Ali Mazrui who was later to become head of policy planning at the State Department.

The third and culminating piece of evidence for an imaginative

American handling of the aftermath of 9/11 was the administration's enthusiastic reaction to UNDP's first Arab Human Development Report. Published in 2002, it dramatically stepped up the program's advocacy of good government in the region.

Up to this point UNDP had not been particularly successful in the Arab world. The last significant initiative UNDP had taken there was to bravely open a program in the Palestinian Territories in the 1970s. The then administrator Brad Morse, a former U.S. congressman, took the organization's commitment to universality very seriously. We were the UN; we should be everywhere we were needed. The Arab world had extremes of wealth and poverty: Saudi Arabia and its Gulf neighbors were at the top of the per capita income chart, and Yemen was at the bottom, with African levels of poverty. At both ends of the spectrum, the World Bank had emerged as a more useful partner, providing better advice for oil-rich, policy-poor Gulf countries, and being a better source of financing for the poorer neighbors.

With the Arab Human Development Report, UNDP seized the region's attention and galvanized debate, becoming for a while the most listened-to voice. The report's principal author was my UNDP Arab regional chief, Rima Khalaf-Hunaidi, a former Jordanian minister of finance and deputy prime minister. A Palestinian by birth, like so many of her diaspora, she saw her region, although not always Palestine's own predicament, with a detachment and clarity that few other Arabs could muster. The corruption and bad government endemic to so many Arab countries is a topic that most Palestinians and Israelis would agree on if they could bring themselves to talk to each other about it.

Khalaf-Hunaidi thought it was time to call a spade a spade: the Middle East was mired in problems of its own making. She and her co-authors concluded that the region was hopelessly entrapped in three interlocking crises: a lack of democracy; the failure to emancipate women and harness their energies; and the absence of any decent secular education system and the internationalist perspective that it would enable.

The indictment shook everybody, and the charge sheet was long. Despite its oil wealth, the economy of the whole Arab region was at the time smaller than that of Spain. Fewer foreign books a year were translated into Arabic than into Greek (a country with a fraction of the population of the Arabic-speaking world). Women were disadvantaged in all kinds of ways by cultural and legal barriers. They could not drive in Saudi Arabia or vote in the countries that had a male franchise. By any measure, the region's democratic indicators lagged behind those of the rest of the world, seeming almost a last bastion of authoritarianism in a world that was embracing democracy.

Our central contention was that no matter how much aid donors went on pumping into favorites like Egypt and Jordan, and no matter how much the Gulf continued throwing off massive oil income, the region, rich and poor alike, would remain hostage to its political backwardness. It had lost its way. Courageously, the authors even added that the Israeli-Palestinian conflict had become an excuse, a fig leaf, for not confronting these devastating domestic failures. It was easier to grumble about Israel and blame it for the region's problems than to confront them honestly.

Certainly, the report balanced these criticisms with strong complaints about Israel's human rights failures in the treatment of its Arab minority. And it noted that Yassir Arafat's PLO rule in the Palestinian territories was no testament to democracy. The report was a refreshingly honest self-portrait of the region by Arab writers, who used the cover of UNDP sponsorship to speak unpalatable truths to their leaders and countrymen.

For me as UNDP administrator, its publication had been quite a risk. The United States seemed likely to seize upon the few pages of criticism of Israel and ignore the rest of the report. Congress and the

White House might call for cutting our funding. The leaders of the Arab world's closed protected political systems never took criticism well, and we were the subject of an apparently furious closed meeting of the Arab League.

At the UN desk at the State Department, the predictable complaints about the Israel material began. The man who was in charge of the UNDP section at State was always anxious to ingratiate himself with his Republican political masters. Typically he would launch tirades and furious incantations that culminated in threats to cut our funding. And Arab complaints said that we had no right to comment on their internal affairs. The report's sponsors and friends suddenly became less visible.

I braced for the worst. I never doubted we had done the right thing because I was convinced that without an honest confrontation of the region's limitations, there could not be development. There was too much alienation and exclusion, too much frustration and suppressed conflict. The Arab world's political failure lay like a fallen tree across the path to its economic development. Until it was cleared, the region would remain in the hands of dictators and terrorists. It would have no progress, no democratic middle class, and no stability.

Our risk-taking paid off handsomely. Uniquely for a UN report, it was a publishing sensation. In the early days, by Khalaf-Hunaidi's estimate, a million copies were downloaded in Arabic. The new Arab cable channel, Al-Jazeera, debated its critique day after day. Even at the end of the decade it was still not forgotten; the *Financial Times* named Khalaf-Hunaidi one of the fifty most influential people of the previous ten years.

The State Department official sulked back to his cage as his superiors seized on the report as Arab validation for their call for democracy in the region. George Bush, Colin Powell, and Condoleezza Rice cited it as confirmation of their calls for democratization of the region. The National War College had asked for complimentary copies for its whole class. They got them. One day Khalaf-Hunaidi called to complain that she was fed up with Washington asking for free copies. She was going to charge the most recent order to my office, she said, as I was always too concerned about maintaining good relations with the administration.

The combined enthusiasm of Washington and the Arab street obliged Arab leaders into a public, teeth-gritted acknowledgment of the report—and even a cold embrace, at least for the cameras. Behind the scenes, however, they were seething, as the Arab League's private session indicated.

Tragically, however, the pursuit of Saddam Hussein turned everything on its head. The opportunity closed as the world concluded that for all its fine words the American objective was simple and militaristic: the overthrow of its old adversary Saddam Hussein. American support for Middle Eastern democracy-building suddenly did not mean providing support to beleaguered democratic activists or interventions to secure intellectuals' right to free speech and free debate. Rather, it was viewed as justification for regime change, the case for war. And with that, the whole democracy project to which President Bush had devoted so much rhetorical energy came crashing down, not just on its American sponsors but also on the brave dissidents who had written, or spoken up, for the Arab Human Development Report. Parts of the region made open war on democrats, who in the public mind were transformed overnight from brave independent voices to agents of American imperialism.

One of Vice President Richard Cheney's daughters, who had headed the State Department office promoting democracy and women's rights, was a great advocate for the report. Paul Wolfowitz's partner, Shaha Riza, a British-Libyan working for the World Bank, was another champion. Wolfowitz himself, as the number two at the Pentagon, was a leading architect of the war. For both women, it became clear, the report was less a case for Arabs to establish open democracies than a justification for invasion. In the eyes of the neoconservative architects of the Iraq War, democracy need not be a home-grown affair; it could be imposed by outside force. That flew in the face of the report's basic argument, which was that people had to win democracy for themselves. The report had called on Arabs, not Americans, to correct Arab failures.

The Bush administration had reached a fork in the road, and with the buildup to war in Iraq, it chose its path. The flood of investigative writing that followed tells us that the decision may never have been in real doubt. Perhaps the invasion of Iraq was ordained from Election Day 2000. A son seeking oedipal redemption by completing a fatally hesitant father's unfinished war, spurred on by a vice president and senior advisers set on reasserting presidential authority and reordering the Middle East, may have seen 9/11 more as pretext than as cause. The slew of articles, books, and even movies seeking motives in psychology as much as in politics has been constant.

What was lost is less recognized: prosecuting the war in Afghanistan with focus and sufficient manpower would have brought early victory; sustained the international coalition that unanimously endorsed action against Afghanistan at the UN; allowed efforts to bring the excluded and marginalized more fully into the global mainstream; and shown that the best war on terror is also a war for democracy, human rights, and a fairer, more inclusive, world. All of these aims were ditched for the pursuit of Saddam Hussein.

Just how thorough was the turn in the road was clouded by the fog of events leading up to the war. The UN's chief weapons inspector, Hans Blix, an elderly rock of a Swede who exuded earnest, steadfast integrity, and the cerebral, fair-minded Egyptian Mohamed ElBaradei who had succeeded him as head of the UN International Atomic Energy Agency (and was later with his agency awarded a Nobel Peace Prize), had resumed inspections inside Iraq for weapons of mass destruction. Saddam Hussein had earlier thrown the inspectors out, but he conceded this round because of the U.S.-U.K. mobilization for war. He gave in under pressure. It was a breakthrough that Kofi Annan and those of us around him at the UN felt needed time to produce results.

If the inspectors could verify the presence of weapons, and Saddam refused to dismantle them, then it would create a casus belli, a justification for war. If they could not, then the United States and its allies could demobilize, confident that Iraqis themselves, frustrated by their continued isolation and the hardship of his rule, would ultimately bring down Saddam Hussein.

The United States and its allies massed troops on his border, but they could not remain there indefinitely. Either they would invade or they would leave. Given the heat, a full-fledged invasion was really possible only during a seasonal window during the first half of the year. If they left, Saddam could reasonably conclude they would not come back and therefore might not even continue his grudging cooperation with the weapons inspectors. So putting troops on the front line limited the options: unless Saddam climbed down, they would invade, on dates dictated by climate and calendar. The diplomatic track never fully recognized the bluntness and urgency of these alternatives. The pace of discussions in the Security Council was slow, with more delays and deadlines than the desert heat would allow.

Further, the inspectors' operation of checking for weapons was like looking for a needle in a haystack. Could they really ever give Iraq a clean bill of health and assert with assurance that it had none? And as the inspectors' own reports seemed to blow hot and cold about the level of the regime's cooperation and the likelihood of discovering weapons, events moved inexorably to war.

The debate in the Security Council was increasingly angry. President Chirac of France headed a group of independent-minded member countries that refused to countenance armed intervention until diplomacy was exhausted. Chirac appeared to indicate he would never support military action against Iraq at all, undermining those who were still trying to find a deal. Friends, including a former president, in the governments of Mexico and Chile (the council's two Latin American members then) have described to me Washington's angry and increasingly frantic pressure to get them to give in and support invasion. Along with the Asian members, Mexico and Chile felt like bewildered bystanders to an Old World dispute.

Kofi Annan and those of us around him never doubted that the war, under the terms it was fought, was wrong. A persistent BBC interviewer later prompted him to call it "illegal," but that is unclear. A current official inquiry in Britain may better establish whether it was illegal or not. Many wars have been fought during the lifetime of the UN without the benefit of a Security Council resolution. The NATO attack on Kosovo proceeded without one because of Russian opposition and secured Security Council endorsement only after the intervention. The political failure was to seek UN support without being able to secure it, then to act (as it had not during the earlier Gulf war) without sufficient international support to provide any cloak of UN legitimacy. We were as unprepared as anyone for the devastating consequences.

The coalition, after early breathtaking successes when the Iraqi defenders seemed to melt away, failed to establish an early victory in Iraq; then the region's widening opposition turned the war into one of the worst disasters in the history of American foreign policy. American wars are in fact rarely wars of choice. Any longtime observer knows that a wariness of unnecessary international engagement lies deep in America's consciousness. Not for it the promiscuous wars that marked long periods of European history or the endless imperial adventures of earlier great powers; history shows the United States to be partial to keeping to itself and usually a late and reluctant entrant into other people's wars. Presidents Kennedy and Johnson were drawn into Vietnam, a disastrous misjudgment, by a French colonial tangle of events from which they could not extract themselves. They did not propel the country into Vietnam as an act of positive choice.

The casualties of this failure, beyond Iraq itself, include American and British standing in the world and the cohesion and effectiveness of the United Nations. The confrontation in the Security Council between the United States and the U.K. and most of the other members was probably the most damaging single event to which the UN had ever been subjected. Earlier differences over the Korean Peninsula, Suez, the Congo, and the Middle East shook the organization to its foundations. But during the Cold War years international affairs were mostly dysfunctional. The UN was not alone in its failures.

In 2003, by contrast, the UN was promoting the Millennium Development Goals, along with human rights and democracy, as the foundations of greater international cooperation. It was this endeavor, not just the institution's reputation, that fell victim to the bitterly acrimonious fight in the Security Council.

Subsequent events only worsened the situation. Annan felt that after the invasion we had to rebuild not only Iraq but also international relations. Once more I pulled together reconstruction planning in New York while Sergio Vieira de Mello, the most talented UN official of my generation and a possible successor to Annan, was dispatched to Baghdad to help with reconstruction. He was to reach out to Iraqi groups that would not talk to the American invaders but might talk to him, and in doing so salve the organization's strained relations with the United States. The American envoy in Iraq, L. Paul Bremer, used Vieira de Mello, asking him to reach out to those Sunni and Shia groups that would not deal directly with the Americans; but when Bremer formed the Interim Governing Council, he discarded Sergio and his advice, concentrating power—almost manically it seemed—in his own hands.

Annan was appalled. The UN was being forced to lend its most precious asset—its good name—to an American enterprise that was doing things in a deeply damaging way. It tainted the UN's role as an honest broker between the coalition and its Iraqi opponents. Among UN staff, we later discovered, a sense of foreboding was growing. Iraqis seemed increasingly hostile, they felt isolated, and the absence of basic security measures like shatter-proof glass in their offices (it had not been installed because of bureaucratic procrastination) added to their fears. Then tragedy struck. On August 21, 2003, a truck bomb was rammed into the UN building below Vieira de Mello's office and killed Sergio and twenty-one colleagues; many more were desperately wounded.

The bombing was a terrible blow to Annan. He was on vacation in Sweden and unable to find a television camera or other means of speaking to the world. To fill the vacuum, I went in front of the TV cameras in New York to express our dismay and sickened outrage. Then followed frantic days of trying to track down and evacuate wounded colleagues and recover the bodies of those who had died.

The American medical response was remarkable and certainly saved lives, but that day was still the most brutal in terms of civilian casualties in the UN's history. On Annan's behalf, I went to the neighboring Jordanian capital, Amman, to receive the wounded and the bodies of those who had died. Adding a macabre element to the scene, a firm of international undertakers arrived to help identify the bodies, complete the paperwork, and provide grief counseling to the relatives. Trained no doubt in state-of-the-art Western techniques of empathy, the counselors would adopt an earnest, I-share-your-pain look, for each encounter with frantic relatives. But rarely have pious grief counselors generated so much extra grief. Their painstaking documentation processes—often, it must be said, at the behest of the American military authorities who held the bodies—delayed the release of the remains to relatives; but Muslim custom requires immediate burial. The grief counselors, with their frozen rictus smiles, seemed deaf to this core complaint.

With ghoulishly comic incompetence, they would also lose vital paperwork, risking further delay. I waited at Amman's military airport for a vast Russian Antonov transport plane to deliver its sad load of fallen colleagues. As the coffins, small against the aircraft's vast size, were carried down the ramp, I saw one of the company's representatives scramble past them, frantically searching his pockets. He had quite literally mislaid a set of documents, and to meet U.S. administrative requirements, one body might have to be sent back to Baghdad. The Jordanians stepped in and accepted the paperless body. Not even death could bring peace, it seemed, from the clash of cultures and misunderstandings that had brought us there.

A Jordanian Palestinian mother, along with her other children, mourned the loss of her beautiful young Muslim daughter, whose assignment as a junior UN spokeswoman in Baghdad had started only a day before the bombing. They were frantic about the religious consequences of the delay in her burial and could not understand the American undertakers' stonewalling as anything other than sacrilege. As our shocked colleagues stumbled through a grief-filled, heartbreaking memorial service in Amman I was presented with the folded, tattered flag that had flown above the UN building on the day of the attack. Later I gave it to Kofi Annan, and it hangs today in a small prayer chamber at the UN, a symbol of our loss.

We mourned the loss not only of our friends and colleagues but of UN innocence. This war destroyed everything it touched. We were now targets. The hope of meeting terrorism with a balanced response was gone. The War on Terror had become a self-declared war of civilizations, and one of its first casualties appeared to be the United Nations.

Kofi Annan tried to apply a brake to the ill-fated American efforts. He sent his senior adviser on Muslim and Middle East matters, Lakhdar Brahimi, to Iraq to try again to build bridges; Brahimi was a Sunni and former Algerian foreign minister who had masterminded our role in Afghanistan. But this time too the Bush administration made selective use of Brahimi's help, jeopardizing what was left of our neutrality. As security crumbled, the human needs in Iraq became so great that we had to help, but each day seemed to condemn us further as little more than tools of the American occupation.

As the 2004 presidential election drew near action against Fallujah, the hotbed of the Sunni insurgency, rose to the top of the agenda. U.S. military impatience seemed to be increasing. Annan was concerned that an indiscriminate air attack might take civilian lives; he was determined to discourage any ill-judged American action. But he did not phone Secretary of State Powell or National Security Advisor Condoleezza Rice. Instead, on the weekend before the election, a duty officer sent a letter, under Annan's signature warning against an air attack in Fallujah. It arrived at an open administrative fax machine, where it lay unnoticed and unsecured for several days. Some in the White House saw it as a flagrant attempt to embarrass the administration just before an election. Annan has steel under his placid exterior, and I suspect he simply wanted his complaint on the record; he may have wanted the Bush administration to know that there was a paper trail showing they had been warned. But he had also rigorously sought to control the UN's every move in those pre-election days to make sure we did nothing that could be construed as interference. He understood the stakes and did not intend it as an election ploy.

The administration did not attack Fallujah until just after the election, and when it did, it did not rely on an aerial bombardment; instead it sought to minimize civilian casualties, even at significant cost to American lives, by going in with ground troops and fighting door to door. I doubt the UN's intervention had much to do with this wise decision; rather, the U.S. military was coming to recognize that its operations must be more surgical and careful about minimizing civilian casualties.

However, the political damage back at the UN was done. Even as Annan confronted the challenge of restoring a broken-backed UN to health, he faced an administration that was distant at best. Speculation had it that after the Fallujah letter the president had washed his hands of the secretary-general. Then the Oil-for-Food scandal erupted. The neoconservatives' ally in Baghdad, Ahmed Chalabi, who hated the UN as much as they did, released files that appeared to show the UN's Oil-for-Food chief Benon Sevan had been a direct beneficiary of Saddam Hussein's oil voucher scam.

Throughout early 2005 I sought to arrange a meeting for Annan with President Bush, to ease the tension. Steve Hadley, a friend of mine who had succeeded Condi Rice as national security advisor, was affable and always available, but he rebuffed my efforts, pleading scheduling difficulties. It was a lonely time.

Later that year we received what many considered the White House's real response to Annan's Fallujah letter: President Bush dispatched a new ambassador to the United Nations, John Bolton. As in Iraq, with Bolton the United States was in the end the biggest loser. The United States has probably never been as poorly represented at the UN, and it happened just at a time when the country's urgent diplomatic priority was to repair bridges, not pull them down. Pigeonholed as a neoconservative, Bolton's beliefs were actually somewhat at odds with the neocon embrace of democracy promotion and, after Iraq, nation-building. He was in fact an old-school conservative who believed America should limit its engagement in the world strictly to what benefited it or enhanced its security, and that it should act without restrictions to protect its own interests. To his eyes, one of the greatest threats to that principle was a meddling UN intent on drawing the United States into a web of international rules and supranational institutions.

Many in Washington sought to block Bolton's nomination, an obvious declaration of diplomatic war on the UN. He finally arrived in mid-2005, when the Oil-for-Food scandal was roiling the UN, and Kofi Annan and those around him were trying to address the management weaknesses that the scandal had exposed with a reform program. The arrival of this cantankerous anti-UN figure as America's chief representative was not a friendly act. Moreover Annan was also trying to push through long-overdue changes in the UN's collective security, development, human rights, and humanitarian structures. This could have been America's moment to come back into the UN fold after Iraq. A leader on UN reform since 1945, the United States could have taken up that role again.

Instead President Bush chose to send a vituperative critic of the United Nations who not only hated the organization and those who worked for it but viewed the whole concept of multilateralism as an unacceptable constraint on American power and freedom of action in the world. Bolton used the Oil-for-Food crisis to shame and tar the organization, and he used the reform proposals as a stick with which to beat the UN, rather than strengthen it.

In the spring of 2004 Annan asked Paul Volcker, an eminent former chairman of the Federal Reserve who had a weakness, as he ruefully put it, for trying to help troubled international organizations, to explore the charges of corruption swirling against the UN, including an accusation that Annan had helped his son Kojo get a UN contract for a company he worked for. A careful and precise former South African judge, Richard Goldstone, joined Volcker on the panel, as did a much less precise Swiss campaigner against corruption and a team of fifty investigators. The job of this Independent Inquiry Committee, as the panel was called, was to examine the Oil-for-Food debacle from top to bottom.

Volcker, in his anxiety to either prove or disprove allegations as quickly as possible so that the United Nations could get on with its job, committed to producing a series of rolling reports. The working method seemed to be that the panel's hard-charging young investigators and the Swiss member would assume the worst in what they charged; Richard Goldstone, and the other more seasoned members of the team, would then require proof; then mere days before publication Volcker and his staff director, a wry, phlegmatic retired Canadian civil servant called Reid Morden, would seek to balance the two approaches. As each report was published, the media viewed it as a potential resigning matter for Kofi Annan, so it would be introduced to a packed press conference, and we would spend days combating, accepting, or clarifying findings that we ourselves had been shown only just before the press conference. I was lead gladiator for the defense, leading our response and more often than not rolling myself out to joust with the press corps.

Annan, on the insistent advice of friends who understood just how hot this was going to get, engaged a formidable legal counsel, Greg Craig. Craig, who bears a physical resemblance to a middle-aged Spencer Tracy, had defended President Clinton during his impeachment hearings and was later to be President Obama's first White House counsel. But Craig was under no illusions where he was operating: in this highly charged atmosphere, there was no chance that justice would get done on its own, let alone that the story would have the Hollywood ending of a Spencer Tracy movie. This was an investigation, not a court, and Greg had to fight tooth and nail to protect Annan against investigators and congressmen eager to make their names by getting his scalp via any means.

UN communications were notorious for their diplomatic circumlocutions, steeped in qualifications and nuance. Mastering that language was normally a survival skill for a UN career, but when Fox News wanted a response for its next news bulletin, the staffers on our UN crisis management team often did not know how to say plainly that something was incorrect. So I turned to a tough Texan, Robert Mead, to help. Mead had grown up on hardscrabble local election campaigns, then come to work for my political consultancy firm,

Sawyer-Miller, in the 1990s on contested corporate takeovers. (We had extended our political combat skills into a more profitable arena.) I asked him to apply a little Texan directness to the responses.

I also added a former *Financial Times* journalist, Mark Suzman, to our UN defenses. Suzman, a South African, had joined me early in my days at UNDP and was fondly known as Little Mark because of my rather larger physical stature. At the UN and at UNDP, people would go to him to learn what the boss was thinking. During that long year of Oil-for-Food investigations and daily media combat, some of us wanted to race out and make ill-considered comments. But Mark, much calmer than me and a model of reflection before action, restrained us from giving in to our first instincts. His ally was Mead, who had a real ear for how our comments would play in Washington.

Contrary to the critics demanding the secretary-general's head, and contrary to the feverish press coverage, Volcker's team did not find the UN to be a particularly corrupt organization. Only very few UN officials were guilty of taking bribes or other unethical behavior. For an organization whose authority rests on its good name as much as anything, even one case of abuse was too many, but the corruption was much less pervasive than had been claimed. Billions of dollars of oil revenue appeared to have been directed toward meeting Iraq's immediate needs, which was the purpose of the program. It had been set up to ensure that ordinary Iraqis could escape the impact of sanctions targeting the regime. It allowed imports of food and other basic goods needed to keep the economy going, including the oil sector; Iraq was allowed to make approved export sales to finance these imports; and the UN was supposed to regulate and monitor both the imports and exports to prevent abuse. Its job was to make sure products bought and sold were approved as being for peaceful purposes. It was not with the buyer or seller where the main corruption lay.

A fair-minded reader of the Volcker reports would see that the principal corruption was not in the UN but between companies that were buying Iraq's oil and selling its goods, on the one hand, and the Iraqi government, on the other. The government had organized an elaborate kickback scheme with those companies that allowed millions of dollars to be skimmed off. The UN was not so much corrupt as incompetent. Its failures were supervisory and operational. Its auditing was inadequate, and in many cases, when an audit found faults, the UN made little or no attempt to rectify them. The muddled lines of responsibility and accountability went all the way to the top. When Volcker and his colleagues interviewed Annan and his then-deputy Louise Fréchette, each thought the other was in charge of the program.

Annan had signed a memo assigning supervision of the program, and of its wheeling-and-dealing Cypriot chief, Benon Sevan, to Fréchette in her first days on the job in 1997. She did not recall having ever seen the memo. The Volcker panel concluded that neither the secretary-general nor his deputy knew who was in charge of Oil-for-Food. It traced payments to Sevan from a beneficiary of oil contracts for whom Sevan had lobbied in Baghdad. He was indicted on that basis. I had considered him a friend and was dismayed that he could have let the UN down in this way—he had betrayed all of us. Sevan is now in hiding from American justice in Cyprus.

Equally distressing, the Oil-for-Food Program had become a major income source for cash-strapped parts of the UN system in Iraq. UNDP wanted to rehabilitate the electricity system in the Kurdish parts of northern Iraq, but arcane administrative rules required us to find another UN entity to implement that program. My predecessors had used a UN Secretariat department whose traditional work was drafting reports and servicing conferences. Rehabilitating the electricity no doubt seemed like a nice little money-earner, but little happened. The lights and power were still out. I put a stop to it and had UNDP take direct charge, under a couple of our strongest field managers. We planted them on site. To acquire the generating equipment, they navigated complicated import procedures and depended on the uncooperative government in Baghdad to acquiesce; nevertheless, results quickly showed.

Iraqi's schools needed chalk for the blackboards, which they could have imported under the Oil-for-Food Program. But one UN agency, eager to grab a share of the action, proposed building a chalk factory. It was done. But officials accustomed to organizing seminars on the perils of illiteracy knew nothing about chalk making. The factory failed to manufacture any chalk that could withstand contact with a blackboard without crumbling, and after some years it was closed. How schoolchildren and their teachers got by in the meantime is not clear. It was a further example of an underfunded UN system plunging into the apparent goldmine of the Oil-for-Food Program to finance their activities elsewhere around the world.

As a result of the Independent Inquiry Committee's investigations, a small number of UN procurement staff, government officials, and agents and staff of companies involved in the racket have lost their jobs, been indicted, or gone to prison. A larger number of other non-UN cases, against companies and their executives who paid off Saddam, remain pending as national governments have proved reluctant to follow up and expose wrongdoing by their own nationals and have been keen to close the chapter. As Annan, and indeed Volcker, had feared, the UN took the fall for a scandal that was much bigger than its own part in it.

The symptoms of management paralysis that Volcker uncovered did not surprise most of us—we had been fighting it for years. But the instances of wrongdoing made the case for UN reform beyond argument, and no manager with a conscience could preside idly over such a poorly functioning system. In the hope of breaking through and moving reform forward, I was ready to throw myself at the problem as many times as it took, no matter how bruising the fight. The world surely could not afford a dysfunctional United Nations.

A World Summit was to be held in September 2005, the successor meeting to the 2000 Millennium Summit, which had produced the Millennium Declaration and the Millennium Development Goals. This summit too would produce a declaration. It included some big new ideas on UN structures. Additionally, earlier that year, at Annan's request, the Deputy Secretary-General, Louise Fréchette, and I drafted a set of reforms for UN procedures; also on our team were Rajat Gupta, a McKinsey senior partner, and Bob Orr, an energetic and inventive American policy planner heading that function for Annan. Our proposed reforms would be part of the summit's declaration; they covered all the critical internal problems: bottlenecks of audit, recruitment, and staff separation; conditions of service for our colleagues in the field; and budget flexibility for managers. UN diplomats screened and debated them.

The summit preparations saw early progress, as diplomats cautiously moved toward agreement on the reforms. Then in early August John Bolton arrived at the UN. He immediately denounced the whole negotiation and insisted on starting over. That and the growing antagonism to the Oil-for-Food inquiry, which was being cast as an American coup against the UN, marked the beginnings of the end for the reforms.

The proposed reforms covering peace-building, human rights, development, and humanitarian relief, and even some of our management proposals made it through the labored preparatory process of drafting committees. But by the eve of the summit, we faced an impasse. Diplomats still had more than a hundred brackets, as they call them, in the text—that is, language they had not agreed to. With impeccable timing, Annan had Bob Orr write a compromise text: the day before the summit Orr reached into the proverbial hat and pulled one out. During the morning we called in key ambassadors in a carefully orchestrated sequence; to bypass the irascible Bolton, I called Condi Rice's delegation at the Waldorf. At lunchtime we were able to release the text. Ambassadors had been alarmed that they would have no text to show their imminently arriving presidents, but they fell into line with relief. They could easily defer to Kofi Annan's compromise. So there was a summit and a declaration. Heads of government made then appearances at the summit and endorsed the declaration.

But as soon as the presidents were gone, the battle resumed. Impassioned divisions between North and South reopened. The North wanted the declaration to address security more, including an unambiguous definition of terrorism; the South wanted more on development, choosing to treat the huge aid pledges just made at the G8 summit in Gleneagles as old news and less important than having extra officials to service their meetings on development. On management reform, we had proposed that the secretary-general have greater authority but also more accountability; developing countries chose to view that as a plot to increase American and Western control over the UN.

The series of reforms that we had carefully crafted allowed mobility and better quality of staff; a more rational budget process; flexibility in hiring, so that every single post did not have to be approved by a committee of 192 member states; topped-up field salaries and contract terms, to overcome high vacancy rates and high staff turnover in our peacekeeping operations; a new outside audit committee to ensure the real correction of financial control problems; and a proper job description for the deputy secretary-general, to make him or her a real chief operating officer for this sprawling, undermanaged organization. But the deputy's position remained undefined (as it did when I took over the post in 2006 from Fréchette), because when we drafted the reforms, Annan concluded that governments would oppose on principle anything on paper as an attempted Western coup. More power for a British deputy would mean less power for an African secretary-general. In truth nothing disempowers a chief executive more than the absence of a clear, accountable management structure. The diplomats' political stubbornness was management folly.

Many ambassadors were also inflamed by the Oil-for-Food investigation and its American chair, Paul Volcker. They saw the Independent Inquiry Committee as part of an American right-wing witch hunt against Kofi Annan and the UN. The U.S. Congress, after all, had undertaken five investigations into Oil-for-Food, and tirades erupted almost daily from Fox News and the opinion pages of *The Wall Street Journal*. Volcker, however, was disquieted by the unproven allegations and the political name-calling. His investigation focused on the facts; disproved grossly exaggerated claims that would have brought down Annan; and in general saved the UN from a Washington lynch mob. But the angry ambassadors missed this fact, and long before Volcker officially presented his final report in October 2005, they had already made up their minds. The report was dead on arrival. Unfortunately, so was his argument about the necessity of major management reforms.

Hardliners on the other side had very much wanted to block UN reforms, not only to embarrass the United States but to prevent the strengthening of an organization that they felt denied them sufficient power. The elegantly saturnine Munir Akram, Pakistan's representative, relished Washington's enemy fire on the UN and considered John Bolton, its New York emissary, to be a gift from heaven.

Washington's choice of Bolton had, I suspect, many such unintended consequences. Bolton had had to be moved from the State Department because he was such a liability in the nuclear security area where his responsibilities lay. Colin Powell took to personally clearing any speech he gave. He had arrived at the UN as a result of a presidential recess appointment because the Senate would not confirm him. When he arrived during the negotiations on the text of the World Summit declaration, his tantrums had left it in tatters. He wanted massive cuts in almost everything that other countries who saw reform as a vehicle for strengthening not weakening the UN furiously resisted. If Bob Orr had not come up with an alternative draft, and the presidents had arrived the next day without one being ready, the blame would have been squarely placed on American shoulders, and President Bush would have had to face the fury of the rest of the international community; on the other hand, Bolton may have been disappointed that he failed to bring the UN down at the first try.

Or perhaps not. I am inclined to think Bolton typical of a certain kind of Washington conservative. An advocate of small government, he has nevertheless spent his whole career living off government. When he has not been in office, he has been a Washington lawyer, lobbyist, or think-tanker living off government indirectly, a major beneficiary of a gold-plated welfare system. Perhaps he did not want to rock the boat in Washington to the point of capsize.

After the World Summit, opposition to reform resurfaced once the government leaders had left town. Bolton insisted that UN member states adopt the reforms that been agreed to by the heads of government and threatened to block the new two years' budget, due to start in January 2006, if they refused. The fact that the budget vote required consensus made his threat real. The United States was also the biggest contributor to the UN and had a history of withholding payment when it did not like what was happening there. But Bolton's sponsorship of reform killed it, because he was thought to intend only harm to the organization. Some of the developing countries were keen to let Bolton provoke a shutdown of the UN, convincing themselves that it would backfire on him in the same way that, a decade earlier, Newt Gingrich's shutdown of the American government had boomeranged on him. Annan and I considered the boomerang effect to be most unlikely, since it was unclear that anyone in New York would miss the UN. Many Americans, not just those on the right, would have regarded its shuttered headquarters on Manhattan's First Avenue as a victory. The field operations that kept the peace, saved lives, and contained massive refugee flows would have carried on much as before because they were funded largely outside the disputed New York regular budget. We brokered a deal to put the budget on a six-month installment while acrimonious negotiations on reform continued.

After the summit the mood in the UN only got worse. The microphone outside the Security Council became Bolton's personal briefing platform, and he used it with considerable skill, often, it seemed, preempting his boss, Condi Rice, in making policy on UN-related issues. He was more in her face here than he would have been if she had kept him in Washington. He would strut scowling into sessions discussing reform, sometimes deliver himself of a few bromides, and then quickly depart. Other than his White House patron Dick Cheney, it was not clear that any senior administration figure relished the public podium that Bolton built for himself at the UN. Most could see that he was doing the United States damage.

Despite this, at the World Summit we squeezed through a couple of important new institutions. One was the Human Rights Council, the result of an effort to revamp the human rights machinery. The old Human Rights Commission had been discredited and politicized; this new council that replaced it was to be more rigorous and dedicated. A second new institution was the Peacebuilding Commission, intended to draw political, security, and economic support for previously failed states into a more coherent approach. Both, however, were pale shadows of what had been proposed. And both have been disappointments in their early years of operation. Negotiations had cut the guts out of both as it did out of the new doctrine of responsibility to protect, intended to give the international community the right to interfere when a country embarked on mass domestic human rights abuse. To those suspicious of Bolton and the Americans, this seemed to be endorsing future Iraq-like interventions.

More successful was a revolving fund for quick response to disasters; otherwise, reform was now largely reduced to what we could press through under our limited executive powers. On issues where intergovernmental approval would later be necessary, we delayed, gambling that the intergovernmental mood would improve. We focused on personnel reform. First, we tried to tackle a running sore at the UN: the backroom deals that surrounded the top appointments. We began to publish short lists of candidates for the most senior jobs, along with job descriptions and criteria for the selection. We also reached out widely to governments and to NGOs for candidates, as well as conducting our own parallel search efforts using headhunters.

This change was quickly noticed. In the summer of 2005 the World Bank board was loyally if grudgingly rubber-stamping the White House's closed selection of Paul Wolfowitz, a neoconservative architect of the Iraq War, as its new president; at the same time Kemal Dervis, a Turkish economist and governmental reformer with decades of developmental experience, emerged as my successor as the new head of UNDP. The contrast could not have been more marked. Soon, we had similarly good outcomes for other top jobs.

But in the middle of 2006, the governments that supported reform threw in the towel. They recognized developing country resistance was too strong and so reform was dead. Bolton's budget cap was lifted and face was saved with a few positive comments by all sides, including pious comments from about the G77's commitment to reform. Then the UN went back to dysfunctional business as usual.

Reflecting on our rocky path, by mid-2006, I had had enough. My frustration went much deeper than John Bolton, who had come to appear the product of an accident of bad personnel policy as much as administration design. I had concluded that, while a strong secretary-general could shape reform with smart proposals, there was no alternative to a real commitment by individual countries to a better UN. If they remained on the sidelines, lobbing grenades at reform to score political points off each other, we could not progress.

And it seemed to me that the United States had to be the indispensable partner in UN reform. It was the founding architect of the institution, and in more than sixty years no major innovations had occurred without its sponsorship and, usually, leadership. Perversely, although its motives and positions often evoked much suspicion and hostility, countries liked to be able to fall in with the United States. They deferred to American leadership and had done so repeatedly over the UN's life.

The United States, long before John Bolton or the Bush administration, had often treated this status as a casual seigniorial right rather than as a unique diplomatic authority to be cultivated. The United States would use the UN when it suited its interests but otherwise did little or nothing to defend or support it; when the UN was not convenient, it was equally casually discarded. We were like a menu from which the United States ordered sparingly, I used to grumble, on an à la carte basis; but to make the UN function effectively, America had to order all the courses, even the ones that were not particularly to its taste.

In the early summer of 2006, when reform was failing, it seemed the time had come to appeal more directly for American support. A forum presented itself in a conference on U.S. foreign policy sponsored by the Century Foundation and the Center for American Progress. The timing was right—it would be the last appropriate forum before the long summer, after which Annan would have just four months left in office and so in terms of rekindling any reform it was now or never—but while the speakers were bipartisan, the organizers had a distinct Democratic Party hue.

Carefully, I laid out the complaint: the United States over many administrations of both parties had taken the UN for granted. Presidents and their administrations had lost the habit of standing up for the UN against its critics and of educating Americans in the UN's usefulness to American foreign policy objectives. What had happened, I asked, to the America of Roosevelt and Truman, the idealistic visionary founders of the organization?

The location, the speaker, and the theme were too much for Bolton, who grabbed his microphone outside the Security Council unleashing a snarling response. His walrus mustache shaking, as the comedian Jon Stewart noted, he furiously demanded that the secretary-general dis-own the speech and that I apologize. Neither happened, and in his closing weeks in office Kofi Annan, six months later, gave a similar, albeit typically gentler and subtler, speech than mine. At the Truman Library he compared American leadership at the beginning of the UN's life with the dismal record of today. What Bolton's outburst did do, however, was make my speech defining in terms of the U.S.-UN relationship. The speech was debated in editorials and blogs across the country—making it on to even Jon Stewart's *Daily Show*. The knee-jerk right resented the criticisms, but many thoughtful Americans ap-peared to ruefully agree: the United States had deserted the UN.

Later in the year the U.S. Senate threw Bolton out—it refused to approve his extension. There was some justice. I told the press I had no comment, but it was noted that I encouraged them to report that I said it with a smile. But it was a hollow victory. Bolton had rained on the parade. There had been a moment when the world could perhaps have come back together after Iraq around an agenda of strengthened international cooperation. Geopolitics and personali-ties combined to cost us the opportunity.

CHAPTER NINE

SAN FRANCISCO II

Officials have been tinkering with the UN since its founding in 1945, the way a family keeps its first car on the road through a mixture of fond repairs and the occasional exasperated kick to the tires. But as the years go by, the old car spends more time in the garage than on the road, and the neighbors wonder why it is not traded in for a new model.

UN secretary-generals are the great home garage mechanics. Each new one has paraded plans to change the organization, whereupon follow-up initiatives cascaded down from his thirty-eighth-floor office. Kofi Annan was no exception. He introduced three major waves of reform: once at the beginning of his term, once when he was re-elected for a second term, and then again in his last two years. The first called for a major restructuring of departments and UN programs, which rather misleadingly is what the semi-independent agencies like UNDP were called. The second was a tidying up to the first one; the third wave of more fundamental reform was what I described in Chapter Eight.

In between came a steady trickle of lesser proposals. The different UN agency chiefs, too, talked of reform incessantly, on the other side of Manhattan's First Avenue, in the UN funds and programs, and at the agencies in Geneva, Rome, and elsewhere.

UN staff were for the most part fed up with reform proposals, doubting their sincerity and seeing them as interfering with the job at hand. But donors demanded reform, so the UN chiefs had little choice but to talk the talk if they were to secure financial resources.

Governments and the UN's other stakeholders and partners felt that our capacity to get results seemed impaired. People wanted more from us. Unable to deliver, we kept trying to fix the machine. It became an occupational obsession, especially for the secretary-general, who, despite his elevated status, had less management power than many of his underlings because member states insisted on shadowing and second-guessing everything he did through a laborious intergovernmental committee structure.

Annan had reluctantly concluded that the UN needed a bigger makeover than mere tinkering. The world rained demands down on us, and we were ill equipped to address them. When I worked for Annan, first as his chief of staff and then as his deputy, I liked to describe my job by listing what was in my in-box that day: nearly always Darfur, often Lebanon and the Middle East, the Democratic Republic of the Congo, several other African crises, Haiti, Kosovo, climate change, avian flu, HIV/AIDS, migration, trade, and poverty. We were constantly being pulled in all directions as global problems and opportunities piled up.

Our twenty-four-hour Situation Center tracked global crises, particularly political ones; often it woke me up in the morning or found me at the train station to impart news of an overnight incident long before I even got to my in-box. The crises never stopped: the center's open-plan room buzzed constantly with phone calls, e-mails, websites, and CNN and BBC news screens. The news and messages that came in and went out became in my mind a distillation of the UN's business. And as governments stretched for solutions only to find them beyond their reach, an ever-wider range of issues came our way.

The UN quite simply had to step up to another level if it was to meet expectations. Annan and I had both talked of a "San Francisco moment" in our discussions about for the summits of 2005, evoking the 1945 conference that had agreed on the UN charter. Our hope was that at Gleneagles in July and then at the World Summit in New York in September, the world might take a collective look at its bleak future, realize it was on the edge of disaster, bury the hatchet, and agree to forge a new and better UN. That was more than better organizational machinery. Indeed, that would only come if there was first a real meeting of minds around how the world might cooperate better to govern itself. We hoped to establish a shared vision of globalization that would offer greater economic security and opportunity to all, as well as wider participation in decision-making on security matters.

The 2005 summits were the fourth, and actually least ambitious, try since the Second World War to establish a system of international cooperation. The first had been the creation of the United Nations, the World Bank, and the IMF, in the mid-1940s. The San Francisco Conference had been more ambitious in substance than ours but every bit as well polished, in public relations terms, as Gleneagles. Politics ambushed it too, in the form of the Cold War, an even more divisive issue than today's War on Terror. Once the Soviet Union and the United States confronted each other, the world was divided—and at odds.

The second try, much less well known, came in 1974, when exhausted UN General Assembly delegates adopted by consensus a declaration establishing the New International Economic Order. As we saw in Chapter Two, this was an ambitious but bitterly contested postcolonial effort attempted to create an international framework to manage economic relations between poor commodity-producing developing countries and their richer Western customers. The NIEO sought to stabilize commodity prices and to regulate multinational companies' behavior, goals that Western governments disliked. The initiative collapsed, a victim of its divided times, the continuing Cold

War, the Arab oil price shock, and a steamy angry postcolonial social-ist rhetoric that the West was having none of.

The third try began in 2000, when Kofi Annan proposed to world leaders that they come to the opening of the UN General Assembly in September 2000 and by their collective presence turn it into a much grander world summit that might set a course for political action in the new century. And indeed more global leaders gathered together than ever before or since. Annan was riding high as a global leader—the moment was buoyant, and he seemed to catch its hope and multicul-tural optimism. In his report he steered clear of controversy or propos-ing big structural changes in the global economy—instead he talked of democracy and human rights and the fight against poverty. The as-sembly might have broken down into individual interests to battle one another over a draft declaration, but it adopted his report wholesale. Glum-faced Chinese delegates went along with the calls for democ-racy, while the Americans and Japanese, the two biggest UN contrib-utors, who understandably got tight-fisted when other delegations talked of spending more money, went along with the idea of fighting poverty, albeit without promising a specific amount of money.

Thereafter reformers called for modifying some of the UN's 1945 arrangements. We didn't want to tamper with the Charter itself: that might open a Pandora's box, and the whole arrangement could end up worse than before. Since little of the vision and statesmanship of 1945 remained, we thought it best to leave well enough alone and tidy up what we could.

The new century's possibilities briefly seemed to dwarf its chal-lenges, and the almost euphoric optimism about globalization and its possibilities inspired greater ambition at the Summit. Political leaders there were thinking about poverty. In a globalized world, poverty lived next door, in Johannesburg and Rio de Janeiro and many other places. In an integrated world, as it had been a hundred years earlier more locally in New York or London, abject poverty was both an intolerable injustice and a dangerous threat. Law and order and middle-class prosperity could not be sustained amid extreme global inequality. Many pundits in newspapers, TV, and online suddenly embraced this maxim: that social order could not indefinitely survive unmanaged extremes of wealth. But the problem of poverty could not be solved by private charity alone. Nor could it be left to traditional development assistance or relief organizations—that would be akin to leaving it to the poorhouses and churches a century earlier. It needed a new level of governmental action.

Similarly, the leaders at the summit considered other issues that had been left to spiral out of control for too long: failing states that became havens for international terrorists; antienvironmental practices, from industrial smokestacks to burning rainforests; and little-researched communicable diseases in the third world. These issues could no longer be brushed under the carpet. They mattered to everyone—global transportation systems and weather patterns made sure of that. Commercial airliners could carry avian flu to New York as easily as they could carry terrorists. Deforestation in Brazil could wreak damage on the U.S. environment. Our fates, and how we managed them, had become enmeshed.

Globalization is a hard issue to get one's hands around—not just in the how-to-manage-it sense but also in the how-to-measure-it. Although numbers cannot tell the whole story, they are striking. World population is now more than six billion and is unlikely to start leveling off until about a third more people have been added. The planet is getting crowded. About 90 percent of births now occur in developing countries, as Western populations decline except where supplemented by migration.[1] But a bigger world is not necessarily a poorer one. Changes in global per capita income have also been gathering pace. According to the historian Niall Ferguson, "The average individual's income, allowing for fluctuations in the value of money, increased by little more than 50 percent between 1500 and 1870.

Between 1870 and 1998, however, it increased by a factor of more than six and a half. Expressed differently, the compound annual growth was nearly thirteen times higher between 1870 and 1998 than it was between 1500 and 1870."

The most noticed dimension of globalization is trade.[2] From 1993 to 2003 the value of world exports more than doubled, to a total of $9 trillion. Exports are now responsible for more than a quarter of world income, and half in East Asia and a third in sub-Saharan Africa. Nor is trade any longer a hierarchical business, in which poor countries sell food and commodities to rich countries in return for industrial goods. Today more than 40 percent of developing countries' exports go to fellow developing countries, and the share of agriculture and primary products in the value of world trade has fallen by a third since 1980, to 10 percent. One of the single most interesting new trade relationships today is China's rapidly growing trade with Africa. The old trade order, mercantilism as economists call it, is breaking down in unsettling ways for some and liberating ways for others. As developing countries add value, through extra steps in production, to what they export, they are creating new and better jobs. But those in the old economies are correspondingly losing them.

A consequence of growing trade is that there are few "national" products left. When the first Model T automobile rolled off a Ford production line in 1908, it was all homemade, so to speak. A hundred years later only about one-third (by value), of each "American" car originates in the United States. But its not anywhere abroad that such parts come from. We are seeing the rise of new export giants. Two-thirds of the computer components marketed in the United States have at one stage or another passed through the single Chinese city of Dongguan.

Thrown together by population growth and our intertwined economic lives, we find that we are bumping up against not only one another but ceilings. In 2005 the UN's Millennium Ecosystem Assessment concluded that most of the twenty-four natural support systems that it studied were in decline. Some two billion people are at risk of not having clean drinking water; there is widespread soil degradation and a high risk of climate change. We are overwhelming the natural systems upon which depend. These problems are a consequence of economic growth, increased global, consumption and population growth.

Today China imports 50 percent of its oil and the United States 60 percent—those two nations alone are responsible for 35 percent of world consumption. Ten years ago China was not even a fuel importer. Across the developing world demand for energy to feed industrial and consumer growth is rising. Inevitably, this scramble for energy challenges the existing political and economic status quo. Hungry new customers are challenging cozy producer-supplier relationships.

Just as energy demand is taking off, some of the world's old oil fields are starting to fall off, and new sources, often in unstable corners of the world, are coming on tap. Hence the scramble for the world's remaining resources.[3] Currently West African oil exports to Asia are up 670 percent over 1997 and to the United States up 30 percent. Caspian energy supplies to Europe are up 280 percent. Russia's own fields, largely because of a shortfall in new investment, are currently flat in production terms, but Russia will need to soften its current nationalistic antiforeign investment mood in favor of attracting outside technology and capital. Production from the West's "safest" sources, North American and North Sea oil, is flattening and facing increasing environmental difficulties. Brazil and other Latin American supplies are, by contrast, growing rapidly.

So the race to control oil supply is taking place in a highly uncertain global market. And the antidote—developing stability and transparency in supply arrangements; taking global steps to reduce consumption; and substituting new technologies and energy sources—is faltering. Energy encapsulates the danger of a world without rules or governance: it could become every country for itself.

Even without the financial crisis, the fluctuations in energy prices in 2008 and 2009 would have been an economic shock.

No less destabilizing than the competition for energy is uneven development performance. Failed states like Afghanistan, Somalia, Iraq, and Bosnia can become home to networks of terrorists. More generally in the globalization stakes, many smaller, isolated island or landlocked nations have fallen further behind. The poorest countries are concentrated in Africa but are also found in Central America, Central Asia, and the Pacific—so whereas large parts of the third world are moving upward in terms of income, "the bottom billion" (as development economist Paul Collier calls them)[4] remain stubbornly stuck. In the 1990s this group's income actually declined by 5 percent. They ended the century poorer than they had been in 1970. Long-term growth rates, although currently disguised by high commodity prices, are now such that the average person in one of Collier's poorest countries has an income only a fifth of the average in the rest of the developing world.

The world's top several billion have seen growing population and incomes—the middle classes of developing countries are growing by about 75 million people a year, according to one international investment bank assessment. But the vast billion-person underclass that lives on less than a dollar a day, and the 2.8 billion who live on less than two dollars, are in many cases being left behind.

If a global executive or parliament existed, it would need to tackle these kinds of strategic questions:

- The problems of growth. Across a fast-growing global economy, with increasing competition for resources, people, and capital, how can we manage the environmental, human, and infrastructural bottlenecks that invariably develop?

- The problems of integration. As communications and trade draw us together and integrate cultures, how can people preserve what matters most to them from their separate identities without entering a ruinous backlash? How can globalization become a stage on which we present and celebrate our differences as well as a vehicle for drawing us into a smoother interdependence?

• The problem of limits. How can we agree on the terms that will allow us to live within our global means? How can we ration fairly our global use of nonrenewable resources, and how can we encourage the invention of new energy-efficient technologies and then share their use?

• The problems of those left behind. India and China, despite their economic success, still have a lot of poor people. By some measures, 40 percent of the world's poor live in India. But the Indians like the Chinese are doing some impressive things to fight poverty. Their success depends on the rest of the world remaining an open market to them. More difficult, how can we support whole countries that have fallen out of the global economy. In an integrated world, letting them sink ever further behind has risks and costs.

Each of these four sets of problems raises pressing questions of social, economic, and environmental policy, as well as security. However, no global policy-making arrangement exists to address them, no individual and no institution to take charge, no parliament or executive.

The international community of 2000 and after eschewed the heavy-handed state intervention model of the 1970s. No one proposed to fix prices or regulate international corporate behavior, except after extreme provocation the financial sector after 2008, or set up new global authorities. Rather, the solutions suggested were partnerships among governments, development agencies, NGOs, and the private sector. And at a time of incremental, rather than radical, ambition, the affordability of change was stressed. On the behalf of Kofi Annan, I commissioned the development economist Jeffrey Sachs to assemble some 250 experts and policy-makers from around the world to calculate what it would cost to implement the eight Millennium Development Goals established at the 2000 UN summit:

- Eradicate extreme poverty and hunger

- Achieve universal primary education

- Promote gender equality and empower women

- Reduce child mortality

- Improve maternal health

- Combat HIV/AIDS, malaria, and other diseases

- Ensure environmental sustainability

- Develop a Global Partnership for Development

In an elaborate multivolume report, Sachs's team concluded that the cost of ending poverty fell within 0.7 percent of national GDP, the long-talked-of aid goal that rich countries should annually aim to give poor countries. Sachs would break this up into the ten-dollar malaria bed net that could save a child's life or the increasingly low cost of AIDS treatment. Many of these interventions, he argued, would cost each of us less than we spend at Starbucks in a week.

The question for the future is how to set up UN reform to achieve real action. The new secretary-general, Ban Ki-moon, is following the path of his predecessors and proposing to move bits and pieces of the structure around. Nothing yet indicates that he understands the scale of change required. But a long period of tinkering with the UN machinery may actually allow the growing gap between performance and need to increase.

Two things are, however, likely to bring matters to a head. First, the growing gap itself will renew calls to address UN weakness more systematically. When politicians reach for a solution for climate change or a war and cannot find it, this absence will build the case for a better UN. And if the direction of global events leads, as it inevitably must, to more such demands on the UN, the call for reform is likely to grow steadily. In that sense, a fresh try at reform remains inevitable. The question remains *when*, not *if*.

The political philosophers Thomas Hobbes and John Locke, whose writings provided the intellectual foundation for the modern state by insisting on the imperative of introducing basic domestic order, might recognize the current international moment. While today there is less war and violent death than at many points in world history, particularly in the twentieth century, the crisis of what might be called governability is growing. We are more integrated than ever before, which constrains the old nation-state's power, but it has left us less governed than ever before. That itch is what draws so many of us back time and again to reforming the international system. But the project is imbued with difficulty because so many of the downsides of global change are laid at its door. Politicians everywhere rail at the big international or regional institutions, notably the European Union, that are taking power away from the people. The UN, World Bank, EU, and others have been so thoroughly painted as antidemocratic and as part of the problem of globalization rather than the solution that it is a brave politician who prominently makes the case for strengthening these organizations.

In 2008, as food and fuel prices soared and the world slumped into a housing and credit crisis, I was working, as a member of the cabinet, of one such politician, the British prime minister Gordon Brown. When trouble hit, his instinct was to pursue common global action: to open food markets by pushing for the completion of the Doha free trade round; to pool international resources to improve agricultural productivity in poor countries; to work with the Gulf countries, Nigeria, and others, to expand oil production while developing international funding mechanisms for oil producers to participate in financing the development of alternative energy sources; to add to the World Bank's role of funding development of a second arm for the environment; and to improve the IMF's ability to predict future financial crashes. He was a fountain of ideas for international action to address these crises.

At home, Britons heard Brown's message in irritated silence. They could not relate to it. They wanted more homespun solutions that dealt with the domestic here and now. Politics, it seems, is always local. What Brown was arguing for seemed far off in time and space. He understood this very well but found it hard to stop discussing an analysis that provided real answers, in favor of pandering to the domestic political impulse.

Brown's dilemma was every modern politician's dilemma. And if national leaders were ever to concede enough power that an effective UN, or other international governance structure, could be made to work, the dilemma would be far worse.

The intergovernmental gridlock, concerning governance and voting, between the big UN contributor countries and the rest of the membership is the core dysfunction. To overcome it, to find a grand bargain to allow a more realistic governance model for the UN, both sides would have to rise above their own current sense of entrenched rights and privileges, the bread and butter of member states.

Reform of the UN must move from tinkering to real restructuring, but achieving it may take a crisis. Only tragic events of some kind seem to bring countries to the table, ready finally to do business and cut a new deal. The year 1945 was a moment of malleability and vision as a result of the war. Today environmental catastrophe, terrorist attack, or breakdown of peace—one wishes for none of them, but such an event may be required now to galvanize reform. In 2008 such a disaster struck in the form of the financial crisis, but as we will see in the next chapter, it provided only a partial and temporary spur to action.

The fact that real UN reform would entail painful concessions of rights and privileges may explain why delegates clutch at almost any excuse to avoid discussing it. Bickering in committee rooms can look like a good option for diplomats scared of being drawn into the issue, say, of national sovereignty, which for now remains impregnable.

Reforming the UN would require the most powerful member states and the weakest to give ground. Room needs to be made for India, Brazil, and South Africa at the Security Council table. This poses a challenge to the existing permanent members. Would their own rights be impaired? How big a Security Council is practical? Britain and France, both permanent members, would face the question of what they must give up, as well as what they should share with Italy and particularly Germany which is presently demanding an additional European seat for itself alone.

Small countries will have to allow the new regional powers a preferred status. Brazil or India's smaller neighbors will feel even more overshadowed. The pretense of equality in the UN General Assembly may recede further. Small countries already resent the new G20 arrangements in the international economic sphere because they feel unrepresented compared to their big emerging-economy neighbors.

As the last decades have shown, countries can rise or fall very quickly. The UN has to be able to correct representation on the Security Council in a low-key way that does not force existing members to dig in and try to save face. That suggests putting the new members on long-term renewable terms, lasting as long as they are felt to be the most effective representatives of their region. Africans are already debating whether the biggest countries could necessarily be the most representative of the continent's concerns. Nigeria and South Africa both have their local critics.

My successor as administrator of UNDP, Kemal Dervis, has proposed a weighted voting system for the Security Council similar to that of the World Bank. A country's vote share could be determined by its relative GDP, population, UN financial contributions, and peacekeeping and aid levels. We slipped in the latter three conditions of global good citizenship—UN contributions, number of peacekeepers, and aid as a proportion of GDP—to the election criteria for the new Peacebuilding Commission. It seems to be creating healthy competition among candidates as they seek to prove their eligibility. The UN has regularly assessed changes in countries' GDP but without providing any incentive for those that are growing richer to volunteer a bigger contribution; most often they try to hold down their payments as much as possible. China and India both pay much too little for membership and vigorously defend their parsimony. Equally as important as membership is who gets to use the veto. Its use has gradually been whittled away as the current Security Council strains for consensus and when that is not possible a vote without any of the permanent members falling back on their right of veto. But a history of United States vetoes of resolutions criticizing Israel reminds both sides how far apart the world remains on some issues and how unready we are therefore to hand over our national fates to a body like the Security Council.

Talking of reforming the Security Council, one soon starts to sound like an institutional chiropractor. If only this critical piece of the organization's spine were properly aligned, goes the hope, then the alignment will spread through the lower spine, arms, and legs, as the whole UN body politic recalibrates itself.

The unhealthy resuscitation of the developing countries' opposition lobby, the G77, owes a lot to this fight for a more representative Security Council. Outcasts like Cuba, Venezuela, and Syria had used it as their own club, in both senses of the word, until India, Brazil, South Africa, and others revived it as a means of confronting the West on UN reform and particularly Security Council membership.

A more representative council might reduce the level of poison in the discussions. The Human Rights Council, the management and budget committees, the Economic and Social Council, the Committee for the Inalienable Rights of the Palestinians, and the rest of the alphabetic cacophony of committees, councils, and governing boards all exhibit the same distorted behavior patterns. Each has become about politics and point-scoring. The proper work has too often been jettisoned.

But if the fever receded, then the Human Rights Council could become a serious deliberative place where delegates of real stature debate countries' performance and behavior against objective human rights criteria rather than crude political targets; the Fifth Committee, which covers budget and administrative matters, might recognize that a group of 192 generally junior diplomats, one from each country, with little management experience, is not the best way to manage the institution's affairs and so begin by reforming themselves, by creating either small professional subcommittees or an external control mechanism like an audit and oversight committee, whose membership would be of the highest professional standards (something we tried); and the Economic and Social Council would end its interminable discussions of abstract development objectives and policies and become a practical interministerial committee for the Millennium Development Goals, tracking progress, identifying problems, and building agreement between donors and poor countries for corrective solutions.

As for the Security Council, if reforming its membership could unblock the obstructionism that has brought so much decision-making to a stop, the deal must involve more than membership. Membership must bring responsibility, be it financial or troop contributions, as well as a commitment to an activist Security Council. India has in the past tried to prevent Security Council involvement in Nepal and Myanmar; South Africa has vigorously sought to keep Zimbabwe off the council's agenda. Until late 2006 China stonewalled on Darfur because of its oil interests in Sudan. I have described the United States and Britain's isolation and ultimate defiance of the council on Iraq. The Security Council's handling of the Palestinian issue has a long and sorry history. Nobody smells of roses.

As a British government minister with responsibility for UN matters, I saw more clearly that Britain and France, because they are declining in terms of global power, take the Security Council much more seriously than do China, Russia, and the United States. In general they respect the role of the council; refer matters to it whenever they can; work hard on negotiating resolutions; and then throw a lot of diplomatic effort into ensuring that resolutions, once adopted, are enforced. It has become a critical part of Britain's and France's world role, and they act usually, although not invariably, as guardians of the council's authority and standing. Other members are much more casual.

New members, if they are to be admitted, will have to be able to show they will match these two countries' track record. Unless the Security Council first demonstrated a long uninterrupted period of sober responsible global crisis management, the United States would never countenance even a discussion of limits on its veto, and Britain and France would never consider giving up their status. At the moment the council often seems more gadfly than problem-solver. So reform of the council's working procedures may be as important as membership. The procedural blocks to bringing a Zimbabwe or Myanmar immediately to its attention must be removed. But equally the weapons, hard and soft, that are available to the council need to be improved.

The council's current arsenal for enforcing its decisions many be characterized, only a little cruelly, as: (1) condemnations, which—like the children's nursery rhyme, "Sticks and stones may break my bones, but words will never hurt me"—are often of little consequence; (2) sanctions, which rarely work and often hurt the poor victims of a regime rather than the regime members themselves; and (3) under-armed peacekeepers (the sticks and stones), operating under restrictive conditions often without sufficient numbers or authority to keep the peace.

Sanctions are, however, getting smarter. The United States has pioneered techniques for pursuing the financial assets of wrongdoers through the international banking system. Iran, defying the council and continuing with its nuclear program, has nonetheless felt the pressure; the same techniques appear to have brought the North Koreans to the negotiating table on their nuclear program. The first thing the North Koreans wanted was access to their funds in a bank in Macau. Money matters.

A controversial new tool is the International Criminal Court (ICC). The Bush administration strongly opposed it, wary of a foreign court that might seek one day to charge Americans with war crimes. The Obama administration appears gingerly to be taking a fresh look but has not dared change the Bush White House's stance. As a consequence the United States has not only failed to sign up to the ICC but has forced the Security Council, which has some political control over the court's jurisdiction, to pass exemptions covering the American military.

But the rest of the world, love it or hate it, is adjusting both to the ICC and to the broader array of international justice measures of which it is the apex. Some courts, international arraignments, and solo operators—magistrates in Spain and France particularly—provide a dangerous global spider's web for dictators contemplating retirement. A Spanish magistrate trapped Chile's former president

Pinochet in London with a European arrest warrant. Bosnia's Serb leader, Radovan Karadzic, who after ordering the deaths of eight thousand Muslims at Srebrenica hid as a bearded faith healer, was caught after ten years on the run, showing there is no escape. Liberia's butcherous former president Charles Taylor, who thought he had safe exile in Nigeria, now finds himself in a cell in the Netherlands and undergoing international trial. As Kofi Annan's chief of staff at the time, I took particular pleasure in overseeing his rather complex handover from comfortable exile to lifetime imprisonment. Very bad rulers are discovering that they are accountable for their actions. Punishment can come this side of the grave.

As with so many innovations in international governance, there have also been setbacks. In Africa an angry rebellion has erupted against the ICC, nominally because of its indictment of President Omar al-Bashir of Sudan for war crimes in Darfur, but in fact because of a sense that international human rights instruments are used casually and indiscriminately against current African governments. President Paul Kagame of Rwanda, who rescued his country from genocide and was a founding signatory of the ICC, told me how, with regret, he had become a critic and opponent of the ICC within the African Union because his own government colleagues faced European arrest warrants when traveling. These were based on what he considered weak and trumped-up cases relating to the period of the genocide and were issued by individual European magistrates, not by the ICC. But he saw them, he told me, as part of a conspiracy of expansionist European human rights meddling.

Prosecution does at certain moments deter dictators from giving up power. If as private citizens they will be constantly vulnerable to arrest and other harassment, they may try to cling on. In such cases the Security Council can, in twelve monthly installments, stay action by the ICC. But the message is now clearly out there: leaders who order the mass killings of their own citizens will live the rest of their lives a step away, at best, from seizure by agents of international justice. Impunity no longer reigns. A little bird is hopefully constantly on their shoulder to remind them of the future personal cost of human rights crimes they might be contemplating.

The Security Council's crucial function, however, is its ability to interrupt or prevent the conflict cycle by authorizing mediation. The UN is strapped for mediators, but it has informal arrangements with NGOs that are skilled in this area. In some ways the most impressive international industry convention I know is that of a small closed meeting of the world's mediators. They gather in their jeans, with at least the appearance of having just emerged from the bush and their last conflict, to meet in Norway. Organized by the Norwegian government and the Center for Humanitarian Dialogue in Geneva, they meet to share the tricks of their curious trade—persuading people who hate and distrust each other to talk and make peace. From the Middle East to Sri Lanka, Afghanistan, Burma, Indonesia, and Darfur, they are active. Needless to say, even the best mediators manage only a mixed scorecard. Moreover the cost and the reluctance of governments to allow UN meddling in their affairs means the UN is not as central as it should be.

The Security Council's main punch comes when conflict ends and there is a peace that needs keeping. Yet resources and governmental timidity constrain the council from deploying international peacekeepers. Peacekeeping expanded fivefold under Annan to more than a 100,000 troops, but what's really needed is a NATO-like capacity to lift the blue helmets quickly into trouble spots to contain trouble or police the peace; a truly effective UN peacekeeping capability would have in place shared training, common equipment, logistics capacity, a unified line of command, and a disciplinary system. But investment for that is missing. As it stands now, each operation is assembled through an arduous process of bargaining, and none of the council's permanent five members are significant contributors of troops, leaving the task, as I mentioned earlier, to less powerful countries.

Little real attention has been given to the changing nature of peacekeeping. It began as the insertion of a thin blue line of peace-keepers between two warring states, tasked with monitoring an agreed frontier or ceasefire line. Today their task is more often to keep warring communities, who live among each other apart, or to protect refugee camps and relief operations. The peacekeepers' military role has therefore changed from infantry to armed police and has put a great premium on mobility, as the area of operations has often hugely increased. Darfur is the size of France, and when a dispute flares up there, peacekeepers need helicopters and planes to move quickly.

The final stage of the conflict cycle is the peacetime reconstruction. More often than not previously warring countries will lapse back into conflict, so the Security Council must support the peace-keeping by moving in effective political and reconstruction assistance. Allowing a country to get back on its own feet is critical to the mission of rescuing a country from war. The peacekeepers may need to help train a national police force and army to replace themselves.

At each stage of this process, however, the Security Council is dogged by political caution, archaic procedures, underfunding, and a sheer lack of ambition. Adding new members will not solve that problem. Rather, we need states to accept again the overriding importance of a global collective security system. The world is challenged by new potential conflicts not just between states but within states, and over issues such as water and oil, nuclear and chemical weapons, and terrorism. If ever there were a time for a "San Francisco moment," this would be it.

But before we can have it, we must address the Gordon Brown problem. The UN has to matter to people, to voters. They have to feel that the organization counts in their lives, so that politicians can become its strong supporters without risking their careers.

Plenty can be done at the national political level to connect countries more effectively to UN decision-making. In the United States, the UN ambassador long had cabinet rank—and the Senate still must always approve the president's choice. No other ambassador faces such a test of accountability. John Bolton and his predecessors frequently reported back to congressional committees. That kind of relationship builds connection and prominence for the ambassador's work back in the capital. In Bolton's case it cost him his job, as despite his president's support, the Senate voted him out by refusing to extend the president's initial recess appointment. No other country has such an accountable arrangement.

These arrangements reflect the United States' unusual division of power between legislature and executive, but other countries could copy parts of this approach. A British Labour government in the 1960s briefly gave cabinet rank to its representative to the UN. Parliament could hold hearings, which would stir civil society involvement.

Parliamentarians join their countries' delegations to the General Assembly. The Inter-Parliamentary Union organizes conferences and briefings at the UN for its parliamentarian members around the time of the annual General Assembly meeting. But the UN has quite enough of these mechanisms and meetings already. They will work only if it can reestablish its global relevance. If its members allow it to address issues of inclusion in the global economy, and if a Security Council emerges that is representative and therefore legitimate and able to effectively address conflict, then the UN will be back in business.

CHAPTER TEN

TWO THOUSAND AND EIGHT
AND ALL THAT

The collapse of Lehman Brothers in September 2008 was an un-mitigated financial disaster, but at first it seemed that it might also be the elusive key to reform of the international system. After all, the demise of that international bank hit one of the world's most powerful stakeholders, the financial community, where it hurt, and appeared to demonstrate the weakness of global financial regulation. As collective panic swept both financial markets and their govern-ment regulators, the crisis spread into the real economy. The world seemed to reach a turning point. Could the financial crisis have a silver lining and be the spur that pushed forward global governance?

A sector that had generally opposed more international regula-tion was suddenly confronted with the costs of its laissez-faire ap-proach. Within days governments rescued the insurance giant AIG from imminent bankruptcy and expensively shepherded American and British banks into the protection of stronger rivals. Then the two countries—the United States and the U.K.—that in earlier days had most stoutly insisted that governments had no business being in the banking sector undertook a wave of state takeovers of banks. Late in the evening at a mid-September birthday party in London, an Amer-ican acquaintance took a call on his BlackBerry, then hastily left our table early to go back to his office. By dawn he was an employee of the U.S. government. His firm had been nationalized. Those were extraordinary days.

I spent this period as a minister in Gordon Brown's cabinet. When he took over from Tony Blair in 2007, Brown had called me back from the United States to lead his work on Africa, Asia, and the United Nations. Or perhaps more accurately, he had summoned me from a plush Mayfair hotel room, where my wife, Trish, and I were just packing up after a business trip to go back to New York. We knew a prime ministerial summons was in the cards and had mixed feelings about it; as I left, I mumbled something to Trish about keeping the room and watching the TV. Little more than an hour later, sitting among our suitcases, Trish watched in disbelief as the television showed live footage of her now-ennobled husband arriving at the door of No. 10 for his first cabinet meeting.

My two-year ministerial run had its share of disappointments—we failed to resolve the conflicts in Darfur, Zimbabwe, Myanmar, or Sri Lanka, or to push through the UN reforms I was still hoping for. Some of the bad blood that I had generated in Washington over my spat with John Bolton followed me to London: upon my arrival in Brown's cabinet, I was greeted as an antiwar figure who had opposed the U.S. invasion. Brown, thrown off guard, had wanted to signal a new distance from the Americans, but he was as fearful as his predecessor of doing anything that might seriously offend Washington.

Coming from the UN, of all places, I was struck by how craven much of the British political class had become in its blind pursuit of the Special Relationship. A prime minister fretted over how much face time he got with an American president, and if he ever thought of assessing the relationship by other criteria, the opposition, the media, and Whitehall would all pour ridicule on him. For postcolonial Britain, access to the American president had become a totem of influence and standing. It was astonishing to see how much it still mattered but equally to see how few British leaders understood how counterproductive it was. As an old Washington hand I felt this kind of diplomatic sucking up cost us respect and hence influence, in America. Further, because this perceived dependence on the United States engendered frustration among many Britons, it also seemed to fan anti-American vitriol of a primitive we-hate-you-because-we-need-you, variety. Staunchly pro-American myself, I longed for a more independent UK relationship with the United States.

So while President Bush was still in office, I was prevented as a minister from getting involved in various issues that I knew something about, lest his administration take offense. I suspect the White House would not actually have noticed much that I did, as it had rather bigger things on its mind. In fact, in my last year at the UN the Bush administration and I made common cause on Iraq, as we had jointly led the efforts to raise funds for its reconstruction.

But my nervous new political masters whispered that Condoleezza Rice, the U.S. secretary of state, had uttered something rather disparaging about me, so I must keep my head down. The most absurd attempt to hide me came early on, in September 2007, when the annual Labour Party Conference coincided with the opening of the UN General Assembly. The prime minister had asked me to cover for him in New York but then apparently discovered that that meant I would be sitting beside George Bush for a couple of hours in the Security Council. I was hastily recalled to Bournemouth to tell the Labour delegates about the outrages under way in Darfur instead.

British foreign policy lost a year or so when an able foreign secretary, David Miliband, and others might have begun some course corrections in the Middle East and elsewhere, but instead they had to wait for the election of President Obama. Nowadays Britain can make a hit on the foreign policy stage only rarely. The long interval between the failure of one American administration and the arrival of one that called for a new direction might have offered the U.K. a rare chance to strike out on its own and lay some of the groundwork. But Britain had lost the courage for such a role. The immediate opprobrium of the Bush administration mattered more than retrieving U.K. foreign policy from its cul-de-sac that association with the Bush administration had placed it in.

Fortunately, British courage recovered during the 2008 financial crisis. By the time Gordon Brown hosted the second G20 summit of the crisis in April 2009, Barack Obama was already in office. Reveling in the honeymoon of the Obama administration and dealing with an issue that he was comfortable with, Gordon Brown could now dare to lead.

When a crisis hits, a sudden malleability results, and briefly anything is possible, including international reform. The global financial system seemed at greater risk than at any time in modern history. Every day brought new surprises. Bankers had compromised everyone, with risky lending and a breathtaking casualness about the instruments that they had devised to recycle profits several-fold for their own gain. The bankers themselves seemed shaken by the global house of cards, and the inherently unstable and now insolvent financial products they had built. Older bankers I knew shook their heads in disbelief at how they had allowed younger colleagues to hide reckless risk behind financial complexity that they lacked the quantitative skills to penetrate. They had thought they were spreading risk by selling mortgages and other assets, but they were in fact selling each other more risk in a manner that now jeopardized them collectively. They were shocked. As the crisis ripped through what had seemed the most impregnable and respected institutions, it revealed breakdowns of management and supervision so extraordinary that they left Alistair Darling, the British chancellor of the exchequer, gaping in incomprehension.

Darling's manner is that of an old-fashioned bank manager. His voice, with its genteel Edinburgh accent, and his face—prominent black eyebrows under a shock of white hair—usually give little away. But at one of our cabinet briefings, his incredulity was plain to see. A senior banker had come up to him at a reception, he told us, and solemnly announced that the most important lesson he and his colleagues had learned was that they should never again allow financial products to be traded that they did not understand. The careful Darling was stunned that the world financial system had to be brought to its knees before that banker learned this simple prudential point.

Lehman Brothers, like all the institutions initially affected by its fall, had raised and lent funds across world markets. When its business stopped overnight, the effects were felt everywhere. Trades were left incomplete, and customers were left hanging from Prague to New York and Johannesburg. As the consequences worked their way through the global banking system, banks rushed to liquidate whatever they could and strengthen their domestic balance sheets by abruptly terminating loans and demanding repayment. Eastern European countries with real estate bubbles financed by Western banks were an early casualty. Letters of credit, the vital instrument of world trade by which exporters securely finance the shipment of goods to customers, were suddenly unobtainable. Almost instantly the world was in recession, as the banking crisis brought world trade to a halt.

As a government minister, I sensed impending collapse everywhere. Discussion of the crisis consumed Britain's annual political party conferences, held shortly after the Lehman collapse. At the opening of the UN's annual General Assembly in September 2008, I heard a hardy few speakers, eulogize world capitalism but a lot more express down-to-earth fears about unemployment, hunger, and protests in the streets. A consensus quickly gathered that governments must act not just to stem the crisis but to ensure it could not happen again. Commentators assumed that that meant international action. Lehman's collapse had rippled out across the world, almost sinking apparently quite separate institutions and revealing that they were actually strapped together by dangerously invisible webs of cross-lending; that alone made it clear that the world needed better global governance of finance.

In the waning days of his beleaguered presidency, George W. Bush called for a summit of the world's top economies, the G20. Until then the G20 had been a little-noticed gathering of finance ministers; now Bush was inviting its heads of government. That he had had to reach beyond the old G8 of developed industrial economies to this newer formation—which included the big emerging economies of China, India, and Brazil—dramatized that the old economies could no longer right the world on their own: the crisis seemed to be ushering in a new order.

That Bush, the longtime skeptic of the rest of the world, had summoned this meeting was an advantage. It was a bit like Nixon going to China or an archconservative Israeli prime minister negotiating with Egypt: only Bush could have gotten away with apparently throwing himself on the mercy of the rest of the world. The fact that the summit was his initiative reassured American conservatives that U.S. sovereignty was not imperiled. As a consequence, one of Bush's more positive enduring legacies may be that he took this major step toward an international global architecture. One of fate's little surprises, it seems.

The G20 also provided the high point of Gordon Brown's troubled prime ministership. He grabbed the hosting of the next summit, as Britain was already slated chair of the finance ministers' meetings in 2009. The G20's London summit in April 2009 became his astonishingly ambitious effort to reshape the global financial order. He was in his element, able to propose ambitious plans to save the world (as he appeared to claim in an inadvertent slip at the parliamentary dispatch box). The truth was a bit more prosaic but nevertheless important. The summit adopted crisis measures: a global stimulus that would reach poor as well as rich countries; a huge reinforcement of financial wherewithal to the IMF; and demands that the World Bank and others extend credits, loans, and guarantees so as to restart trade, head off further banking collapses, and take the worst edge off the economic downturn. A series of longer-term undertakings would change the governance of global finance through better regulation, pressure tax havens to comply with new codes of behavior, and strengthen the various institutions tasked with shaping these changes.

We wanted to reach beyond the solemn officials who were the traditional audiences for such gatherings and address the broader civil society. So we used the new electronic communications tools and staged the event so as to seize the imagination, deploying branding, marketing, and press relations in ways that were eye-openers for much of Whitehall. When we determined to call it the London Summit, rather than a longer more formal title, the cabinet office lawyers came back worrying about copyright and precedent. They were overruled.

More significantly, the G20 vindicated my view that in government today it is the global that matters. It was a career-affirming lesson: I had spent all those years abroad in the right places, after all. Britain had come to understand that it had to make its influence felt with the global institutions. Badly run banks were now not just a national headache but a global one. Taxpayers everywhere were exposed, if not to the crisis of the bailout, then to the indirect impact on their economies. Politicians and bankers who had been wary of more international regulation were suddenly falling over themselves to propose it. Finance had become too big to fail but also too global to police at the national level.

Governments had become the banks' default owners and guarantors. Politicians' caution about messing with the golden calf of the financial sector ended. The fabulous money machine that had become the U.K.'s single biggest source of corporate tax income was suddenly revealed as a casino. The critics and reformers were out in force.

The public sector is risk-averse at the best of times. As the new owners, government officials' instinct was to tie the banks up in regulations that would prevent similar crises in the future. But the passage of time has brought complexities and trade-offs. While politicians wanted higher reserve capital requirements and more conservative lending policies, they were making the contradictory demand that banks help the economy recover by extending mortgage and business loans as aggressively as possible. As the economy started to right itself, reform has visibly slowed.

Further, the debate about bankers' compensation has distracted everyone from broader reform. Just as blue-collar and middle-class job losses in the real economy were mounting, bankers were returning to pre-crisis levels of reward, much to public outrage. Moreover, the fact that banks profited from trading on the loose money, the so-called quantitative easing, that governments had had to introduce, at great cost to the public finances, to fight the crisis that the banks had caused, added insult to injury. The American, British, and French governments frantically attempted to blunt the anger by limiting or taxing bonuses; banks then committed to pay the taxes for their employees, thereby shifting the cost to the shareholders. Bound up in their own competitive universe, bank chiefs seemed unable to grasp that their behavior posed a broader risk to their political situation.

In early 2010, as the G20-led reform process was slowing, a populist grassroots demand to take the bankers down a peg was growing. Goldman Sachs was the best-run and most successful of the international investment banks, with its political connections to Washington; two recent treasury secretaries, including Hank Paulson (who was in charge during the crisis) and a White House chief of staff, among others, were Goldman alumni. But its apparent arrogance in the face of criticism made it the lightning rod. The populist anger may yet revive politicians' interest in global financial reform, because its logic still holds: reform must be global, because if you squeeze bankers in one jurisdiction, they will move to one where regulations and taxes are significantly lighter.

Many of those who advocate tough treatment of bankers would be suspicious of international regulatory action, but that is what tough treatment is likely to require. The London Summit offered a foretaste of populist internationalism. In advance of the summit, French president Nicolas Sarkozy thundered against tax havens, like Hong Kong and Macau, arguing that there must be no dark corners for bankers to hide. The Chinese leadership took offense. Along with a rather coy German chancellor Angela Merkel, Sarkozy threatened to walk out of the summit if his grievances were not addressed. The British press thought Sarkozy's threat could jeopardize the whole meeting, but in a series of briefings, I argued otherwise. I thought the dispute showed the new importance of such meetings. They were no longer esoteric affairs conducted behind closed doors with little public interest; they were now real politics. It mattered to French voters if, as their government got tougher on bankers, the bankers moved off shore to more congenial jurisdictions. That became one of the lessons of the summit.

The other lesson was that older Western institutions will not be able to solve the problem of tax havens. As chair, Gordon Brown sought to turn over responsibility for naming and shaming tax havens to the august and venerable Organization for Economic Cooperation and Development (OECD). This international institution, based in Paris, has only a couple of non-Western country members and therefore little credibility to run a policy aimed at countries that are in the South. The latter would suspect a likely double standard: how would OECD treat Western tax havens compared to them?

Memorably, the Chinese president was heard asking his aides what the OECD was. It seemed he had never heard of it. An institution based in Paris was no longer at the center of this new world.

In the end an emollient President Obama resolved the dispute. Ironies abounded: a Chinese Communist president was defending tax havens against a right-wing French president; peace was brokered by an American president, whose own vice president hails from one of the greatest of all tax havens, Delaware, where many American corporations choose to be registered for tax purposes.

But the incident also highlighted that ordinary people's anger is more likely to reanimate international institutions than reform led by politicians, and that these organizations will have to be remade in terms of membership and function. Forecasts have said that over the next couple of years Western countries will lose 25 million jobs, and the rest of the world will lose more; that is likely to light a fire under reform. In the U.K. one in five young people joining the employment market did not find a job in 2009. Unfortunately, new jobs will probably be postponed for several years more.

In the West, massive public debts may overhang economic performance for a generation or more. The likely consequence: an American friend, a successful commercial real estate investor, rather melodramatically announced to me that he was liquidating his U.S. portfolio of shopping malls and office buildings and moving his money to emerging markets.

The crisis has accelerated the speed at which the burgeoning economies of Asia and Africa and Latin America and Eastern Europe are catching up to Western economies. Brazil and China escaped the worst of the crisis and emerged with their confidence intact. They shortened the West's GDP lead and sharply increased their trade with one another and in their own regions. International dependence on the American consumer has started to fray. This growing confidence asserted itself at the G20.

The crisis sent the poorer countries a more ambiguous message. Along with energy and food price spikes, it reminded them of their dependence on Western economies and their lack of say over the global economy. In mid-2009 I attended a rather sad UN summit on the global economic crisis. Its conference paper was rather good. But the West, having bet on the G20, was unwilling to concede one iota of power over economic matters to the UN. Nobody's heart was in it, except for one or two Latin American rabble-rousers and the Sandinista Nicaraguan priest who was then president of the General Assembly.

That summit revealed to me, however, the G20's vulnerability. Unlike UN membership, membership in the G20 is not universal. The G20 is young and new and represents more than 80 percent of the world economy and a majority of the world population, and has burst onto the world stage as the preferred crisis management mechanism of the powerful. But being left out of the G20 was a poke in the eye to countries such as Poland, Pakistan, Egypt, and Chile. Each had to swallow the fact that local rivals were invited to sit at the table while they were not. Smaller poorer countries were equally alarmed: they had no pretensions to membership but worried that this club of the powerful, based on no treaty and with no substantive formal connection to the UN, would make decisions that should not be made without them.

At the London Summit, at Brown's behest, I had invited additional representatives from Africa and Asia, both to guard against G20 envy and to make sure their point of view and needs were on the table. In wider consultations, we invited a group of African leaders and finance ministers and central bank governors to Lancaster House, the government's elegant central London conference center, to brief the prime minister in advance. I met with the Asian foreign ministers in the rather different setting of a holiday resort in Thailand where the Association of Southeast Asian Nations was meeting, far from Bangkok demonstrators, who were besieging the meeting's originally intended site.

The selection of African leaders to attend the G20 posed a particular challenge. The current chair of the African Union was the mercurial Muammar Gadhafi of Libya, famous for disrupting any meeting he attended, sometimes through tendentious interventions but more often through his circus-master-cum-cabaret-performer skills. When he entered a room, his bodyguards, famously often female, would push delegates aside, cutting a wide swath for him. While he was chairman of the African Union, he met with African leaders in his home town of Sirte to discuss continental unity; he became so irritated with those who disagreed with him that he briefly locked them on a ship where they were staying, to try to force agreement without them.

Brown's message on Gadhafi was uncharacteristically blunt and colorful. The gist without the expletives was: *I do not want that man setting up his tent in Hyde Park during my G20 meeting.* Some suggested hand-picking a favored African leader who was considered a model economic reformer and good democrat to boot. I warned that such a personalized choice would damage the individual we chose and undo all that we were trying to achieve. The time for this kind of patronizing selection of Africa's representative was past. Working with the officials—conveniently, all friends—who headed Africa's main regional organizations, they settled on Meles Zenawi, the Ethiopian prime minister. That choice had a clear logic, as Zenawi chaired the economic side of the African Union, which is headquartered in Ethiopia; further, he was a tough fighter, an ex-guerrilla chief, and his fellow leaders would trust him to stand up for them.

The London Summit attracted the normal general demonstrations against globalization to the Docklands conference center, where the meeting was held; but amusingly, the only leader who seemed to have earned his own protest was Zenawi: a small band of Ethiopian exiles kept a vigil against him.

The selection of Zenawi was ad hoc; the G20 will have to find a way to achieve balance in its formal representation. Perhaps constituency-based representation would work, in which each region has seats allocated by population size and GDP, then chooses its representatives on a rotating basis. Whatever the means, Europe, which characteristically snared too many seats, will have to give some up.

As traditionally rich countries lose power and investment to the developing and emerging economies, the governance of global institutions is becoming a real tug-of-war. As the G20 envoy for Gordon Brown, I was told all over the world that the G20 was an improvement over the G8, and that China, Brazil, South Africa, Russia, and other countries were determined to ensure an even more fundamental shift in who gets a place at the table. The more I pressed for renewal of the United Nations, the World Bank, and the IMF, the more I heard that in the eyes of those countries, reform will be meaningless without a significant change of ownership.

The Chinese, and more frivolously the Russians, have started to press for unseating the dollar from its role as sole global currency. They argue that the dollar's dominance has left others, particularly China with its large dollar holdings, too much at the mercy of American economic policy. During the financial crisis the dollar, perversely, was strengthened as bank credit dried up and companies raced to acquire dollars to manage their global cash flow.

Despite the revolt against the greenback—the symbol of American global economic leadership—the United States remained the indispensable power. Influence may be shifting toward Asia and other regions, but still the United States bears a disproportionate cost of underwriting the global economy and maintaining global security. So far the newcomers speak the language of rights and claims, not of shared responsibilities. China is wary of being pushed into a global role for which it does not feel prepared. Brazil and India are still primarily regional actors. All three, unlike the United States, pay only a tiny portion of the costs of the United Nations. America remains the reluctant global sheriff. A new global sharing of power will also require a sharing of responsibility.

Could the global financial meltdown that began in 2008 usher in a new era of global cooperation? The worst days of the crisis have receded, and the business and financial community has lost much of its appetite for reform. Once again it is criticizing politicians for meddling in the vital business of wealth creation. But four trends that favor reform have emerged from the crisis and are growing irrevocably stronger.

First, as ordinary people pay the price for the bankers' crisis, they are going to get angrier and demand action. Second, as business opportunity shifts southward, as multinational companies move into new territory, they will want level playing fields and transparent laws and markets. That is, they will become a stronger voice for global regulation. For a group that has usually resisted regulation, that will be a sea change. Third, as emerging economies take a bigger share of global power and wealth and as poor countries fear greater marginalization, both will press for a stronger voice in the international system. Finally, the G20, and more generally the events of 2009, have been a master class in global cooperation. They have proven that we need global rules and arrangements as we integrate our economies. What is true for finance is surely true for public health, poverty, and international security.

We are embarked willy-nilly on a dramatic transformation of how we govern ourselves. The old arrangements do not work anymore. Yet the financial crisis reminds me that even global catastrophe brings only a brief opportunity of reform. The G20 world leaders, herded together by fear, went further than ever before in committing to global cooperation, but the impulse has slowed as economies have righted.

Most significantly, the cost of the crisis is being borne not by bankers but by governments and taxpayers. Banks were nationalized, and fiscal stimulus rescued the global economy. We will all be paying for these rescues for decades. National governments will struggle to justify the austerity that lies ahead, courting domestic failure. Ironically, while a burst of global political activism was the early response to a truly international crisis, it is domestic politics that have taken the strain.

CHAPTER ELEVEN

COMPASS POINTS

After the fall of the Soviet Union in 1989, the historian Francis Fukuyama famously observed that history had ended: the ancient grievances that had kept countries and classes apart had been buried, he thought, and the world was on course for a single, happy middle-class market economy. Fukuyama has long repented making this claim.

My years in international development have provided me with my own repudiation of Fukuyama's claim. Conflicts that had been suppressed during the Cold War flared up, once the superpowers were no longer focused on keeping lids on them to further the bigger geostrategic game. Yugoslavia had been held together because the Soviet Union did not want a country at the European end of its empire to crumble into its constituent parts. Assorted corrupt African dictators were kept on their thrones because losing one or another of them would have left the Russians or the Americans with a loss to their regional standing. In the Horn of Africa or in the Democratic Republic of Congo, the consequences have since been reflected in refugees, poverty, and conflict.

This Cold War legacy is the least of the post-1989 conflicts. The process of globalization has created its own backlash, and two points of view that seem likely to contest each other for decades to come. In one corner stands globalization and its promise of rising affluence and a greater integration of everything, from trade to ideas. In the other corner stands nationalism.

After the exuberance of 1989, now a distant memory, nationalism returned. Russia exhibited a nationalist reaction in the form of anger at its humiliation and loss of influence. Vladimir Putin has set about recovering influence by supporting Russian minorities in Russia's near neighborhood; he has also sought to play a world role by allying with countries that share suspicions of liberal democratic values. We have also seen Chinese nationalism: Chinese bloggers have employed a new global technology to express frustration with the West's support for Tibet and its criticism of China's undemocratic government.

Osama Bin Laden, al Qaeda, and radical Islam represent a different manifestation of the nationalist backlash. They seek to conserve their religion and nations against the spread of Western culture and power in the form of globalization. Their nationalism is a distant cousin, a virulent deformed version, but still a cousin.

A much milder strain of the backlash is found in the political debates of every country: every society fears the perceived leveling character of globalization and the loss of the special attributes that define a society as different. Nationalism among many developing countries is fueling the resistance to Western reform of the international system. India objected to the Doha trade round, causing its collapse in 2008, because of the absence of sufficient protection for its farmers. This same issue made France a reluctant participant in liberalizing agricultural trade. In both cases protection of farmers was a cultural as well as an economic issue. The small farmer is an iconic part of both French and Indian culture. In India, farmers continue to comprise a huge portion of the real political economy, though they represent less than one percent of GDP in France. In a perverse way, as states fail, nations are growing stronger. Globalization undermines governments because they no longer own the solutions, whereas it revives nations, which provide the cultural shell to deflect the homogenizing impact of globalization.

Globalization seems to have left its fingerprints everywhere. It has challenged governments and states, churches, political parties, old-line businesses, and other organizations, and in many cases unprecedented levels of change have pushed them aside even though as I argued at the start most have kept their trappings if not their power. The internationalization of public health, the environment, and security leaves the old ways of doing things wanting. Officials and institutions desperately spin their wheels, seeking some kind of traction on problems, but unable to get a grip on them.

Globalization often takes the blame for what is actually a broader set of changes. In the past few decades, we've seen growth in population, incomes, consumption, diet, affluence, and aspiration. And as growth and integration take place, we are also bumping up against limits in natural resources and therefore patterns of consumption.

The late twentieth century offered a Houdini-like escape from limits; market economics suggested that if the price incentive was right, there would be no shortages of energy or raw materials. A highly technological knowledge society implicitly seemed to need fewer physical resources for its sustenance. We substituted manmade materials for natural ones; we found new sources of energy; we cut down rain forests to increase food production; and we enabled populations to shift from countryside to city to reduce their apparent direct dependence on land.

But not all the knots, it seems, were slipped. Rates of energy consumption are not sustainable, as the modernization of India and China places huge extra demands on sources of oil and gas as well as iron and steel and basic foodstuffs. As families by dint of growing incomes move up the food chain, from cereals to meat, the pressure on grains, water, and other inputs grows rapidly. As biofuels based on soy and sugar enter the market, energy and food compete for the same land. We are told that the market and new technologies provide solutions, but the market seems dubious in this regard: it seems unlikely to sensibly allocate resources between different uses and between rich and poor users, or to encourage new technologies when they make energy or food more expensive in the short term.

Ironically, as the market is being exposed as an unfair way of allocating resources in a constrained world, market approaches are being adopted to battle climate change. Europeans have strongly promoted the so-called cap and trade system, in which carbon credits can be traded so that polluters pay lower carbon-emitters for part of their spare carbon allowance; they have advocated public guarantees of different kinds to encourage private investment. So market principles are central to the new thinking about solutions. But what has been rejected in many quarters is market fundamentalism, the throwaway assumption that we can leave globalization's course to the markets, that no governance is needed.

That does not mean we do not need smart market-based thinking to answer questions such as: What are the incentives, and who provides them, to convert economies from high-energy-cost technologies that have years of cheap life left in them because they are already paid for? And what if only some countries or companies make the expensive conversion to new clean technologies? Won't that leave those who stick to the old with an unfair advantage, what economists call the free rider problem? In 2000 at the UN Millennium Summit, we had to work hard to get any real discussion of the environment. At that moment of globalization fever, environmental constraints seemed a distraction.

In handling each of these three great drivers of our century's change—integration, growth, and limits—the questions get more pressing every day. Integration throws up myriad issues from taxation to migration and security, yet we chronically lack any adequate global policy or regulatory framework to handle them. Growth raises acute questions of human welfare and growing inequality between rich and poor. Limits pose the challenge of how on a crowded globe we maintain a platform for growth and integration. How do we share finite resources? There is almost no sensible debate about how to manage a runaway world. Endless difficulties have beset climate change negotiations, and even smart market schemes cannot work unless they are set within an agreed global regulatory framework, firmly stipulating the degree of carbon adjustment that each country will make. Without that framework, we have no practical basis on which to trade carbon emissions, and the whole move toward a lower-carbon world may well stall.

These three factors—integration, growth, and limits—are the context for policy-making on just about every issue that has an international dimension. But what is missing is a meeting place where people can make public policy around them. The global level has largely been a laissez-faire space, allowing those operating in it to choose which, if any, national jurisdiction they will subject themselves to on what issue. The government owners of the UN, the World Bank, and the IMF, for example, keep those organizations well away from international tax issues, which are at the heart of any functioning global system.

A deep phobia against global regulation prevails in almost every arena. The antiglobalizers are not alone: it is a strong feature of U.S. policy particularly. The United States makes every effort to prevent its citizens or companies from being subjected to global regulatory systems. The hostility is deeply ingrained, whether it is a human rights court or a taxation system. On the other hand, the United States has little compunction about trying to extend its own national jurisdiction overseas. U.S. tax legislation and U.S. corporate disclosure and reporting requirements have long arms.

Nevertheless, in the absence of a global regulatory system, markets fill the vacuum. Markets alone determine not just levels of wealth but also levels of welfare and dislocation. As global economic forces play themselves out, politicians seem sidelined. They allow the argument to stand that if they show interest in international issues, it means they are putting these matters ahead of domestic concerns and their voters.

But even the most local problem may need an international fix, because the world is too integrated for our own solutions to school, health, and job problems. As Tony Blair acknowledged as he left the British prime ministership: "Ten years ago, if you had told me I would spend a significant part of my premiership on foreign policy, I would have been surprised, a little shocked and probably politically somewhat alarmed. Even today, we all run for office concentrating on domestic issues. 'Foreign' policy rarely wins votes, and can easily lose them. Yet nowadays the reality is increasingly that we are obliged as leaders to think, work, and act internationally."[1]

His successor, Gordon Brown, perhaps because of his ten years as chancellor of the exchequer, was from the first instinctively internationalist. Hit in his early months in office by credit, food, and energy crises that were clearly international in origin, he publicly sought international solutions to them, only to be confronted, as I observed earlier, with complaints that he was not sensitive enough to people and their problems. Why, the British people asked, was he talking about all these irrelevant international matters?

The dilemma of the modern politician is that the answers are abroad but the votes are at home. And so Brown, like Blair before him, had to find a language and narrative of politics that is deeply rooted in the at-home. Among political leaders, neither the natural globalizers nor the nationalists are able to cut themselves free from the strings of domestic politics. That is the forum to which they all remain beholden.

And local is a tough taskmaster. Coming back to the U.K. as a minister to help Brown drive his internationalist agenda, I was brought down to earth by the first weekend's newspaper headlines that blamed the government for uncollected garbage in London's streets. It does not get much more local than that.

. . .

As political leadership wrestles with these tensions, certain cat-egories of leaders are up and others are down. The world looks good for mayors and other local leaders. The fortunes of cities like Moscow, Cape Town, and Chicago have often been countercycli-cal to those of their region or country, often due to the leadership of strong mayors.

Mayors appear to be beneficiaries of two things: demography and globalization. More people in the world now live in cities than do not. Across Asia, Latin America, and even Africa, urbanization has been rapid. While globalization has pulled national politicians in contrary directions, it has let mayors find their feet. Nowhere is this clearer than the two cities where my family and I have most recently made our homes. Young MBA recruits, one of the world's most mo-bile work groups, think of New York and London as the interchange-able twins of the world financial system. As places to work and live, these recruits are comparing cities, not countries.

The mayors in both capitals, Michael Bloomberg (and before him Rudy Giuliani) in New York, and Boris Johnson (following the long reign of Ken Livingstone) in London, are national, even interna-tional, figures. Their success in fighting crime, improving public ser-vices, and keeping their cities business-friendly is not only a domestic victory but a vital point of international comparison because the rivals for those high-end internatonal financial service jobs and the capital they manage are not principally local rivals such as Chicago and Man-chester but Geneva, Paris, Singapore, Tokyo, and Hong Kong.

However, unlike their national counterparts, mayors solve prob-lems that are close to home: violent crime, drugs, public infrastruc-ture. They have to care about schools, social services, police, and public investment. Where the drugs or crime have international roots, they are problems of the occupant of the White House or No. 10 Downing Street. The buck gets passed up.

· · ·

Another set of leaders who are riding high are the chiefs of nongovernmental organizations and foundations. Members of a remarkable generation of new wealth have set up foundations, on the model of the Fords and Rockefellers of a hundred years earlier. The astonishing partnership of Bill and Melinda Gates with Warren Buffett has created the most financially powerful of these institutions. Depending on the appreciation of its three contributors' wealth, its endowment will be in the order of $60 billion, and it has big ambitions in public health, education, and development to match.

Perhaps as significant, the Gates Foundation has begun to merge business and not-for-profit cultures. The language of the MBA, with its emphasis on business plans, start-up strategies, testing, and refining results, has crossed over into the world of development. It is a mixed blessing, as these foundations place great emphasis on an empirical businesslike approach to development that can overlook local cultural realities. Nevertheless, the model is breaking down barriers and attracting new blood to the NGO community. Applying a little financial engineering or some market incentives to development problems has often produced dramatic tipping points. The Gates Foundation's promotion of new drug development for the diseases of the poor, or for the growth of microfinance, both illustrate this point.

Nor is the entry of business culture into the not-for-profit world a one-way street. George Soros's Open Society Institute (OSI) and Ted Turner's United Nations Foundation (UNF) represent a slightly older (twenty-plus years and ten years old respectively) generation of foundations. Soros, by funding freedom in Eastern Europe before and after 1989, has scored a spectacular success and deserves equal billing with Gorbachev, Reagan, Thatcher, and Kohl in the fall of the Berlin Wall.

Soros cultivated the early seedbed of civil society in Eastern and Central Europe. He awarded scholarships, support, and stipends to

Russian scientists, medical programs, and the independent media. Unlike the more rigorous Gates business model of piloting and testing concepts before rolling them out, Soros, the consummate financial speculator, was all instinct and big bets.

OSI, whose board I am on, and its network of grantees such as the International Crisis Group make it still very much the leader when it comes to results. Few other foundations can lay claim to having changed societies as profoundly as OSI has. The role of Rockefeller in India's Green Revolution in moving Indian agriculture to the point where it could economically transform that country may have been the last comparable foundation success.

The people who have made up OSI are drawn from the much wider and growing gene pool of civil society. Many of them, before joining the foundation's staff in New York, London, and Budapest, had been OSI grantees. In most countries where OSI operates, a board of local civil society leaders directs the foundation's local activities. It seems much more indigenous than the button-down Gates model—which is still very centrally directed from Seattle—if at times less strategic.

The genius of Soros, though, is that he is frequently right, and he can often exact the most dramatic results with the smallest bets. In his political funding he probably started an earthquake, he says, with the $2,300 (the maximum individual contribution) that he gave to the Obama campaign early on, when it was a long shot. Soros's contribution signaled that Obama could attract serious money, so it served as a tipping point. By contrast, the millions that Soros gave to Democratic organizations in 2004 probably had less of an effect on Democratic Party fortunes. I was in his New York living room when it became clear John Kerry had lost Ohio and hence the election. The political workers and guests such as Hillary Clinton were devastated and soon headed off into the night disconsolate. George was more phlegmatic. Tomorrow was another day. He had lost bigger bets.

The key issue for foundations or civil society organizations, however large their endowments, is how to find the level of change, the tipping point. Although donors like Soros and Gates appear to have all the financial means at their disposal, each acknowledges that his resources are modest compared to his ambition for social change and the scale of the problems he is tackling. Melinda Gates has said to me that she still finds it hard to reconcile being co-chair of the richest foundation in the world with the reality that the resources fall far short of the needs.

Both foundations need partners and entry points that will encourage governments to follow them or markets to pick up on their innovations and draw in the for-profit sector. Foundation money alone rarely does the trick. Rather, they see themselves as the providers of seed capital, and success as an idea or project that takes off and brings in others; that is, the idea exerts a power many times greater than the dollars that went in.

Ted Turner's United Nations Foundation was a billion-dollar bet on a single idea—that creative funding which offered more flexibility than government money could help the UN live up to its potential. Turner is still at it, and the UN is still struggling to live up to its side of that bargain. But he has had extraordinary influence well beyond that of foundations of similar size. His UNF has given him, like Soros and Gates, a second act at least the equal of his first business career.

During the last twenty years civil society has emerged as a global third leg, beside the public and private sectors. It is no longer left outside importuning for funds but is recognized as a necessary partner. If a business is to embark on a major expansion in a country, winning the approval of key civil society groups may be as important as gaining formal government agreement. The potential consequences of not doing so—the environmental sit-in, the corporate boycott, the human rights protest—can become embarrassments at the global shareholders' annual meeting. Conversely, with active civil society engagement, businesses can reach whole new market segments among the poor and the emerging middle class and enjoy a partner that is more dynamic, innovative, and often trustworthy than government.

Concluding these local and global partnerships is bringing out a new kind of business leader. A global business cannot be run within the narrow parameters of hometown stakeholders. Today's business operates within a web of countries; political and regulatory and labor systems; and civil society activism. The goals of these constituencies are unlikely ever to match neatly with the home team's objective of profit maximization.

Business schools are changing the education they offer. Particularly in emerging countries, they seem to train MBAs as social workers as well as business leaders. Students are often taught to recognize employee health and well-being and the broader economic and social condition of the country's consumer as key to corporate success. So businessmen are becoming politicians and social workers. They are accustomed to heavy involvement in the home country to smooth their way, and to contributing to the local congressmen's reelection campaign, but a company operating globally today faces political challenges that are of an altogether different magnitude and complexity.

Compliance with EU, U.S., and a host of other national regulatory regimes covering everything from taxation, antitrust, transfer pricing, and environmental, social, and labor standards is a challenge for legal, accounting, and planning staff. It is a still bigger strategic challenge for corporate leaders as companies are starting to run up against globalization's backlash. Western energy interests in Russia have encountered its resurgent nationalism, and at this writing, they have not found a compelling way of telling Russians that even from a nationalistic point of view, increasing their energy production requires Western know-how and capital. For now Western corporate involvement seems in the Russian mind to be tied to a Western political agenda that uses globalization as a cover to undermine Russian economic and political power.

Global business is going to have to find ways of sidestepping increasingly acrimonious clashes between globalization and nationalism without forgetting which side they are on, as their own shareholders will not allow them to. Business activities will be kept under the civil society spotlight. The challenge will be now to square the circle of operating in nationalistic semi-closed corners of the world—often, it seems, where the oil, gas, and minerals are—without betraying the broader values a corporation must increasingly subscribe to if it is to protect its reputation and its share price.

In a world of blogs, cable news, Twitter, and twenty-four-hour global news cycles, corporations are under extraordinary scrutiny. A union-organizing issue in Colombia threatened to mushroom into a global human rights problem, throwing worried Coca-Cola executives off balance. In India an NGO cheekily sought to break down scientifically the contents of both Pepsi and Coke and declare them a threat to Indian health; the public health campaign had an incipient global appeal. CEOs used to the more regular pace of quarterly or annual earnings announcements find it unsettling when a media-Internet storm breaks over his or her head because of an action taken by a faraway subsidiary, and they must defend the corporate reputation. But on issues ranging from soft drinks to energy, financial services, movies, and software (where copyright protection is a major issue), international trade and local politics have clashed. As a consultant and then international official, I often found myself drawn into trying to find ways through.

All is made much harder by the incessant media attention that political and corporate decisions face. The media themselves are not immune to the beast they have created. Rabidly conservative Fox News, either loved or feared by many as America's most potent cable news channel, planned in 2007 to hold a debate of Democratic presidential candidates. Then an Internet viral video campaign showed clips of how biased the channel was when covering Democratic politicians. After hundreds of thousands of viewings and many complains, the candidates pulled out.

Yesterday's insurgent is today's besieged establishment institution. The new information technologies allow people not only to combine globally but also to bypass established power centers. As hard as the old media giants try to win a foothold in the new technologies and so leverage their global distribution strength, many will fall by the wayside, their competitive advantage overwhelmed by creative new media able to gain a free ride on new information platforms. Rupert Murdoch has bought MySpace and now Dow Jones, publisher of *The Wall Street Journal*. An Internet world where we can all be owners has old proprietors running scared. But Murdoch may have the last laugh, because *The Wall Street Journal* seems better placed than most other old media properties to secure a fee base for electronic content. But as this old bruiser goes one last round, it is worth asking what kind of leadership works in this new context.

Today mayors, other local political figures, civil society leaders, and some CEOs are on the up, while traditional national politicians and a lot of business leaders are victims of forces beyond their control. Inevitably leaders do better when they are aware of the new forces at play; understand the global dimensions of decision-making; and recognize that power is more dispersed not just between nations but between the new stakeholders. Today's dynamic leaders can operate within the three poles of the policy framework—growth, integration, and limits—and understand that the changes they are living through are neither straightforward nor always benign. Globalization has raised incomes but it has also triggered nationalism, exacerbated inequality, left many in poverty, and has thrown us up against environmental limits. Leaders of cities, NGOs, countries, companies, and international organizations need an internal compass that guides them across this map.

Kofi Annan's apparently easy mastery of this context showed personal traits of leadership that work in today's world. A nonauthoritarian personality, he expended huge emotional intelligence in trying to understand the people he dealt with. He declared at one point, to much subsequent ridicule, that he could do business with Saddam Hussein. I suspect he meant that he understood the insecurities, fears, and vanities that drove the dictator—not that he was to be trusted.

With his upbringing in Ghana, his university education in the United States and Europe, and his UN career, Annan is steeped in internationalism. Along with Nane, his Swedish wife, he made it all seem easy. If he had a fault as secretary-general, it was that he was probably too cautious. I hesitate, though, in even that criticism as his decades-long knowledge of the international system allowed him to identify and seize opportunities that others missed. But his long UN career left him convinced that risk-taking was not always possible. Successful secretary-generals may always be better balancers than drivers of policy. Other global leaders with whom I have worked lacked his natural international touch but were still able to drive things through the complex of stakeholders that is modern international decision-making. Jim Wolfensohn at the World Bank was much too much of an activist to take no for an answer, but his career in investment banking made him astute enough to know when to stop. In his old business, clients hired investment banks for energy and alternative thinking but ultimately did not expect to be repeatedly crossed.

Cory Aquino was always underestimated and always used that fact to her advantage. Using the power of her gentle intuition, she continuously assessed the largely male and very macho political class that surrounded her. She had listening skills. She was a poor communicator and a passive decision-maker but she understood emerging Filipino civil society. She would wait the old politicians out, knowing that they would come up with some chest-beating demand to change her government or resign, and each time they did, it seemed to leave them exposed and isolated. She defeated the consummate Asian autocrat Ferdinand Marcos and as president survived six turbulent years and repeated coup attempts. At the end she explained how she did it by saying: "It was God's will."

By no stretch of the imagination was Aquino charismatic—she had a great speechwriter, Teddyboy Locsin, and soldiered through her speeches as he wrote them, with little resort to adlibbing. Kofi Annan had a similarly perfect meeting of minds with his speechwriter, Edward Mortimer. A fellow of Oxford's All Souls, the white-haired Mortimer was a tall, stooping ex–leader writer for *The Times* and former columnist for the *Financial Times*. Having written so many columns, I worried he would be too clever and too opinionated for the straightforward but intuitive secretary-general, but theirs was a speechwriter-leader union made in heaven, as Cory would want it put. Edward found his master's voice.

As CEOs and NGO chiefs find themselves ever more public figures, the ranks of their public relations advisers and speechwriters expand. But wordsmiths get a modern leader only so far. The intense media spotlight on a leader, as in the revolution against Marcos or in Annan's diplomacy with Saddam Hussein, irrevocably brands that leader. And for all the best speechwriting, the informal, unscripted word on a decisive political action often becomes the defining moment.

George Soros is an enigmatic media figure. He is not a particularly powerful public speaker, although the intensity and spareness of his prose hold the reader or listener. But by any measure he has done more to establish open societies in Eastern Europe and now Africa and South Asia than any of his furious critics on the American right have done. In the NGO community, where he now spends much time, he is properly a legend for the causes he has taken up. Yet when it comes to the press, he remains an unrepentant free speaker, willing to drop mischievous asides that send currencies into free fall and induce governments to see plots. As his aides have found, he is unscriptable. He is a splendid throwback to life before the scripted soundbite.

Each of these individuals operates naturally (perhaps with the exception of the late Aquino) across borders. They network industriously. Each keeps a clear set of goals, without diluting or losing sight of them, even as they are buffeted by the difficulties of building global alliances.

Perhaps my years as a refugee worker left me skeptical that an inspirational leader can somehow swim against an underlying tide in the affairs of men that is flowing in the other direction. Soros succeeded in Eastern Europe because the region, he discovered subsequently, was in ferment. But more often political movements billed as liberating had time after time proved to be less inclusive than promised and to produce refugees. Sitting on the front lines of the Cold War as a refugee worker, I saw how easily whole populations can get caught up in volcanic political eruptions. That it has continued since, from Kosovo to Darfur, is no surprise.

The War on Terror now imposes a logic on conflict, much as the Cold War once did. The old lines of communication between humanitarian workers and guerrilla groups, however gruesome their ideology, are gone. Western humanitarian groups and the UN are condemned as having taken sides.

Russia stokes proud old claims to status and shakes off the humiliating loss of empire and prestige in 1989; Islamic terrorism strikes disproportionately at civilian targets and excites visions of holy war among both supporters and opponents. Both are extreme and cancerous manifestations of the new more general fault line of politics. The embrace of globalization or resistance to it: these are the most elemental attitudes of modern political life. They are creating strange new bedfellows in the established politics of all countries.

In the United States, the Republican Party has remained bravely in favor of free trade, at least at the presidential level, while the Democrats ceded a lot of ground on the issue in the Clinton-Rubin years. Now the damage that free trade inflicted on blue-collar job security and incomes is driving the Democratic Party toward an apparently more ambiguous position: President Obama ritually declares his commitment to free trade, but nobody expects him to act, given the political obstacles he faces.

In Britain, by contrast, Labour governments have been resolutely committed to free trade. Both Brown and Blair strongly believe that Britain remains a trading nation, as do the Conservatives and the Liberal-Democrats. But in opposition the Tories seemed much less internationalist. Today in government with the Liberal-Democrats they are again internationalist. Their leaders nevertheless are by background more insular than their Labour counterparts. They oppose strengthening the European Union and in general exhibit discomfort with many aspects of globalization. Britain's global culture may be stronger than most, but so if there is an antiglobalization party in the U.K., it may always be the opposition! In government, politicians confront the fact that Britain's opportunities are global. In opposition they fall back on simpler stereotypes. Now in opposition, Labour for example seems likely to follow its Tory predecessors and turn its back on the world.

In the fierce resentment of immigration in both the United States and the U.K., and in Britain's bitter opposition to Europe, the resistance to unimpeded global integration is making itself felt. Few politicians anywhere can appear to undermine national defenses against unfettered immigration or the swamping of the home economy by cheap imports that destroy jobs.

Thus the true globalist remains an unlikely candidate anywhere. In Mongolia, young Western-trained economists came to power and took their country, wedged between China and Russia, on an implausible journey toward what they saw as Western-style capitalism. That journey brought real economic gains for the country, but voters chafed at two developments: the changes disrupted and dislocated long-subsidized services and protected jobs, and the handling of mineral concessions. Russian and Chinese business interests proceeded to dig shallow mines for low capital investment; the mines produced quick profits but wrecked the environment. The damage soured Mongolians against all foreign investment, and the Westernizers were voted out. The new government renegotiated the concessions. When I was there in 2008, an embarrassed leader of the opposition, a self-described Thatcherite on economics, had to explain to the visiting British minister that electoral expediency required him to support the renegotiations. He too had to pose as a nationalist.

Tacking close to globalization without allowing it to swamp the boat is the principal challenge of governments everywhere today. The debate will be whether to tack or head straight into the wind. The tackers likely have it right, allowing politicians to manage change in a way that protects their citizens.

The process will continue to be tumultuous and disruptive. Politicians will struggle to institute reforms quickly so that they can show enough results to prevail at the next election. Those who appeal to fears of change will resist those who move boldly. Time after time, in my years as a political consultant, when I stripped away the local campaign issues to the core, I found that a given election was about embracing change versus retaining the safety of the status quo. That choice can only become sharper as change accelerates. Future elections will be broadly about whether countries embrace or hold back from the world economy. The ostensible issues may be migration, jobs, prices, or schools, but the underlying choice will be this primal one.

The international system must cope with threats to peace from this clash of approaches. For if globalization and its nationalist reaction were not difficult enough, they are compounded by our era's limits. Disputes over energy, water, food, and land hold potential to escalate into further conflict. Ancient ethnic and religious grievances will combine with resistance to change. The world is getting to be a trickier, not a simpler, place, as Fukuyama now acknowledges.

Managing these volatile dynamics will require strong international institutions that are perceived as fair and legitimate and that carry authority. The need for peacekeeping and conflict prevention will grow. The world will need shared systems to manage climate change and migration. It will need to commit resources to ending poverty and create a global safety net, and some kind of transnational framework will be necessary to handle international commerce in all its aspects, from copyright to taxation to labor standards.

Practical international arrangements will steadily nudge forward. But will open, cooperative political values triumph in the world and accommodate traditions that people want to conserve? Or will nationalism break up this surge of international integration, as it did in 1914? The stakeholders in global openness, as they might be called—governments, civil society, and businesses—need to stand up for the values that underpin this agenda: the rule of law, democracy, human rights, opportunity, and sufficient security for all.

The Millennium Development Goals, the international human rights movement, and new concepts such as the Responsibility to Protect are among the foundations, however uncertain, of a new global society. But they will prevail only if the world makes a real commitment to rebuilding an international framework of rules and institutions that all can rally around. How much the UN can lead depends in large part on the success of its reforms. If it can become representative in a changed world and operate effectively, then its global legitimacy will make it the first port of call for those promoting new arrangements. If it does not, then an alternative, more ad hoc architecture may emerge to replace it, in the G20 and in informal networks.

The United States remains the key nation in creating any such system. As I argued in the speech that so upset John Bolton, Roosevelt and Truman understood this in a way none of their successors fully have. At a time when the UN dominated the global economy and international security much more than it does today, these two presidents sought to pool U.S. sovereign efforts within a broader system of collective security.

But for now the UN is stranded. Many in the developing world, as well as major powers like China and Russia, view it as hopelessly partisan. They think it is driven by double standards and is still under the control of the Western victors of the Second World War and their chosen partners.

But in truth the U.S. has become disengaged. Frustrated by Iraq, unwilling to make the concessions that a superpower would have to make to pool sovereignty at the UN, its leaders have doubted the gains of UN engagement. President Obama, while evidently more multilateralist, has evinced caution about an institution that he may believe has lost its progressive energy.

The post-1989 world is crowded and riven by deep disputes; the fear of change has breathed new life into historic enmities; and travel and technology have enabled new threats that challenge our traditional defenses. Under these circumstances, the world has a pressing need to strengthen and improve the UN.

After World War II, in the first decade of the nuclear age, the world seemed too dangerous for anything less. But as the hopes first espoused in San Francisco in 1945 were dashed, the world has muddled through with less for more than sixty years.

How much longer can it continue?

CONCLUSION:
THE GLOBAL PROMISE

This book is about uncertainty, not inevitability. I make my case for stronger global arrangements based not on the inevitable rise of China or the fall of the United States or Europe. Rather, I argue for strengthening international institutions because the world needs to have rules in place that allow for peaceful adjustments between states. I imagine that violent showdown, the historically preferred means of change management between states, can be replaced by negotiation. I assume that states will fall as well as rise—more often than not in unexpected ways.

I have already ticked off the factors that set off this dizzying period of global change and hence uncertainty: global integration that is doubling the size of the global economy every twenty years or so; and innovations in technology that have expanded health, life expectancy, education, and opportunity at an unimaginable scale and rate, even as world population has grown by almost a third in the last twenty years.

Sustaining the world's ability to absorb new people and provide them a decent life is the political issue of our times. Some hark back to the earlier, easier times of small-town America, Europe, Africa, or Asia where people may have had less but life was allegedly better, and many politicians still win elections on such appeals. But they deny the reality that by 2050 the global population is expected to grow by a further three billion. And most of those people will live in cities.

But the exuberant alternative, a market-led globalization that lacks rules and favors the strong, is equally unsustainable. The global financial crisis that began in 2008 underlined the injustice that inequality is not limited to income but also applies to behavior: bankers got away with it because they were not subject to the same rules as the rest of us. They did so, not because, as the left has always grumbled, the rich and powerful always do get away with it, but because globalization seemed to have set them free: the exotic global level where they operate has no apparent laws, no financial enforcement offices or systems to stop them. They escaped national controls.

Bankers have mounted stout and savvy defenses in the committee rooms of Congress and European parliaments, and in the media. They have thrown millions of dollars into lobbying to resist regulatory reform; but it seems their time is up, at least for now. Some further national and international regulation will be established even if it is, as I suggested in the last chapter, likely to be, tentative and insufficient.

Another reason global government may begin to form is that we all now live in an underregulated hell where deteriorating earth, rivers, oceans, and climate go unchecked. Growth consumes nonrenewable resources like energy, forests, water, commodities, and clean air at a staggering pace. We share the impact globally, but the solutions remain blocked at the national level.

The formation of a new global political order, however, is unlikely to occur just because bank regulators and environmentalists demand it. The nation-state may have begun as a system for preventing its citizens from harming one another, but it grew because it offered a further value proposition: services that advanced citizens' well-being.

Individual democratic nation-states provide a social contract between government and people. Today, as states run up against their limits, international society is surely ready for a global social contract. The Millennium Development Goals are a modest half-step in this direction, promising the achievement of basic levels of welfare over the coming years. But their vision is limited: they offer access to primary education but not secondary or tertiary, for example, and they propose minimal environmental obligations but not democratic accountability.

Further, the MDGs lay out minimum basic outcomes but not the means of achieving them. Although this omission has given governments freedom to set their own economic course, it works less well at the global level. For example, the eighth goal's commitment to providing assistance to poor countries goes largely unmet. Economic and policy responsibilities remain jealously guarded at the national level. But to achieve the MDGs, the world needs a coordinated global policy.

Issues like climate, trade, and international economic policy all have negotiating forums—climate in a meandering UN process, trade in the World Trade Organization, and economic policy in the G20. But none are backed by the political will needed to get effective outcomes that bind countries into policy commitments.

Aligning policy behind a united global purpose is vital if inequality and poverty are really to be tackled. Aid alone will not solve these issues; rather, inclusive global economic policy is now vital, targeting jobs, opportunity, training, health, and education in persistent pockets of poverty, as governments have done at home for a century or more.

Poverty can be beaten, but the network of private activism and cautious governmental engagement that is taking on the task needs the reinforcement of real commitment to international action. What lags is a shift in the compass points of our political culture to embrace global responsibility and meet global objectives.

The spur may be finite natural resources. Water and energy may force global sharing arrangements, indeed a globally orchestrated process of managing down consumption to live within our limits. That effort may have dramatic implications for our values and how we measure the good life. Perforce we will have to seek more fulfillment from nonmaterial pleasures and recognize that out of mutual obligation, on a shared resource-stressed planet, our consumption is rationed.

Globalization, if associated with a more moderate, less consumption-oriented life, would be less a threat to local cultures than their quiet supporter. Global solidarity, if defined as living by rules and limits suitable to our fragile shared habitat, would encourages finding value in our history. We cannot go back to a quaint rural past; our numbers and our economy condemn us to cities. But we can make those cities human by exhibiting a greater respect of our past and thereby dampening future consumption.

The MDGs were written hurriedly in a UN office building, using the language of earlier global agreements. They are no Declaration of Independence or Magna Carta. Rather, as one of their drafters I can ruefully acknowledge, they are a poorly worded, incomplete stab at a global commitment among all of us in the global community. Their drafting is not the stuff of great history, but they are a start. And like any healthy contract between governors and governed, they consist of mutual obligations and responsibilities.

Meeting those goals would do more than require richer governments to fund social services in poor countries. In the longer run it will require that we establish the right global policies covering finance and economics, trade, migration, and environmental management, all of which and much else will determine the opportunities for the poor.

As the momentum toward a fairer and more inclusive world gathers speed, we can add other ambitions. The need to keep peace and protect citizens is becoming a global rather than a national task.

Today terrorism targets civilians, and much of international trade is criminal, through narcotics, people-smuggling, money-laundering, gun-running, illegal logging, and other commodity-smuggling. If history is any guide, security will become another driver of the modern global order.

Technology and growth have not only abetted global integration; they have also enabled people to take more control over their lives. Democracy has spread in part as a means of resisting change to the precious traditional way of life, and yet the tide that has carried it forward has been globalization. Closed countries are left with ever fewer places to hide.

These two trends—global integration and greater personal control—can combine around a global social contract to allow the emergence of a political culture that sustains it. Indeed, if they do not align, both are jeopardized. Of course, integration and personal control are not easy allies; people react to the apparently dehumanizing aspects of globalization by holding on more tightly to the familiar and to what sets them against the others. So even as shared goals for a common humanity emerge, politics will likely remain at least as fractious as ever. Each step toward a more integrated future will be contested.

That political fight will remain national, and even local, as politicians have to show that nations have not been bypassed but rather have been incorporated into the decision-making of increasingly powerful global bodies. Leaders will want to show that these institutions' accountability to governments has been preserved. At the same time, civil society will be challenging that preeminence of states, calling for new models of advocacy and representation that empower them to speak for people on a cross-border basis.

If this gargantuan struggle for political power in our global century is to become allied to popular concerns, then the creation of a global contract (probably never to be captured in a single document, name, or even concept) is critical. It will be the anchor by which new and strengthened institutions will remain attached to a global purpose that makes sense to people. It will become the anchor for our shared future.

Sometime in future, we will pause and look back at the feverish years of writing agreements to reduce poverty, regulate banks, and fight terrorism. We will see in retrospect how a new set of commitments among people, states, and international institutions came into being. When we look back, we will see the revolution.

AFTERWORD

The hardcover publication of this book in February 2011 followed the early triumphs of "the Arab Spring" revolutions in Tunisia and Egypt. The convulsions that shook the region prompted interviewers and reviewers to frequently ask whether this sudden outbreak of democracy was a big step toward finishing the Global Revolution of my title.

Since the book calls for a more comprehensive global democracy where we all have more say over our local, national, and our global affairs, the Arab Spring is evidently a step in the right direction. The Arab Human Development Reports,[1] which I had sponsored at UNDP, pointed out that of the world's seven regions, the Arab countries had the lowest freedom scores.[2]

As I argued earlier in these pages, the three Arab deficits of political freedom, woman's participation, and secular education—combined with political drift and a corrupt, aging leadership—had led to such an unequal economic performance that it was in a way remarkable that the streets of Tunisia and Cairo had not filled with angry demonstrators years earlier. This was a social time bomb that had been set to go off for a while. Yet revolution is not easily sparked in a world where rulers govern with an iron hand. The examples of successful revolt in the Arab world were few and far between.

The different reactions of the Arab "Street" and the Arab elite to our report in 2002 dramatically demonstrated the political explosion that was nevertheless building. Though it was condemned in private by Arab League ministers as discourteous meddling, the report became the region's runaway bestseller. In the coffee shops and on the new cable TV channels, they loved it. The old men in power had to bite their tongues.

And indeed those leaders were to enjoy nine more years in power and perhaps many more for some. For as I write these words the Arab revolutions are still unfinished. In Egypt and Tunisia elections are scheduled to happen shortly. In other countries the conflicts remain unresolved with ruling groups exercising an ever more heavy-handed oppression, and with the cost-benefit of NATO's intervention in Libya uncertain.

To a reader of these pages, however, the notion that the force of street protests that begins a revolution subsequently loses its way in the long, less glamorous, sequel of taking power will not be new. Indeed in my experience, the completion of the shift from overthrow of the old to a more stable democratic order is on average a ten-year project. Much beyond the ballot box has to change. The old elite's grip on absolute economic power has to be prized open, a culture of democratic openness and minority rights forged, a civil society given the political oxygen to breathe and grow, a justice system people respect and trust established. Nearly always new governments struggle to make these changes while also battling a legacy of economic failure and pent-up popular demands for jobs and basic services that they have inherited from their failed predecessors.

In Egypt and Tunisia, all these conditions for a long, difficult journey to a "finished" revolution are present. Elsewhere the challenges are more difficult still. Whereas Egypt and Tunisia already have middle classes that offer the basis for a pluralistic political system, states like Bahrain, Saudi Arabia, Libya, and Syria still have family-

and clan- or sect-based power structures where the economic patronage of government, rather than markets, have determined people's economic standing. And the ticket for access to, or denial of, state support in most of these countries is family or religion. This is not a promising foundation on which to build a competitive secular democracy.

Yet the message of this book is that despite the obstacles it can be done. The little club of once struggling democracies that recruited me to help push political and economic reforms forward have, after a usually floundering start, mostly done well. Even if it has often taken a decade or so to get there.

The Arab spring began with an auspicious, if tragic, start: the self-immolation of a Tunisian street seller, Mohamed Bouazizi. On December 18, 2010, he set himself alight because he felt threatened and ignored by corrupt, bullying local police officers. The power of his protest came from the fact that his desperate frustration was shared by so many others. His act lit the dry timber of latent anger against a line of corruption and privilege that stretched from the local female police constable, who ignored his complaints, to President Ben Ali, his wife, and his family. By the time Bouazizi died from his burns on January 4, 2011, the region was catching fire.

The act was auspicious because such apparent futility and weakness brought down an apparently all powerful political order. And indeed this David and Goliath theme of weakness confronting strength and prevailing was a steady part of the early months of the Arab spring. Peaceful protestors, drawing courage from the links to each other and the outside world that Facebook, text messaging—particularly Twitter— and other social media communication provided saw off heavily armed government forces.

Force and power have been given a new asymmetric twist by the organizing tools of the new communications media. Before, a dissident rarely knew if he or she was alone or whether there were tens, or hundreds, or hundreds of thousands prepared to come out onto the streets. Social media has reversed the old monopoly of Arab regimes' hold on power through their control of the military and police.

Just how much new technology was a game changer initially went largely unnoticed by the outside world. Yet it took only from December 18, Bouazizi's burning, to February 11, 2011 for the two neighboring dictators, Ben Ali and Hosni Mubarak of Egypt, to be driven from office.

Mubarak's appointment of Omar Suleiman as his vice president might in more normal times have been enough to stabilize the situation and enable a managed transition from an aging and failing military man to a slightly younger and more vigorous one. I had gotten to know Suleiman, the country's spy chief, during my years in Gordon Brown's administration, since we were our governments' principal contact points on Sudan among other places.

Over a long Saturday morning in his office in 2009, I remember how perplexed he was that despite his repeated visits to South Sudan, the construction of an Egyptian hospital and many other overtures to the new leadership of the south, nothing could deflect it from its determination to break from the Arab north of the country and find its own destiny. He understood every twist and turn of the south's complex ethnic makeup and its tortuous civil war with the north, but still he could not get his mind around the transcending demand of southerners for their freedom.

So despite all his skill it was in the end no surprise to me that he could not steady the ship in Egypt. Mubarak's time was up because the people of Egypt had now drunk at the same well. They too would stop at nothing to win their freedom. This was something men of the president's generation just could not comprehend. Perhaps they had when they were ambitious young officers in Nasser's and Sadat's Egypt but that was a long time ago.

Some months after the revolution, an interim military sponsored government in Egypt has slowed political change, encouraged the fragmentation of the opposition, and promoted the rise of religious parties as both a scare tactic and as possible allies. Despite show trials of front men of the old regime—most notably Mubarak himself humiliatingly held behind a cage in the courtroom—it has left much of the old economic power structure in place. Indeed the military itself was, and is, the major shareholder in much of the web of state-controlled companies that still dominate the economy.

Yet the very reasons why Suleiman and Western experts failed to anticipate the revolt in the first place suggest that it may still get a second wind. In January 2011, an able ex-MI6 station chief in Cairo paid me a visit. Quickly the conversation turned to Egypt, still free of the major demonstrations that had convulsed Tunisia, and we speculated whether there would be consequences in other countries. He thought it most unlikely since Egyptians enjoyed greater liberty than others in the Arab world; there was healthy economic growth and a strong middle class was emerging. He assumed there would be change when an elderly Mubarak departed the scene, but that it would be evolutionary and controlled. It seemed most likely that Gamal, Mubarak's son, would succeed him, and if not then probably Suleiman. Days after his visit, protestors occupied Tahrir Square.

Not much later, Gamal was in Tora prison on the outskirts of Cairo facing corruption charges and Suleiman was gone from office. My British spy friend's false diagnosis was shared by many other experts. The sheer political inertness of Mubarak's Egypt, combined with a late flowering of a spate of economic reforms that belatedly generated real growth, blinded them to the country's instability.

Egypt's emerging middle class, accelerating economic growth, and the economic reforms, particularly privatization and the limiting of basic subsidies, far from being the bulwarks against revolution, were its triggers. I am struck again by the analogy to the Philippines and

Cory Aquino's successful campaign against Ferdinand Marcos. The World Bank had prevailed on Marcos to revive the economy by cutting subsidies and beginning to privatize state enterprises, and while this was the correct economic prescription, it was toxic politics. It amounted to a corrupt regime removing one of the few economic benefits it gave the poor. In Egypt's case bread prices soared even as the regime's well-connected friends were making fortunes out of privatization. The most dramatic score-settling the military has so far allowed against the old order in Egypt is the trial and imprisonment of members of the ministerial privatization team and their business friends. The World Bank has also been seriously damaged in ordinary Egyptians' eyes as a central member of the team, the former minister of investment Mahmoud Mohieldin, is now one of the bank's three top deputies. He was a controversial reformist ally of Gamal Mubarak. As a consequence, the interim government has turned its back on the bank's money.

In the wake of Egypt's revolution, politics and economics will be buffeted by popular demands for jobs and affordable goods and services. The political system seems likely to be fragmented with weak parties. Islamic-oriented parties, with their longer history of organization and opposition, are likely to do disproportionately well in early elections, despite the fact that Arab protestors' concerns were far from the manifesto of such groups. The Arab protests had very secular demands—freedom and jobs—which were also domestic-oriented. Yet brave years of opposition and a real record as providers of social services have given the Muslim Brotherhood a head start in Egypt.

Islamic groups tend to be not just socially conservative but economically conservative as well. In Iran, I saw how the Mullahs allied themselves with a powerful trading class that has left the country bereft of the competitive modern manufacturing and domestic service sector that it might otherwise have developed.

Given the complex religious and ethnic mosaic, the Arab region would be wise to lead the world in entrenching minority rights in its new constitutions. It is hard to imagine a stable and consensual government emerging without a strong framework of basic rights. It is equally important that a wider civil society quickly emerges at the grass-roots level. Presently, Islamic groups seem much more deeply embedded in communities and devoted to their welfare than the more secular and middle class groups which have more of a salon, rather than a street, agenda of political rights.

Many of the old regimes hung on because they offered protection to minorities who had often lacked power in the past or feared for their futures when majorities would rule. In Syria, an Alawite minority regime sustained itself on the back of other minorities fearful of the Sunni majority. In Bahrain, the Sunni ruler and their allies fear the Shia majority in the slums and countryside. In Egypt, many Coptic Christians continued to support the Mubarak regime to the end seeing him as a guarantor of interfaith peace. Members of their community have been at the top of government and business circles. Now they have noticed with alarm that the revolution coincided with a sharp increase in attacks on Christian churches. Yet protecting such minorities' rights, when it includes wealth and privilege, will be an affront to many in the new majorities.

So struggling Democrats will have their hands full. It is unlikely that there will be quick and easy transitions to fully functioning governments that can pick up the economic reform agenda where their failed predecessors left off. We should expect a long period of ducking and weaving, such as the period of Cory Aquino's rule, as systems struggle to find political stability and economic consistency.

Elsewhere in the region, at the time of writing, most countries have not emerged from the pre-phase: the overthrow of the old order. It would be nice to say it is only a matter of time and all will be happily resolved by the time you read these pages. But in countries such as Syria and Bahrain regimes have dug in, bloodily. In Yemen, a discredited regime held on even after the president was injured and had to flee. In Morocco and Jordan, their kings responded to protests with reform. Whether it is sufficient remains to be seen. And in Libya, the old terrorist Gaddafi clung on against Western air attacks and rebels for much longer than expected.

This resistance is challenging a number of comfortable Western assumptions. First, that the power of the people, when right is on its side, is always unstoppable. Perhaps this is still true in the end, but often a lot of lives later. And usually a regime's political base is less denuded than the triumphant prose of foreign correspondents implies. Clans, beholden to and linked by family to Gaddafi, remained an important power base, as have Syria's Shia and other minorities to Assad and the Sunni minority to Bahrain's ruling family.

More troubling still, violent oppression often works. The conditions required are an unfaltering military. If it is a citizens' army and they are being asked to oppress kith and kin then maintaining troop discipline, as in Egypt, can be tough. It is easier if the army draws largely on members of the ruling group supplemented with outsiders, as in Bahrain, and trickier if the officers are from the ruling group but the troops are from the oppressed majority, as in Syria.

A second condition for successful suppression of revolt is keeping it out of the international news. This has become progressively more difficult in general because of the global rise of social media which means even when the formal international media are largely barred, as has been the case in Syria, photographs and accounts are still smuggled out electronically. In 1982 Bashar Assad's brutal father massacred up to 20,000 people in Hama. It took a while for the news of the killings to leak out and by then it was too late; without the photographs or footage there was no international outrage at the time and not much later. Today, a crackdown in Hama may remain in the media shadows but it cannot be kept secret. And indeed in August 2011, it was what finally provoked condemnation of the regime's violent behavior from the UN Security Council and finally a call from Obama and other Western leaders for Assad's departure.

Yet there is a significant minority of what might be called the global internal security establishment who, with quiet glee, point to the current successful revival of oppression as a tool of government. During the time I was a UK minister, my colleagues and I looked on hopelessly as the Sri Lankan regime ignored all international calls for mercy to civilians and brutally destroyed the Tamil insurgency. Media access was limited and the Sinhalese military seemed to have had little compunction in cleansing out their Tamil ethnic rivals.

Reportedly an informal annual gathering of like-minded security officials centered on Russia and its Central Asian neighbors gave a standing ovation to the Sri Lankan delegation at its following meeting. The experience of Chechnya's violent suppression by Putin had been successfully repeated.

Nor would such people agree that the communications revolution is a one way street that empowers only protestors. Increasingly, electronic eavesdropping and surveillance is extending its tentacles. Last year China spent more, according to its published budget, on internal security than on its military. Less alarmingly Sri Lankan government blogs have had a go at those such as me who have criticized their human rights record. The electronic media is predictably a tool for all sides. And in its last days the Egyptian regime sought to cut all international Internet access which reputedly ran through a single fiber-optic cable, a stranglehold if ever there was one. When a British Prime Minister responded to looting in the UK in 2011 by suggesting that the police should close down the BlackBerry messenger service that was thought to be the main electronic organizing tool of the looters, the vulnerability of the right to freedom of electronic communication was widely noticed. It is no twenty-first century entrenched human right.

A further Western assumption about modern international affairs is also on trial in the Arab spring. The doctrine of the Responsibility to Protect, or R2P as it is popularly known, was one of the most important, but precarious, achievements of Kofi Annan's time as UN Secretary-General.[3] Drawing on the shared international shame of the world after the genocides in Rwanda and Bosnia, the doctrine is intended to allow the world to intervene to prevent such acts of mass abuse.

When Colonel Gaddafi threatened the rebel citizens of the eastern Libyan City of Benghazi with violent retribution, France, Britain, and a more reluctant United States saw the case for R2P. An even more reluctant Security Council went along with them. Their fears were partly the ever present double standards: much more extensive civilian killings at government hands were concurrently taking place in Côte d'Ivoire and at that point no one was citing R2P.

The council's anxieties also, however, revolved around what France, Britain, and the United States might get up to armed with such a mandate. For a doctrine codified in the aftermath of Bush and Blair's Iraq War, it had been critical that it was limited to humanitarian protection of civilians. Diplomats did not want the mission creep of Blairite Liberal interventionism or of a trigger happy Bush.

The Libyan operation quickly stumbled down this slippery path as Western politicians appeared to acknowledge their real war aims of Gaddafi's departure, and as they did so, so international agreement on the Arab spring was lost. The first heady months, when the world had pushed together for protestors to be treated properly and their voices be heard, descended into a failure by the Security Council to even condemn Syrian Government brutality until August. Chinese and Russian delegates warned that any Syrian resolution might, like Libya's, be taken advantage of by the West. So mission creep threw a wrench into the spokes of international cooperation and cast a shadow over the honorable intentions of saving the civilians of Benghazi.

But what should be the limits of international action on behalf of my unfinished revolution? The Iraq War confirmed, in my view, that democratic change must come from within. Imposing it and using it as an excuse for war negates its very purpose. Democracy does not flow easily from the barrel of a foreigner's gun. Gaddafi may be gone but Libya will almost certainly provide further proof of this.

Yet in the emerging global political society, the world does matter. Politics is not just local. Egypt and Tunisia were internal uprisings but helped by deft pressure from President Obama and others. Violent crackdowns were prevented and the will of the people was allowed to prevail. There was a united international community not least because the Obama administration finally found the courage to follow Obama's Cairo speech in which he had made the case for why America must align itself with aspirations for change in the region. That this would entail breaking so soon with longtime allies such as Mubarak had certainly not been foreseen by him or his speech writers.

And democratic protestors have another large global card to play. The world is moving on; does the Arab region want to get on the train or be left behind? When a former imperial power like Turkey, or a far-off Islamic nation like Indonesia, have seized the future, the failing regimes and societies of the Arab world have been exposed. By any lights they have been left behind.

That invidious global comparison will not go away, and so neither will the demand for change. A global society is a hard task master as it holds up the mirror to how we do, in our own societies, versus others. And as much as anything, the Arab spring was its people's verdict on where they stand in that global league table of self-determination and opportunity. For Arabs, that remains unfinished business.

ACKNOWLEDGMENTS

A book that describes how the world is changing, offers judgments about it, and includes fragments of memoir inevitably involves many people. I owe intellectual debts as well as friendship to many, starting with my extraordinary schoolmasters at Marlborough College, dons, and fellow students at Cambridge and then my professors and fellow graduate students at the University of Michigan. Let me mention two from those early years in particular, who taught me then and remain friends now: Martin Evans and Ronald Hyam.

Outside these institutions, many more encouraged me to raise my sights, from the remarkable late Launcelot Fleming, explorer, churchman, and environmentalist who was such a direct influence on me in my teens and twenties, to my extended English family and then our American one, too.

I have been lucky enough to enjoy the friendship of wonderful colleagues in the different organizations where I have worked: *The Economist*, the office of the UN High Commissioner for Refugees, the Sawyer-Miller Group, the World Bank, the United Nations Development Program, the United Nations, the British government, particularly the Foreign Office, the World Economic Forum, the Monitor Group, and now FTI Consulting. It seems invidious to single out individuals given that I have worked with so many people as I rose through the ranks. At UNDP I had literally one of the world's best jobs, with real power and means to make a difference and a group of colleagues who were as passionate about that opportunity as I was. UNDP allowed me the magnificent freedom to act on behalf of humanity, such as I had last enjoyed twenty years earlier as a young UNHCR refugee officer on the Thai-Cambodian border. Both the UN proper and the World Bank provided excitement and challenge, even though both were more tied down by politics.

For support in this book's preparation, I feel a special debt of gratitude to Mark Suzman, who worked with me through my UNDP and UN years, read an early draft, as did Nick Van Praag, another old friend and colleague. Additionally Ed Reilly, my old political partner, friend, and summer neighbor, deserves thanks for his support and comradeship. George Soros and I have discussed much of what is in these pages twenty-five years of conversations over long lunches, dinners, and weekends in different parts of the world. I have both an intellectual debt and an accumulated dining debt to him, one of the most influential change agents of our times.

I have been lucky in my bosses. Kofi Annan was certainly the greatest UN secretary-general of recent times; his grace and decency under fire were an example to all of us who were privileged to work for him. He and his wife, Nane, modeled the values of tolerance, care for others, and sensibility that will one day be the foundation of a successful global society. Before that I had struck lucky at the World Bank with Jim Wolfensohn, who exhibited a very different leadership style but offered a young lieutenant important lessons about embracing those you work with and building real friendships, and about cutting through, in an international world of often muddy compromise, with a real focus on results. My other notable chief was Gordon Brown, who, despite his domestic political difficulties, on the issues of Africa, Asia, multilateralism, and the G20 that comprised my ministerial portfolio, cared deeply and threw himself into the detail.

I thank Ernesto Zedillo, the director of the Yale Center for the Study of Globalization, for early support for this book. When I left the UN, the center provided a home, intellectual companionship, and financial support for a few critical months as I got this book under way. Ernesto also appears in these pages as a reformist president of Mexico. His deputy at Yale, Haynie Wheeler, helped get me set up as a visiting fellow, and among her most important gifts were three great part-time research assistants, Aniket Shah, Alexis Arieff, and Robert Berschinski. She also found an editorial assistant, Susanna Cover, who made brisk sense of my scribblings.

A number of friends who have labored at similar writing projects, Samantha Power, Strobe Talbott, Kemal Dervis, Jeff Sachs, and Robert McCrum, have encouraged me at various points in this enterprise.

I have been lucky too in my publishing associations. Twenty-five years ago Andrew Wylie first told me I should write a book. For an agent not used to waiting for anything, this wait required superhuman patience. He has been friend and conscience (about the book) throughout. At Penguin I found an old friend at the helm, John Makinson, and two great editors, Laura Stickney and earlier Vanessa Mobley, both of whom worked under Ann Godoff. The copy editor Janet Biehl did a wonderful job. In London, Will Goodlad was also very helpful.

Just before the publication of this book, Richard Holbrooke, a friend for thirty years, died. He was once more in harness as a senior US diplomat seeking to find a way out of the morass of Afghanistan. Re-reading these pages I was surprised he had not been featured more. Our lives as officials, fumbling fortune seekers when we were out of office, inveterate do-gooders, and close friends had criss-crossed across the decades. He and his wife, Kati, were devoted to the same lost causes and great causes as Trish and I. Nobody was more resilient about getting back off the ground and heading back into the fray than Richard. I miss him enormously as a personal inspiration and an example of a rugged revolutionary.

Let me add thanks also to Camilla de Caires who has helped me manage my working life and the logistics of book launches with great calm and order. To Jack Dunn, the CEO of my day job, who has been a big supporter even when he must have wished I were calling on a client and not at another book event. And my thanks to all my FTI colleagues who have been so supportive as well as to William George-Carey, my much-adored godson, who helped me with the afterword, and to Rosalind Steele who picked up the grammatical errors that a more attentive author would have found on his own.

My last and deepest thanks are to Trish and our children, Madison, Isobel, George, and Phoebe: this book's regular resurrection over a number of summers kept me too frequently from family activities. More profoundly, my global life has meant frequent changes of home and school. Thank you.

NOTES

INTRODUCTION
1. George Bush, Inaugural Address, January 20, 2001, online at http://www
   .whitehouse.gov/news/print/inaugural-address.html.
2. Nayan Chanda, *Bound Together: How Preachers, Adventurers and Warriors Shaped Globalization* (New Haven, Conn.: Yale University Press, 2007), 246.
3. Ibid.
4. Andrew Kohut and Bruce Stokes, *America Against the World: How We Are Different and Why We Are Disliked* (New York: Henry Holt, 2006), p. xvii.
5. "Country Briefings: France," *Economist*, February 5, 2007, online at http://
   www.economist.com/countries/France/profile.cfm?folder=Profile-
   Economic%20Structure.

CHAPTER TWO
1. The Charter of the United Nations

CHAPTER THREE
1. UNHCR, *The State of the World's Refugees 2000: Fifty Years of Humanitarian Action* (New York: UNCHR, 2000), 105.
2. William Shawcross, *The Quality of Mercy: Cambodia, Holocaust, and Modern Conscience* (New York: Touchstone Books, 1985).

CHAPTER FIVE
1. Sebastian Mallaby, *The World's Banker: A Story of Failed States, Financial Crises, and the Wealth and Poverty of Nations* (New York: Penguin, 2004), 63.
2. Ibid.

CHAPTER SEVEN
1. Dominic Wilson and Roopa Purushothaman, *Dreaming with BRICs: The Path to 2050*, Global Economics Paper 99 (Goldman Sachs, October 2003).

2. Lee Kuan Yew, *From Third World to First: The Singapore Story 1965-2000* (New York: HarperCollins, 2000), 50.

CHAPTER EIGHT

1. Mark Malloch-Brown, "Human Security and Human Development in the 21st Century: A Post-September 11 Agenda," speech to the Centre for Global Governance, London School of Economics, October 25, 2001, in *Mark Malloch-Brown at the United Nations Development Programme* 2001, 281.

CHAPTER NINE

1. U.S. Census Bureau.
2. Niall Ferguson, *The Ascent of Money: A Financial History of The World* (New York: Penguin Press, 2008).
3. Petroleum Finance Company (PFC), internal presentation, 2007.
4. Paul Collier, *The Bottom Billion: Why the Poorest Countries Are Failing and What Can Be Done About It* (New York: Oxford University Press, 2007).

CHAPTER ELEVEN

1. Tony Blair, signed essay in *The Economist*, June 2007.

AFTERWORD

1. See pp. 155–58.
2. Arab Human Development Report 2002, *Creating Opportunities for Future Generations* (UNDP 2002) p. 27.
3. See pp. 75, 234.

FURTHER READING

To the reader who wants to learn more about the events and issues raised here, let me make the following very selective book recommendations:

ON THE HISTORY OF GLOBALIZATION:

Chanda, Nayan. *Bound Together: How Traders, Preachers, Adventurers, and Warriors Shaped Globalization.* New Haven, Conn.: Yale University Press, 2007.
Talbott, Strobe. *The Great Experiment: The Story of Ancient Empires, Modern States, and the Quest for a Global Nation.* New York: Simon & Schuster, 2008.

ON REFUGEES:

Shawcross, William. *Sideshow: Kissinger, Nixon and the Destruction of Cambodia.* New York: Simon & Shuster, 1979.
———. *The Quality of Mercy: Cambodia, Holocaust, and Modern Conscience.* New York: Simon & Shuster, 1984.

ON POLITICAL CONSULTING:

Harding, James. *Alpha Dogs: The Americans Who Turned Political Spin into a Global Business.* New York: Farrar, Straus & Giroux, 2008.

ON THE WORLD BANK:

Mallaby, Sebastian. *The World's Banker: A Story of Failed States, Financial Crises, and the Wealth and Poverty of Nations.* New York: Penguin, 2004.

ON UNDP:

Murphy, Craig N. *The United Nations Development Programme: A Better Way.* New York: Cambridge University Press, 2006.

ON DEVELOPMENT AND POVERTY:

Collier, Paul. *The Bottom Billion: Why The Poorest Countries Are Failing and What Can Be Done About It* (New York: Oxford University Press, 2007).

Malloch-Brown, Mark. *Statements, Speeches and Commentary 1999-2005*. New York: UNDP, 2005.

Sachs, Jeffrey D. *The End of Poverty: Economic Possibilities for Our Time*. New York: Penguin, 2005.

ON THE UNITED NATIONS:

Malone, David M. *The International Struggle Over Iraq: Politics in the UN Security Council 1980-2005*. New York: Oxford University Press, 2006.

Power, Samantha. *Chasing the Flame: Sergio Vieira de Mello and the Fight to Save the World*. New York: Penguin, 2008.

Schlesinger, Stephen C. *Act of Creation: The Founding of The United Nations*. Westview Press, 2003.

Traub, James. *The Best Intentions: Kofi Annan and the UN in the Era of American World Power*. New York: Farrar, Straus and Giroux, 2006.

ON THE INTERNATIONAL FINANCIAL CRISIS:

Soros, George. *The New Paradigm for Financial Markets: The Credit Crisis of 2008 and What It Means*. New York: PublicAffairs, 2008.

INDEX

ALLEN LANE
an imprint of
PENGUIN BOOKS

Recently Published

Dominic Sandbrook, *Seasons in the Sun: The Battle for Britain, 1974-1979*

Tariq Ramadan, *The Arab Awakening: Islam and the New Middle East*

Jonathan Haidt, *The Righteous Mind: Why Good People are Divided by Politics and Religion*

Ahmed Rashid, *Pakistan on the Brink: The Future of Pakistan, Afghanistan and the West*

Tim Weiner, *Enemies: A History of the FBI*

Mark Pagel, *Wired for Culture: The Natural History of Human Cooperation*

George Dyson, *Turing's Cathedral: The Origins of the Digital Universe*

Cullen Murphy, *God's Jury: The Inquisition and the Making of the Modern World*

Richard Sennett, *Together: The Rituals, Pleasures and Politics of Co-operation*

Faramerz Dabhoiwala, *The Origins of Sex: A History of the First Sexual Revolution*

Roy F. Baumeister and John Tierney, *Willpower: Rediscovering Our Greatest Strength*

Jesse J. Prinz, *Beyond Human Nature: How Culture and Experience Shape Our Lives*

Robert Holland, *Blue-Water Empire: The British in the Mediterranean since 1800*

Jodi Kantor, *The Obamas: A Mission, A Marriage*

Philip Coggan, *Paper Promises: Money, Debt and the New World Order*

Charles Nicholl, *Traces Remain: Essays and Explorations*

Daniel Kahneman, *Thinking, Fast and Slow*

Hunter S. Thompson, *Fear and Loathing at Rolling Stone: The Essential Writing of Hunter S. Thompson*

Duncan Campbell-Smith, *Masters of the Post: The Authorized History of the Royal Mail*

Colin McEvedy, *Cities of the Classical World: An Atlas and Gazetteer of 120 Centres of Ancient Civilization*

Heike B. Görtemaker, *Eva Braun: Life with Hitler*

Brian Cox and Jeff Forshaw, *The Quantum Universe: Everything that Can Happen Does Happen*

Nathan D. Wolfe, *The Viral Storm: The Dawn of a New Pandemic Age*

Norman Davies, *Vanished Kingdoms: The History of Half-Forgotten Europe*

Michael Lewis, *Boomerang: The Meltdown Tour*

Steven Pinker, *The Better Angels of Our Nature: The Decline of Violence in History and Its Causes*

Robert Trivers, *Deceit and Self-Deception: Fooling Yourself the Better to Fool Others*

Thomas Penn, *Winter King: The Dawn of Tudor England*

Daniel Yergin, *The Quest: Energy, Security and the Remaking of the Modern World*

Michael Moore, *Here Comes Trouble: Stories from My Life*

Ali Soufan, *The Black Banners: Inside the Hunt for Al Qaeda*

Jason Burke, *The 9/11 Wars*

Timothy D. Wilson, *Redirect: The Surprising New Science of Psychological Change*

Ian Kershaw, *The End: Hitler's Germany, 1944-45*

T M Devine, *To the Ends of the Earth: Scotland's Global Diaspora, 1750-2010*

Catherine Hakim, *Honey Money: The Power of Erotic Capital*

Douglas Edwards, *I'm Feeling Lucky: The Confessions of Google Employee Number 59*

John Bradshaw, *In Defence of Dogs*

Chris Stringer, *The Origin of Our Species*

Lila Azam Zanganeh, *The Enchanter: Nabokov and Happiness*

David Stevenson, *With Our Backs to the Wall: Victory and Defeat in 1918*

Evelyn Juers, *House of Exile: War, Love and Literature, from Berlin to Los Angeles*

Henry Kissinger, *On China*

Michio Kaku, *Physics of the Future: How Science Will Shape Human Destiny and Our Daily Lives by the Year 2100*

David Abulafia, *The Great Sea: A Human History of the Mediterranean*

John Gribbin, *The Reason Why: The Miracle of Life on Earth*

Anatol Lieven, *Pakistan: A Hard Country*

William Cohen, *Money and Power: How Goldman Sachs Came to Rule the World*

Joshua Foer, *Moonwalking with Einstein: The Art and Science of Remembering Everything*

Simon Baron-Cohen, *Zero Degrees of Empathy: A New Theory of Human Cruelty*

Manning Marable, *Malcolm X: A Life of Reinvention*

David Deutsch, *The Beginning of Infinity: Explanations that Transform the World*

David Edgerton, *Britain's War Machine: Weapons, Resources and Experts in the Second World War*

John Kasarda and Greg Lindsay, *Aerotropolis: The Way We'll Live Next*

David Gilmour, *The Pursuit of Italy: A History of a Land, Its Regions and Their Peoples*

Niall Ferguson, *Civilization: The West and the Rest*

Tim Flannery, *Here on Earth: A New Beginning*

Robert Bickers, *The Scramble for China: Foreign Devils in the Qing Empire, 1832-1914*

Mark Malloch-Brown, *The Unfinished Global Revolution: The Limits of Nations and the Pursuit of a New Politics*